This is the
Henry Holt Walks Series,
which originated with
PARISWALKS *by Alison and Sonia Landes.*
Other titles in the series include:

LONDONWALKS *by Anton Powell*
JERUSALEMWALKS *by Nitza Rosovsky*
FLORENCEWALKS *by Anne Holler*
ROMEWALKS *by Anya M. Shetterly*
VIENNAWALKS *by J. Sydney Jones*
RUSSIAWALKS *by David and Valeria Matlock*
VENICEWALKS *by Chas Carner and Alessandro Giannatasio*
BARCELONAWALKS *by George Semler*
NEW YORKWALKS *by The 92nd Street Y*

BEIJINGWALKS

Don J. Cohn

and

Zhang Jingqing

An Owl Book

Henry Holt and Company • New York

Library of Congress Catalog Card Number: 91–58796
ISBN: 0-8050-2105-1

Henry Holt books are available at special discounts
for bulk purchases for sales promotions, premiums,
fund-raising, or educational use. Special editions
or book excerpts can also be created to specification.

For details contact: Special Sales Director,
Henry Holt and Company Inc., 115 West 18th Street,
New York, New York 10011

First edition—1992

Designed by Claire Naylon Vaccaro
Printed in Hong Kong by Sing Cheong Printing Co. Ltd.
Production House: Twin Age Limited, Hong Kong

Recognizing the importance of preserving the
written word, Henry Holt and Company Inc
by policy prints all of its first editions
on acid-free paper.∞

1 3 5 7 9 10 8 6 4 2

Front cover by Keith Macgregor, Cameraman;
back cover by Magnus Bartlett.

Photography courtesy of Don J. Cohn: 58, 59, 66, 80, 84, 94, 99,
111, 129, 163, 184, 196, 201, 209, 214; Magnus Bartlett: opening
picture, 20, 29, 38, 42, 73, 76, 78, 118, 145, 151, 156, 222, 239, 246;
Xinhua News Agency: 14, 40, 52 86, 104, 122, 134, 167, 176, 180,
190, 204, 233.

(Opening picture) White Dagoba, Beihai Park

To my father Theodore and my Chinese
uncle H.Y. Lowe a true gentleman of Old
Peking and to those who lost their lives in
June 1989 and with thanks to Qing, Mo,
Geremie Barmé, Sang Ye, Fergus
Bordewich, Lo Zhewen, Li Zhiliang
and the supportive staff of
the Guidebook Company.

Grateful acknowledgement is made to the following
authors and publishers for permissions granted:

John Murray Publishers Ltd for *The Book of Ser Marco
Polo* by Sir Henry Yule

Les Editions Nagel for *Nagel's Encyclopedia Guide: China;*
Derk Bodde for *Peking Diary: 1948–49, A Year of Revolution*. Reprinted by kind permission of the author

Henri Vetch for *In Search of Old Peking* by L.C. Arlington
and William Lewisohn (Peking 1935). Reprinted with an
introduction by Geremie Barmé. Oxford University Press
1987

Peking by Juliet Bredon, first published by Kelly and
Walsh, Shanghai 1919. Reprinted from the 1931 edition
with an introduction by H.J. Lethbridge. Oxford University Press 1982

The Moon Year by Juliet Bredon and Igo Mitrophanow,
first published by Kelly and Walsh, Shanghai, 1927.
Reprinted by Oxford University Press 1982

The Adventures of Wu by H.Y. Lowe, first published by
The Peking Chronicle Press in 1940 and 1941.
Reprinted by kind permission of the author

Excerpt from *The Soul of China* by Richard Wilhelm,
copyright 1928 by Harcourt Brace Jovanovich Inc., and
renewed 1956 by John Jolroyd Reece. Reprinted by kind
permission of the publisher

Contents

Contents

Introduction

The city of Beijing is probably as old as Chinese civilization itself, as Peking man inhabited the caves at Zhoukoudian in the suburbs some 500,000 years ago. Written records attest to local settlements dating from around 1000 B.C., and for all but a few of the last 800 years, Beijing has been the capital of the empire—be it Mongol, Han Chinese, Manchu, republican or communist. Ever since Marco Polo reported on the splendour of Cambaluc, as he referred to the 13th-century Mongol capital Khanbaligh, Peking has captured the Western imagination like few other ancient cities.

The contents of the vast curiosity shop known as Old Peking, stocked with the customs, manners, language and material culture of centuries of inhabitants, remained remarkably undisturbed by the ravages of time until the beginning of the 20th century. But the collapse of the Qing Dynasty in 1911, the Japanese occupation (1937–45) and the subsequent communist takeover in 1949 took their toll on some of the more fragile contents of the shop and its gentle proprietors. In the 1950s the communists had little trouble transforming the city in their own image, developing a proletarian sprawl relieved occasionally by pockets of imperial pomp and socialist privilege.

While the current regime cannot be held entirely responsible for the transformation of Old Peking into New Beijing, the post-1949 government, with Mao at the helm, created the vast Tiananmen Square in the very heart of Beijing; dismantled the monumental city walls and gates (*the coup de grâce* of Old Peking); commandeered scores of imperial places and gardens, Buddhist and Taoist temples, and Manchu princes' mansions—many of them formerly opened to the public—for use as their private homes, offices, military barracks, and *dachas*; and reduced the more than 3,000 restaurants in 1949 to several hundred soup kitchens. But on the last two points there have been significant improvements over the last decade.

Despite these changes, some of them the inevitable consequences of modernisation, the visitor to today's Beijing can experience much of the former grandeur of the places, temples and gardens of Old Peking, once equipped with a modicum of history, folklore and imagination. *Beijingwalks* was written to provide a stimulus for such visions.

Rather than dwelling on the sins of the past, this guide provides clues to help the visitor rekindle the aura that once surrounded Old Peking. There are maps and detailed instructions of where to go and what to see, as well as enough fact, legend and rumour to forge some of the missing links between the past and the present. In the chapter on the Forbidden City, for example, some curious details of the emperors' private lives are included, while the description of the former Legation Quarter quotes the strikingly candid observations of a Dutch diplomat from the turn of the century. Our approach has been eclectic and our intent to inform as well as to entertain.

We would have liked this book to have been twice as long, given the wealth of available information, but then it would be a book for sitting rather than walking.

Beijing is an elusive city, where the dreamlike is constantly clashing with the everyday. Much of what matters still takes place behind walls, with the fate of a billion people balancing in the trembling hands of a few elderly gentlemen. Given this quirk of history, the true personality of the city will not reveal itself readily to the uninformed. *Beijingwalks* encourages the visitor to break down the intimidating walls, to look behind the millions of bricks encircling the Forbidden City, to bask in the sunset over the Western Hills, and to weather the spring dust storms blowing through Tiananmen Square. Beijing presents a challenge to all, but a challenge worth taking, for sooner or later, the city touches all who come close to her.

Don J. Cohn
Zhang Jingqing
Chek Nai Ping, Hong Kong
October 1991

Information
and Advice

VISAS

All holders of foreign passports need a visa to enter China. Visas can be obtained at Chinese embassies and consulates abroad, through travel agents, and with proper documentation (such as a letter of introduction from a Chinese company or a confirmed reservation at a hotel in China) at the Beijing, Shanghai and Guangzhou airports.

Tourist visas are generally valid for two months after the day of issue, for a single visit of one month's duration. Tourist visas can be extended for an additional month at the Foreign Affairs section of any office of the Public Security Bureau.

If you are travelling to China with a group of ten or more people, a group visa will usually be issued. With group visas, individual passports will be sighted but not stamped by Immigration officials upon entry and exit.

A tourist visa gives you access to over 500 'open' cities in China. In Beijing you are free to go anywhere in the city except for those places where armed guards with nasty looks on their faces stop you from proceeding further. In the suburbs you may encounter signs in English (and sometimes Russian) stating that foreigners are not allowed to travel beyond this point. Though these checkpoints may not be manned, you face being kicked out of China if you are caught beyond them, as they often mark the limits of a military base.

CLIMATE AND DRESS

Although Beijing can claim to have four seasons, the finest days of the year are limited to a few fleeting weeks in spring and fall.

Winters are bitterly cold and dry, summers hot with varying humidity. The famous dust storms of March and April that have plagued the city for centuries colour the atmosphere yellow and sometimes orange with silt from the Mongolian plains. They can be depressing, terrifying and choking, as well as a great bother, as the dust lands everywhere, even seeping its way into sealed closets. Peking dust is so fine it seems to be able to penetrate glass.

For the winter, a hat, gloves and long underwear are strongly recommended in addition to warm outerwear. The interiors of many buildings are barely heated in winter and are uncomfortably cold by Western standards. Many Chinese office and factory workers wear their overcoats while they work.

For fall and spring the best advice is to bring layers that can be peeled off and replaced as necessary. Shoes should be light and sturdy. Running shoes are a fine choice.

Informal dress is the rule except for business meetings and banquets, where you will be judged by what you wear as much as by your title. Business cards in Chinese stating your title are as important in making a good impression as anything you wear.

You can buy a wide range of clothing in the small to medium size range in shops all over Beijing. The Friendship Store has some larger sizes and provides quality tailoring.

STAYING HEALTHY

The following suggestions may sound extreme to some, but I prefer to err on the side of caution. I know of few people who are adventurous purveyors of street food who have not on occasion paid with stomach pains for their pleasures.

On the other hand, few foreign tourists get sick in China in the first place, and those who do usually contract a relatively small range of illnesses. The most popular ailment in dry, dusty Beijing are upper respiratory infections (URIs), better known as throat colds. Chinese people believe these can be prevented by dressing warmly (most Chinese think Westerners wear too little clothing, particularly in the transitional seasons of fall and spring) and by drinking lots of (boiled) water. URIs can be treated with vitamin C and *Yin qiao jie du wan/pian*, available at nearly all chemists in China.

Two cardinal health rules for travel in China:

1. never take a drop of unboiled water into your mouth, and
2. wash your hands before every meal.

When you brush your teeth, you should try to rinse your mouth with boiled water rather than tap water. Peel all fruit, and avoid all unpeelable raw vegetables unless they are scrupulously washed and dried. Salads at the best joint venture hotels are unlikely to create stomach problems.

The reasons for the above: human nightsoil fertilizer is widely used on Chinese farms and food transport and handling is not up to Western standards.

In restaurants try to avoid using chopsticks that could be carrying germs from a previous user. Painted (with unscratched tips) or heavy plastic chopsticks that can be dried completely are preferable to absorbent bamboo chopsticks. Consider acquiring your own set of chopsticks or bring along a few dozen pair of disposibles, readily available in department stores.

The first thing to avoid in restaurants with questionable sanitary standards is cold dishes. Anything that is cooked and still hot is likely to be safe.

China has no vaccination requirements for short term visitors, but people planning to work or live in the country for six months or longer must submit the results of a recent Aids test or be subject to a Chinese test. For the latest rules consult Chinese consulates or embassies.

The U.S. State Department has at various times recommended a long list of vaccinations for long term residents or travellers to some of the border districts, particularly in the southwest and northwest: gama globulin (for hepatitis A), hepatitis B, Japanese B encephalitis (not available in the U.S.A., but in China and Hong Kong), cholera, tetanus, polio and malaria. Consult your physician or the appropriate health authority concerning these vaccinations.

EMERGENCIES

In case of medical emergencies of a life threatening nature, call 120 for the Beijing Emergency Centre, which operates a fleet of ambulances. You will naturally save time if a Chinese speaker makes the first contact, but if none is available, you could begin with 'Speak English?' and wait until someone who does comes on the line.

If you are staying in a joint-venture foreign managed hotel, the front desk or assistant manager would probably be able to get an ambulance faster than you could. If you are in a small native hotel where the staff does not speak English well you would do just as well to call the Centre directly.

If an ambulance seems unnecessary or is unavailable, take a taxi to the emergency rooms of one of the following hospitals:

Peking Union Medical College Hospital (P.U.M.C.)
Xie he yi yuan (comprehensive hospital with a large
clinic for foreigners)
Dongdan beidajie
Telephone: 5127733

Sino-Japanese Friendship Hospital
Zhong Ri you hao yi yuan
Hepingli Beijie
Telephone: 4221122

Sino-German Policlinic *Zhong De zhen suo* (privately
run 24 hour ambulance service; performs minor
surgery)
Basement, Landmark Tower, 8 Dong Sanhuanlu
Telephone: 5011983, 5016688, ext. 20903
Beijing Friendship Hospital
Yong'an Lu, Tianqiao
Telephone: 3014411

It is impossible to generalize about the quality of Chinese
medical services, but in Beijing doctors tend to be thorough
and reliable. Most foreign residents prefer to travel abroad
for major medical and dental treatment.

A handful of foreign embassies provide medical
service for their nationals, but as a rule embassy medical
staff are not permitted to practice in Chinese hospitals. In
case of emergency they should be sought out on a consulting
basis only.

DIRECTIONS

Most directions will be given as compass points, in traditional Pekinese style. Much of the city is laid out on a north–
south axis, which makes this quite practical. If seems this
difficult to manage, bring a compass along, follow the sun,
or keep a map handy.

MONEY

The principal unit of currency is the *yuan* (pronounced like the letters UN sounded in quick succession) which is divided into 100 *fen* (pronounced like 'fun').

There are two systems of currency, soft and hard. The RMB (renminbi or 'people's money') is the domestic unit, and Foreign Exchange Certificates, known as FEC, is what the bank hands (or throws, as bank clerks can be quite rude) to you when you exchange your hard currency.

FEC has an English message printed on the back of each bill. It is issued in denominations of 10 and 50 *fen*, and 1, 5, 10, 50 and 100 *yuan*. The coins, worth 1, 2 and 5 *fen*, are RMB, but perversely while the bank will hand out these coins when you exchange your foreign money, banks and hotels refuse to accept them for payment in FEC. Rmb notes start at 1, 2, 5, 10, 20 and 50 *fen*, and leap to 1, 2, 5, 10, 50 and 100 *yuan*. China's C-note features portraits of four deceased veteran revolutionaries—Mao Zedong, Zhou Enlai, Zhu De and Liu Xiaoqi, while the 50 *yuan* whopper carries stereotyped mugshots of a peasant, soldier, worker and, thanks to Deng Xiaoping, a Shanghai-style intellectual.

You will enjoy precisely the same exchange rate everywhere in China—at banks, stores, and hotels. Traveller's cheques will fetch you about one percent more FEC than cash.

Until recently there was a brisk black market for FEC and foreign currency in China, but recent devaluations of the *yuan* have brought the official and black market exchange rates to within a 10 percent spread. The short term visitor is unlikely to encounter or need to use Rmb unless he or she receives it in change. Rmb can only be exchanged back to foreign currency in small amounts at the Bank of China at airports at a very heavy discount. When you leave the country, an exchange memo must be presented to the bank when exchanging FEC for foreign currency. The most convenient place to do this is at the Bank of China counters at the airport. At the Beijing airport there are exchange counters on both sides of customs and immigration.

Some hotels require payment in FEC but now many goods, including imported cigarettes and liquor, can be bought with Rmb. Otherwise Rmb is the currency of the realm.

Rmb notes can be extraordinarily filthy. In food shops, they are handled with tweezers by clerks who also handle food.

TRANSPORT

The six walks described in this book will take you to some of the far corners of Beijing. Taxis are the fastest way to get around the city especially if you time your movements to avoid rush-hour traffic jams, particularly on Chang'an Boulevard. Taxis can be hailed in the street, and most hotels have their own queues and/or fleets. Taxis can be booked for half a day, an entire day, or for longer durations. Extra charges are assessed for overtime, going beyond the city limits or waiting. Deals can be made with individual drivers. Hotel taxis booked through the hotel usually charge the highest rates. Fares average 2 *yuan* per kilometre, with a four km flagfall, though a 4 *yuan* surcharge raises the minimum charge to 12 *yuan*. A taxi to or from the airport will cost about 80–100 *yuan*.

The Beijing Underground (metro), built beneath the scars left when the city walls were demolished, is useful for several of the walks. Buses (painted cream and red) and trolley-buses (painted pale green) can be extremely crowded during the day, but they are cheap and convenient. Make sure you have small change—10 and 50 *fen* notes, or coins. Beijing, being monotonously flat (otherwise the emperors would not have built their own mountains in the city), is ideal for bicycle riding, and most major thoroughfares have bicycle lanes. Bicycles can be rented in many places. Be sure to watch your pockets, purses and luggage on public transport and in all public places.

HOTELS

The number of joint-venture hotels in Beijing has mush-roomed—no, exploded, over the last ten years due to a combination of ambitious officials on the Chinese side and starry-eyed hoteliers on the foreign side. Competition is fierce, discounts are commonplace and quality can be high, although even the best hotels grow shabby fast due to the harsh climate and rough treatment by both staff and guests. It's an old joke that a hotel in China is two years old by the time it opens. At least a dozen hotels in Beijing can provide their guests with an oasis of comforts and conveniences that will enable them to forget they are smack in the middle of the Third World, if they wish: bowling alleys, beauty and off-track betting parlours, wine cellars, swimming pools and gold Roll Royces.

At the other end of the spectrum, several budget hotels provide perfectly adequate accommodation for those who intend to spend most of their time exploring the city rather than, for example, peddling an exercise bicycle to disco music in an air conditioned solarium. Many of the guests in these basic hotels are Chinese business people from out of town, who may be renting a room in the hotel on a long term basis.

Sandwiched in between the luxury properties and the budgets are the older Chinese run standbys that were the backbone of the local tourist industry during the late 1970s and early 1980s. The Qianmen, Friendship, Xinqiao Huadu, Xiyuan and Minzu, to name a few, have been upgraded to keep up with the joint-venture competition, but still seem unwilling or unable to shake off the symptomatic afflictions and affectations of socialism Chinese style. One advantage (some would say) of staying in this class of accommodation is that you always know you are in China, a fact all too easy to forget once you are ensconced in a luxury joint venture hotel.

Electricity in China is 220 volts, and wobbly at times, so computer users should bring a voltage stabilizer. Plug compatibility can be a problem, and as there is no standard in China, you might bring along a conversion device. The lavatories in the better hotels are equipped with hair dryers.

Security is not a major problem, but in the more modest hotels it is wise to leave no visible temptations, such as cameras or electronic devices, in the room. Cash and valuables should be placed in a safety deposit box at the front desk.

Because Beijing has no single downtown area and thus no cultural or business center, the location of a hotel is not an important factor in deciding where to stay, unless of course you will be conducting business in a particular place. All joint venture hotels have high quality restaurants serving Chinese, Western and other cuisines, often at reasonable prices.

Because power is habitually concentrated at the top in China, seek out the hotel's general manager if something goes wrong. Assistant managers are often rather helpless when it comes to dealing with the staff beneath them.

RESTAURANTS

Now that three Colonel Sanders Kentucky Fried Chicken outlets have blown away the mystery of dining in Beijing once and for all, it may be easy to forget that excellent Chinese food can be had at reasonable prices in small restaurants throughout the city.

The cuisine at the top notch hotels can be relied on to be excellent, but food ordered a la carte at the Chinese-run hotels, such as the Beijing Hotel, Minzu (Minorities) and Qianmen, usually runs to the mediocre. On the other hand, a pre-ordered banquet from the same kitchen at one of these hotels can be a marvellous culinary experience. This

is because the hotels are constantly training new kitchen staff.

Another factor influencing the quality of the food in certain cases is who you are. Banquets hosted and ordered by Chinese officials or businessmen tend to be more satisfactory than similar banquets ordered by a foreigner. One way around this is to ask your Chinese host or a Chinese acquaintance to do the booking and ordering.

Ordering a meal at modest, non-tourist establishments presents the problem of language. One solution is to give the waiter/waitress a fixed amount per person, say 20 to 50 *yuan*, and let the chef pick a meal for you. Of course you can always point to what others are eating, carry a bilingual dictionary with you, or ask someone who knows Chinese to write down the names of a few dishes on a piece of paper.

All Chinese restaurants high and low provide diners with chopsticks and a spoon. Very few restaurants stock forks and of course knives are not needed for Chinese food (Confucius said it was uncivilised to have knives on the dining table). If you cannot wield chopsticks, bring along a supply of disposable plastic forks unless you plan to confine your dining to tourist hotel restaurants.

Many restaurants in China operate on rather restricted hours. Lunch is served from about 11:00 A.M. to 2:00 P.M. and dinner from about 5:00 to 8:00 P.M.. If you arrive at a restaurant one half hour before the posted closing time, you are very likely to be refused a table. The closing time indicates the hour when the staff wants to be locking the front door of the restaurant from outside, having cleaned the place up and changed their clothes, etc. Much of Beijing operates according to the principle of early to bed, early to rise, early to stop working.

Every restaurant in Beijing will arrange banquets, but tables should be booked at least one day in advance. A standard table can accommodate from eight to eleven or twelve diners, but the standard is ten. Prices will range from 30 to 500 *yuan* per person. Fifty *yuan* per capita is the bare minimum for foreigners at a quality local restaurant, while 80 to 100 *yuan* per person is what you will pay at a joint-venture hotel. When booking, you can specify that you do not want to eat certain ingredients, such as the notorious sea cucumber or fish maws, as most banquets include precious items like these as a matter of course. Specific dishes can also be requested.

Peking roast duck is available at a dozen restaurants in Beijing. It is usually served at the climax of a lavish meal, as few people can handle more than two or three servings of the rich fatty flesh. Most of the roast duck restaurants in Beijing serve an all duck banquet that includes the liver, heart, brain and webs as well as a soup of duck broth and milk.

To sample traditional snacks, have lunch or dinner al fresco on the shore of Front Lake, north of Beihai Park, where around two dozen small shops run a very clean and economical operation. There is a night market offering similar snacks on Dong hua men Street near Wangfujing.

Chinese working folk often buy and consume their breakfast in the street. Peddlars sell large hunks of deep-fried bread that resembles an elephant's ear, long deep-fried crullers, and crepes wrapped around a fried egg, all freshly made before your eyes. These are nicely washed down with warm sweet soy bean milk.

TIPPING

Tipping is officially discouraged in China but has become a way of life on the tourist circuit: guides and bus drivers expect tips from foreign tourists travelling in groups.

Joint venture hotels and restaurants add a service charge to the bill and no tip is necessary above and beyond that, although there is no reason not to reward extraordinary service. When taking a taxi in Beijing, drivers do not expect tips. On the other hand, if you book a taxi for the day and the driver is extraordinarily helpful, you might throw in a few *yuan* beyond the fixed rate.

Needless to say, Chinese people never tip and some find the idea of tipping difficult to understand.

ENTERTAINMENT

'Beijing nightlife' was once a contradiction in terms. The situation has improved considerably since the early 1980s.

For cultural events in the city, consult the *China Daily*, the only English daily newspaper published in the country. Standard fare includes Peking opera, acrobatics, magic shows, dance dramas, Western operas sung in Chinese, and films. There are several dozen cinemas in Beijing, but all films are dubbed in Chinese. Consult the cultural section of your embassy for further suggestions about what's on.

International concert artists and the occasional rock band show up in Beijing from time to time, however most of the tickets for world-class performers are distributed through the back door and the performances are announced after as a matter of public record only—in other words, as a feather in the regime's Mao cap.

Watching Chinese television is a good way to learn the language and/or bore yourself to sleep at night. Western movies (and those from Albania and Uruguay) shown on television are always dubbed in Chinese, so everyone from Shirley Temple to Rock Hudson can be heard jabbering away in crisp standard Mandarin. With over 80 percent saturation, watching television is the most popular form of entertainment for local residents.

Most of the joint-venture hotels have discos which stay open till the wee hours. Some of the most popular are the Talk of the Town at the China World Hotel, Juliana's at the Holiday Inn Lido, Rumours at the Palace Hotel, Xanadu at the Shangri-La and the Amigo Disco at the Yanshan Hotel (a favourite hangout for foreign students, near the Friendship Hotel in the Haidian district). For dancing to live music, there is Cosmos at the Great Wall Sheraton and Point After and Picadilly at the Palace Hotel.

Popular bars include the Brauhaus in the West Wing of the China Trade Centre, Charlie's Bar at the Jianguo Hotel, the Peacock at the Shangri-La, and the Red Lion on the top floor of the China World Tower. For a casual, American-style bar serving heartwarming hamburgers and french fries, visit Frank's Place near the Worker's Stadium, where owner Frank Siegel tends the bar. Frank's Place is an oasis of familiarity with a regular crowd of businessmen, diplomats, journalists and foreign students.

Walking around the city at night is safe and pleasant. The parks are open until sundown in summer, and are popular among Chinese families. The night markets for local snacks at Dong hua men da jie and the Front Lake behind Beihai Park are excellent destinations. Tiananmen Square is slightly unreal at any time of day, and at night it takes on an even more unworldly aspect as the ghost of Chairman Mao in his mausoleum confronts the spirits of the innocent souls killed in the vicinity of the square on the night of 4 June, 1989.

SHOPPING

Beijing cannot claim to be 'the shopping capital of Asia,' but there is a wide range of goods for sale.

Contemporary Chinese arts and crafts are not to everyone's taste. The range of goods includes cloisonne, cork carvings, papercuts, puppets, kites, embroidered blouses, crocheted table cloths, batik printed cottons, toys, combs, artists' materials, jewellery, bamboo ware and lacquer ware.

But for inexpensive goods Beijing offers many shopping opportunities. Excellent and curious buys, particularly in the housewares and stationery departments, can be found in the huge Beijing Department Store (Beijing bai huo da lou) in Wangfujing Street about a ten-minute walk north from the Beijing Hotel, the Dong'an Bazaar further up the street, or in Xidan Shopping Complex. Remember that the average Chinese family in Beijing makes do with about U.S.$30 a week at least half of which is spent on food, which should suggest the sort of bargains available.

Every tourist hotel devotes large plots to shops or shopping arcades, but the range of goods in such places tends to be what the sellers think foreign tourists ought to buy, rather than what tourists actually want.

The Beijing Friendship Store *(You yi shang dian)* occupies four floors of a huge building near the embassy quarter in Jian guo men wai. It is more like a socialist Sears Roebuck than the Bloomingdale's or Harrod's the Chinese may have been dreaming about. There are sections devoted to jewellery, tailored clothing, rugs, fresh and canned food, silk, cashmere, leather, books and imported periodicals, tea, medicine, imported booze and smokes, flowers and a complete range of arts and crafts. While the atmosphere is not remarkably friendly, it is an efficient place to shop for gifts or practical items. The Friendship Store has a shipping department that will arrange transport (reliable but costly) of goods purchased at the store or elsewhere. Major credit cards accepted, but inquire about the commission you may have to pay.

There are free markets in every corner of Beijing, most of them selling food. The bargaining and haggling over prices that takes place at these markets provides a treasure trove for linguists and anthropologists, whose erudition is often essential to distinguish the cackling of ducks, geese and chicken from the squabbling of housewives. Two popular clothing outlets aimed at the foreign tourist and resident market are the narrow alley near the Jianguo Hotel, and the smaller market in Sanlitun near the Workers' Stadium. In both of these markets and in every shopping venue in Beijing you will see entrepreneurial tourists from Eastern Europe and the Soviet Union buying up cheap Chinese goods, especially silk and down clothing, to sell when they get back home. You can also see bottles of Russian vodka on sale in these markets, evidence of micro-economic barter trade between China and the Soviet Union.

Bronze vat, used for fire protection, the Forbidden City

There are great bargains to be found in the antiques shops but caution is advised. A new generation of antiques traders carefully read all the latest Sotheby's and Christie's sales catalogues, and know world prices for their goods. Chinese customs forbids the export of a remarkably broad range of cultural relics, although these rules are difficult to enforce. Generally speaking, Hong Kong is a better place to buy fine Chinese antiques, but as the rule goes for shopping everywhere, if you see something you like and can afford it comfortably, buy it without further consideration, because you may never see it again—at least not until you get to Hong Kong.

Chapter 2 treats Liu li chang, sometimes called Antiques Street, where there are both official and privately run stores. The antiques market near the north gate of the Temple of Heaven *(Tian tan bei men)* on Tiantan lu, the furniture market at Chaowai (near the northwest corner of Ritan Park) and the expanding facility at Jingsong are worth visiting, if only to observe the revival of the civilised art of antiques dealing.

A few favourite shopping items:

' Mao' hats and 'Mao' suits
> Swiss-army style knives
> Cotton goods of all sorts
> Chinese art books
> Woven straw boxes
> Fountain pens and hard bound blank books
> Silk long underwear
> Flat-soled cotton shoes
> Blue and white covered teacups
> ' Purple' stoneware teapots from Yixing
> Political posters (Xinhua Bookstore)

ESSENTIAL TELEPHONE NUMBERS

Note: When calling or faxing from abroad, the international dialing code for Beijing in 861.

Beijing tourist hotline (24 hours)	5130828
Beijing Emergency Centre	120
International Operator	115
Domestic Operator	113
Beijing Directory Information	114
Domestic Directory Information	116
Beijing Suburban Operator	118
Time	117
Weather	121

Air China Ticket Office	6016667
Air China Domestic Reservations	4014441
Air China International Reservations	6013336
Capital Airport	555402, 552515, 557396
Beijing Railway Station	5128931, 5129515
Capital Taxi Company	863661
Beijing Taxi Company	8322561
Visa Department, Public Security Bureau	553102
Foreigners Section, Public Security Bureau	5128871, 555486
Bank of China	338521
Embassies: U.S.A.	5323831
U.K.	5321961
Australia	5322331
Canada	5323536
New Zealand	5322731
France	5321331
Germany	5322161
Italy	5322131
Japan	5322361
India	5321856
U.S.S.R.	5322051

INFORMATION

It can be surprisingly difficult to obtain information in Beijing. On the one hand, a history of secretiveness growing out of Chinese political practice makes the local people reluctant to share information openly with strangers, be they Chinese or foreign. Under Chinese socialism, information is capital, and is doled out by the state as a reward for obedience. Chinese ministries and bureaus are notorious for keeping their activities to themselves, or at least within the confines of their own vertical hierarchies. China suffers intensely from a crippling, feudalistic lack of horizontal interaction between 'work units' and people.

On the more mundane level, a pretty telephone operator in an large organization will even be reluctant to tell you the name of the organization you have dialed. Thus, for instance, getting an airline schedule often requires a major effort, and the airline itself only makes information about flight changes available to the public at the very last moment, as if by keeping it to themselves they can earn more 'interest' on it.

It is worthwhile seeking out information from more than one source in China, since the situation described above makes it easy for people to give out false information with impunity. You asked me a question, I didn't ask you anything. I answered your question for you, what does it matter if the answer is correct or not?

Visitors should also be wary of depending on local residents, be they Chinese or foreign, for accurate answers to questions about the city. Most Beijing residents, for example, have not visited the Forbidden City for at least ten years, and few long-term foreign residents know the nuts and bolts of getting around Beijing as a tourist, since they have their own lavish flats and cars and often their own cooks.

HISTORICAL AND CULTURAL BACKGROUND

Culture Shock

As a third world country and the most densely populated nation on earth, there is much about China to assail the senses and the mind of the first time visitor.

Many first-time visitors are stunned by the crowds in Chinese cities. An endless sea of black hair about five and a half feet off the sidewalk rises and falls in gentle peaks and waves and there is more inadvertent physical contact than most Western folk are accustomed to. You will encounter dazzling heights of human density in buses, shops, popular tourist sites and train stations, to mention a few places, but both the people and the venue somehow manage to cope.

Garlic breath is a common winter phenomenon in Beijing, as the bulb eaten raw is an essential part of North Chinese cuisine as well as a folk remedy for colds.

Many public toilets reak to a degree rarely experienced in the West and few are provided with toilet paper. Beijing boasts a number of pay toilets (10–20 *fen*), many of them in the sites described in this book, which can be rated tolerable. Women's rooms are often little more than a row of holes in the floor with no dividers between them. In China privacy of any sort is a luxury only few can enjoy. It is advised to bring your own toilet paper and premoistened tissues with you wherever you go in China.

It sometimes appears that Chinese people have a greater tolerance for noise than Westerners, and certainly few pedestrians flinch when a brain splitting bus screeches as it passes by.

In some places in Beijing you may be stared at by the locals, but certainly less so than in a small town in China. As a rule, such stares are curious rather than hostile, and you could ignore them, enjoy them or simply stare back. In the early 1980s, young Chinese would fix their gaze on a foreign visitor to catch up on the latest fashions; today the foreigner is just as likely to be astounded or amused by something a Beijing teenybopper is wearing or doing with his or her hair.

CHINESE LANGUAGE

Mandarin Chinese, or *pu tong hua*, is spoken by nearly everyone in Beijing. Natives of Beijing, who represent perhaps 65 percent of the population of the city, speak the patois of the hutongs, *Bei jing hua* (Beijing speech), which is to standard Mandarin Chinese what taxi-driver Brooklynese is to Chicago English, or cockney to B.B.C.

English. *Beijinghua* can be distinguished by its drawled 'r' at the end of words and a twang that sounds distinctly Texan. Many people get the impression that speakers of *Beijinghua* are forever trying to swallow their tongues. An angry Beijing coloratura in a Beijing market can scare the feathers off the chicken she is haggling over.

One obvious reason Chinese is difficult for English speakers to learn is that it is entirely lacking in cognates except for a few words such as coolie and kowtow. The four tones of *putonghua* create havoc for many beginning learners, and the writing system, with some 8,000 characters in common use, extends the elementary learning time by about two years beyond that required for an alphabetic language.

The good news is that English is now China's second language and it is easy to find someone who speaks it in most situations in Beijing. Visitors should make an extra effort to speak slowly, simply and without idioms or colloquialisms if they wish to be understood.

Listening to Chinese people speaking English presents similar challenges. The numbers 13 and 30, 14 and 40, 15 and 50, 16 and 60, 17 and 70, 18 and 80, 19 and 90 sound exasperatingly similar when pronounced by many Chinese speakers of English, so beware and write prices down on paper, particularly when dealing with thousands and millions.

Learning a few Chinese phrases can be useful, as well as fun even if it only gets you as far as evoking the occasional smile from a taxi driver or sales clerk. In the following, a question mark indicates a rising tone and an exclamation mark a falling tone.

	pinyin	**phonetic**
Hello	*Ni hao*	Knee how?
Goodbye	*Zai jian*	Zigh g-n

Thank you	*Xie xie*	Syieh syieh!
How much?	*Duo shao*	Dwaugh show (shower)
No	*Bu*	Boo!
Good	*Hen hao*	Hun how
Bad	*Bu hao*	zBoo! how

Names

Place names, using the official Chinese pinyin system of romanization, will be divided into syllables upon first appearance, and written in the standard form thereafter: Liu li chang, then Liulichang.

Emperors' names, such as Yongle (Yung Lo), Kangxi (K'ang Hsi), and Qianlong (Ch'ien Lung) are not these gentlemen's personal names but rather designations for their reign periods. However, for the sake of convenience, we will follow the popular convention and refer to the emperors by their reign titles.

What's in a name

Pekin? Peking? Peiping? Beijing? Beiping? The world remains divided on this sticky issue. Some see the *pinyin* 'Beijing'—pronounced like 'paging' with a 'b' instead of 'p'—as a pedantic intrusion into the domestic affairs of the English language. But no matter how you spell it, the present name of the city means 'northern capital.' In 1935, seven years after the capital had been relocated in Nanjing (southern capital) and Beijing renamed Peiping (northern plain, or peace), a guidebook published by the *Peiping Chronicle* devoted an entire page to this issue:

Why 'Guide to Peking' when this is Peiping?

Because:

1. The average tourist is not so much interested in the city of today, which is Peiping,
   as he is in the city of past—Peking.

2. Peiping is so new a name that many of the tourists still feel more familiar with the name Peking, and are more apt to buy a 'Guide to Peking' than a 'Guide to Peiping'.

3. What's in a name, anyway?

Borrowing this logic, in this book 'Peking' will be used to designate the city of the past and 'Beijing' to indicate the present-day capital.

Dynasties and Republics

Several dynasties and imperial reigns figure prominently in the city's history. The bone structure of Beijing is predominantly Ming, laid over a Yuan blueprint; most of the vital architectural organs are Qing; the city's complexion today, warts and beauty marks included, is Republican and People's Republican.

From about 1000 B.C., a series of small states made the area around Beijing their capital. While the emperors of the Han, Tang and Song dynasties built their capitals in central and eastern China, Beijing was under barbarian rule or served as a northern outpost of the empire. In the 10th century, the Khitans, a non-Chinese horde, founded the Liao dynasty and established their capital Yanjing here; in the 12th century, the Jurchen Tartars conquered the Liao and named their Jin dynasty capital Zhongdu (central metropolis). The Mongols sacked Zhongdu in 1215, and in 1260 Kublai Khan established the capital of the Yuan dynasty on the same site, calling it Khanbaligh, or Dadu (big metropolis). This was the Cambaluc Marco Polo so lavishly described in his famous travel book. Oddly enough no mention of the Venetian or anyone like him appears in contemporary Chinese records.

In 1368, the Ming dynasty, a Chinese house, succeeded the Yuan and built their capital in south China at Nanjing. And in 1403, Zhu Di, one of the sons of the founding emperor, Zhu Yuanzhang, unseated his nephew, the second Ming emperor, from the throne. Ruling as the Yongle emperor, Zhu Di then began to build his greatly expanded capital Beijing—so named for the first time—on the ruins of Khanbaligh. Yongle's masterpiece, completed in 1420, provided the city with the stately geometric pattern that remains little changed today.

The Qing, or Manchu dynasty (1644–1911), embellished their Ming inheritance by building grand gardens in the western suburbs and erecting a number of splendid mansions, Lamaist temples and dagobas throughout the capital. No expense was spared in the elaboration of the imperial properties, which were off limits to all but members of the imperial clan, officials attending audiences and the thousands of maidens and eunuchs who served the Son of Heaven and his concubines high and low. The most creative Manchus were Kangxi, Qianlong and the notorious, quitschy Empress Dowager Cixi.

During the Republican period (1911–49) scattered attempts were made to create a style of modern Chinese architecture that combined Chinese essence with Western permanence. Examples of this can be seen at Qinghua and Beijing universities. The Kuomintang Nationalists, or K.M.T., moved the capital to Nanjing in 1928, and when the war with Japan broke out in 1937, Old Peking, then renamed Peiping (northern plain), entered into a twilight period of decline.

The People's Liberation Army 'peacefully liberated' Peiping from the Nationalists in 1949, and established it as Beijing, the capital of the People's Republic of China. Documenting the fate of Peking under the communists is made exceedingly difficult by the cloak of secrecy under which the authorities appropriate large plots of land and individual sites, build high walls around them, and in some cases continue to pretend they no longer exist.

The Tiananmen Gate, southern entrance of the Forbidden City

Post liberation architecture during the 1950s is an odd hodgepodge of Soviet wedding cake fantasies, such as the Beijing Exhibition Hall near the zoo, Stalinist neo-classical piles, like the Great Hall of the People, Museum of Chinese History and Beijing Railway Station, and Chinese flavoured buildings like the Friendship Hotel, which was criticized for the high cost of its glazed tile roofs.

During the 1960s, cheap pre-fabricated housing blocks, bland to the eye and depressing to inhabit, went up to accommodate the population explosion, and many of these eyesores dot the main avenues of the city. More fallout shelters and underground tunnels than buildings seem to have been created during the decade of the Cultural Revolution (1966–76).

Beginning in the late 1970s, a slight improvement could be seen in the design of tower blocks and offices, although no building of character was built at this time. A notable exception is I.M. Pei's Fragrant Hills Hotel, which incorporates elements of Suzhou gardens in the hotel's forest setting. Only in the mid-1980s, once the many joint venture hotels and office towers had come on stream, did the authorities in Beijing permit architects to dabble in international styles. At present, the most impressive new buildings in the city are still the joint venture hotels and commercial towers, many of which were designed by architects abroad. The new People's Bank of China building, shaped like a traditional Chinese silver 'shoe' ingot, is an essay in cuteness, but no one can claim it is not Chinese.

Cast of Characters

The following figures have made significant contributions to Peking, and are referred to frequently in the text. Each represents an age.

Yongle: (reigned 1402–24) Third Ming emperor who usurped the throne from his neplew and laid down the pattern of Beijing as it basically stands today. Yongle also restored the Grand Canal to supply the capital with grain and cloth from the south. He dispatched the great Moslem enuch admiral, Zheng He, on seven expeditions into the Indian Ocean, thus establishing China's naval supremacy in Asia for the only time in history; he forced the Japanese into vassal status for the first time, and exacted tribute from as far away as Africa.

Kangxi: (reigned 1661–1722) Son of the first Qing emperor and second emperor of the Qing dynasty. He built gardens in the western suburbs and a summer palace at Jehol (now Chengde), patronized scholarship and the arts, and assigned foreign Jesuits to the Board of Astronomy. He fathered 20 sons and eight daughters who grew to maturity.

Qianlong: (reigned 1736–96) Kangxi's grandson and the fourth Qing emperor. Successful in military affairs, prolific poet and writer, patron of the arts, garden builder, launched a literary inquisition, rejected England's petition for relaxing trade restrictions, tolerated Jesuits in his court. He had 17 sons and 10 daughters, and joined a military campaign at the age of 85.

Cixi: (1835–1908) whose name looks, and nearly is, unpronounceable, was the virtual ruler of China from about 1865 to her death. The old spelling, Tz'u Hsi, is of little help for the uninitiated. Try *Ts'i* (vowel sound as in 'his', like 'hist' pronounced backwards) Schee. Cixi was the:

– concubine of the Xianfeng emperor (reigned 1850–61)

– mother of the Tongzhi emperor (reigned 1861–74)

– aunt, and regent of the Guangxu emperor (reigned 1874–1908) from 1874 to 1888; Guangxu was three years old when he became the emperor in 1874, but only married and began his reign in 1888.

Mao Zedong: (1894–1976) great helmsman of the People's Republic who condemned the city walls and ensconced himself and his cronies in imperial palaces. Mao, who was 13 when Cixi died and 16 when the Qing dynasty fell, spawned the Cultural Revolution (1966–76) that ended with his death.

The Four Cities of Peking: The names of the four contiguous walled cities date from the Qing dynasty and Republican period. The only 'city' standing today is the Forbidden City, the walls of which are intact. Multi-lane highways—including Beijing's Ring Roads—were built where the walls once stood. The four 'cities' during the Qing dynasty and early Republican period were:

– **Tartar (Manchu, or Outer) City, includes the Forbidden and Imperial Cities**; residence was restricted to the imperial troops and the bannermen, who were originally Manchu, Mongol and Han Chinese soldiers organized into eight groups represented by different coloured banners.

– **Imperial City**; home to the members of the imperial clan. Today portion of the Qing-dynasty Imperial City wall surrounds the south and west borders of Zhongnanhai.

– **Forbidden City**; the palace itself, inhabited by the emperor, his female entourage, and thousands of eunuchs.

– **Chinese (or Inner) City**; Chinese residential area and principal urban commercial and entertainment district.

Fengshui Goemancy: *Fengshui* (wind and water) is as scientific, in the modern sense, as astrology. But the history of city planning and architectural design in China cannot be understood without reference to this ancient art. *Fengshui* experts investigate the shapes of bodies of water, hill configurations, and nearby structures to determine the ideal location, size and orientation of a building (or grave, bank, or parking lot) with the aim of enhancing the welfare of its inhabitants. Negative influences that cannot be modified, such as mountains or skyscrapers, can be mollified just as positive influences can be reinforced.

The layout of Peking demonstrates several basic principles of *fengshui*. The major buildings in the Forbidden City rest on a north–south axis that forms the backbone of Beijing. Because evil influences emanate from the north, all of these buildings face south. Prospect Hill (Jing Shan, or Coal Hill), the artificial mound that stands immediately north of the Forbidden City, prevents these evil influences from infiltrating and polluting the palace. According to legend, when the Yongle emperor was planning his new capital in the early 15th century, a geomancer presented him with an anatomical blueprint according to which key locations in the Forbidden and Imperial cities corresponded with the vital organs of a mythical being named Nozha. Like Chairman Mao's embalmed corpse in his mausoleum in Tiananmen Square, Nozha's imaginary head lies to the south with his feet pointing north. Thus, according to contemporary geomancy, Mao's *membrum virile* corresponds to the Memorial to the People's Martyrs.

Hutongs

Pronounced with an 'r' after the o, accent on the second syllable: *hu-torng* is a Chinese transcription of a Mongol word, *hotlog*, that means 'water well'. Many Beijing *hutongs* have colourful names with interesting historical connotations, though in recent decades some of these names have been purged of their 'feudal' content.

The worst historical abuses in this regard were perpetrated during the Cultural Revolution, when lanes and alleys took on names like Red-to-the-End Road, Great Leap

Street and People's Commune Street. Some street names changed many times during this decade.

Altogether some 600 streets and *hutongs* were renamed after 1949. One reason for this was to avoid duplication. According to a 1944 street guide, Beijing had 16 Shoulder Pole (*Bian dan*) Hu tongs, 14 well (*Jing er*) Hutongs, 11 Flower Blossom (*Hua zhi*) Hutongs and seven Arrow Shaft (*Jian gan*) Hutongs. There were also a good number of *hutongs* with names that the local inhabitants found objectionable. Stinking Skin (*Chou pi*) Hutong became Longevity (*Shou bi*) Hutong; Pants Crotch (*Ku dang*) Hutong became Warehouse (*Ku cang*) Hutong; Hang-up-and beat (*Diao da*) Hutong became Perfect Filial Piety (*Xiao da*) Hutong. A small sampling of present-day names suggests their variety: Fried Beans, Bean Sprouts, Split Beans, Big Stone Tiger, Iron Bird, Sheepskin Market, Sesame Seeds, Tea Leaves, Antique Cash, Lamp Wick, Soldiers and Horses, Sound the Drum, Sweet Well, Dog Tail, Big Ears and New Fur Warehouse.

Ethnology

Beijingers, or Pekinese, like most Northern Chinese, are a great mixture of ethnic types. Though most locals identify with the Han majority, their taller-than-average (in China) stature and facial features attest to early intermixture with Mongols, Manchus and other Central and Northern Asian peoples. Beijing has a large population of Moslems (Hui), some of whom are physically indistinguishable from the Chinese population, some with prominent noses and deep sunk eyes. The distinctly Caucasian men selling shashlik in the street (and often found changing money on the black market) are Uighurs, most of whom come from Xinjiang Province. You may observe a wide range of Chinese types and hear their various languages in such popular tourist spots as Wangfujing Street, Tiananmen Square, the Forbidden City, the Summer Palace and the Temple of Heaven.

Chinese Architecture: A few recurring features
Lion-dogs: These playful creatures, always in pairs, guard

entrances to important buildings. Lions are not native to China, but Han-dynasty (206 B.C.–A.D. 220) annals record emperors receiving lions as tribute offerings from Parthian and other Central Asian missions to China. The king of beasts has been considerably domesticated over the years after numerous incarnations in bronze and stone. The female (with mouth closed) is always shown with her cub; the male (roaring, or yawning) is playing with a ball, perhaps representing the sun or the earth. Legend has it that mother lions feed their cubs milk through their paw, and that the ball is a storage place for milk, which can be extracted and used by humans as medicine.

Marble terraces: Following a tradition at least 3,000 years old, all major religious and ceremonial buildings and the residences of the emperor and imperial clan are built on marble terraces, with the height of the terrace indicating the importance of the building. The tallest terrace in Beijing is the foundation of the Three Great Halls in the Forbidden City, 7.12 meters (23.3 feet); the tallest circular terrace in the Temple of Heaven is nearly two meters (six feet) shorter. The Round Altar in the Temple of Heaven is an example of a terrace that is a building in itself. The Chinese name for these structures is 'Mt. Sumeru terraces' (*Xu mi zuo*); according to Indian mythology, Mt. Sumeru is located at the centre of the universe and is trillions of feet in height.

Pailou: A freestanding multi-roofed gateway or arch of wood or stone erected in streets or on the axis of a temple, tomb, or palace. Peking had several dozen street *pailous* in 1949; only a handful remain. On our walks, *pailous* can be seen in Beihai Park, the Summer Palace, on Guozijian Street, and in the Guozijian and Lama Temple. Some scholars suggest that the design of the *pailou* is of Indian origin. Compare the stone gateways at Sanchi with the *pailou* immediately to the north of the Round Altar in the Temple of Heaven.

Roof creatures: Examples of glazed ceramic roof creatures guarding the eaves of important buildings are plentiful in the Forbidden City, where they appear in groups of as many as ten. Often the first 'creature' in the queue is a man mounted on a phoenix. This is Prince Min of the Warring States period (475–221 B.C.), who was rescued from his death by the giant bird on which he is seated. The other animals are auspicious: the dragon and phoenix symbolize harmony and nobility; the lion, ferocity and majesty; the heavenly horse and sea horse, good fortune; the two mythological lion-like creatures, justice; a member of the dragon family wards off fire; a monkey-like creature with wings brings up the rear. The large figures at each end of the ridge of the roof are the offspring of the dragon, responsible for making ocean waves and rain.

Roof tiles: The colour of roof tiles indicates the status of the building. Yellow was reserved solely for imperial ceremonial buildings and dwellings. After imperial yellow, the pecking order descends as follows: blue, green, black, unglazed.

Staircases: In imperial buildings, all of which face south, the terraces usually have three sets of staircases corresponding to the three openings in gate towers. The central staircase, like the central opening, was reserved exclusively for the emperor; looking north, the left (western) staircase was for military officials, the right (eastern) for civil officials. The central imperial staircase was again divided into three sections. The emperor was carried in a sedan chair over a long marble slope, set between two staircases, elaborately carved with the imperial symbols of dragon and phoenix disporting in the waves and clouds. The sedan chair bearers ascended the staircases to the side. Strange though it may seem, the carved marble slope was often covered with a rug.

Lake Taihu stones: The Chinese term for large chunks of limestone that are placed on the bed of a lake or stream to be eroded by the flow of water and time. A crucial decorative element in every Chinese garden, these miniature mountains are typical of the Chinese taste for aged, bent, and grotesque forms (compare two other Chinese inventions, bonsai and bound feet). Because these rocks were produced in the Yangtze delta area they were an exotic luxury in the north. Before they were shipped to Peking on Grand Canal barges, Taihu stones were covered in mud which, when dry, gave them a protective husk.

Walls: In his book on Chinese architecture, D.G. Mirams wrote: *The Chinese wall is not only a wall but a design. It protects and at the same time it embellishes.* The Chinese word for wall, *cheng,* has 'city' as its secondary meaning. Walls divided the city from the country in traditional China, just as the Great Wall was built to protect the agricultural settlements of the Han from the nomadic barbarians. The height of a wall indicates the status of those who live within, but in Peking even the most humble *hutong* hovels had their walls. Domestic luxury in China was inconspicuous.

ZHOU (JOE)
7 WARRING STATES
481 - 221 BC

Simplified Table of Chinese Dynasties

Old Name	Pinyin	Dates
Hsia	Xia	c. 2100 B.C.–1600 B.C.
Shang ANYGAN	Shang	c. 1600 B.C.–1066 B.C.
Chou XIAN	Zhou JOE	c. 1066 B.C.–1071 B.C. 221 B
Ch'in GRT WALL	Qin	c. 221 B.C.–206 B.C.
Han PEKIN JOE	Han	c. 206 B.C.–220
Three Kingdoms		c. 220–280
Sui	Sui	c. 581–618
T'ang	Tang	c. 618–907
Sung	Song	c. 960–1279
Liao	Liao	c. 907–1125
Chin (Khitan)	Jin	c. 1115–1234
Yüan (Mongol)	Yuan	c. 1279–1368
Ming	Ming	c. 1368–1644
Ch'ing (Manchu)	Qing	c. 1644–1911
Republic of China		c. 1911–1949
People's Republic of China		c. 1949

ANCENT EGYPT

ROME

MID AGES

Table of Ming and Qing Dynasty Emperors

Ming Dynasty (1368–1644)

Traditional Spelling	Pinyin	Dates
Hung-wu	Hongwu	1368–1399
Chien-wen	Jianwen	1399–1403
Yung-lo	Yongle	1403–1425
Hung-hsi	Hongxi	1425–1426
Hsüan-te	Xuande	1426–1436
Cheng-t'ung	Zhengtong	1436–1450
Ching-t'ai	Jingtai	1450–1457
T'ien-shun	Tianshun	1457–1464
Ch'eng-hua	Chenghua	1465–1487
Hung-chih	Hongzhi	1488–1505
Cheng-te	Zhengde	1506–1521
Chia-ching	Jiajing	1522–1566
Lung-ch'ing	Longing	1567–1572
Wan-li	Wanli	1573–1619
T'ai-ch'ang	Taichang	1620
T'ien-ch'i	Tiangi	1621–1627
Ch'ung-cheng	Chongzheng	1628–1643

Qing (Ch'ing Dynasty (1644–1911)

Shun-chih	Shunzhi	1644–1661
K'ang-hsi	Kangxi	1662–1722
Yung-cheng	Yongzheng	1723–1735
Ch'ien-lung	Qianlong	1736–1795
Chia-ch'ing	Jiaqing	1796–1820
Tao-kuang	Daoguang	1821–1850
Hsien-feng	Xianfeng	1851–1861
T'ung-chih	Tongzhi	1862–1873
Kuang-hsü	Guangxu	1874–1908
Hsüan-t'ung	Xuantong	1908–1912

Walk · 1

Tiananmen Square and the Forbidden City

The defensive moat surrounding the Forbidden City

Duration

Minimum six hours. If you have the time, divide this walk into two and go on different days. For example, on day one, start with **Tiananmen Square** and explore the south half of the **Forbidden City**. Go back to the Forbidden City a day or two later and see the living quarters and museums in the north section, and conclude by ascending **Prospect Hill**, an ideal place to contemplate the twilight of the empire.

Description

This walk provides an orientation to central Beijing beginning in **Tiananmen Square**, the world's largest public plaza, and takes you into the **Forbidden City**, the world's largest imperial palace. The Forbidden City is open from 8 A.M. to 4 P.M. in winter and from 8.30 A.M. to 5 P.M.in summer.

Starting Point

Monument to the People's Heroes in the centre of Tiananmen Square.

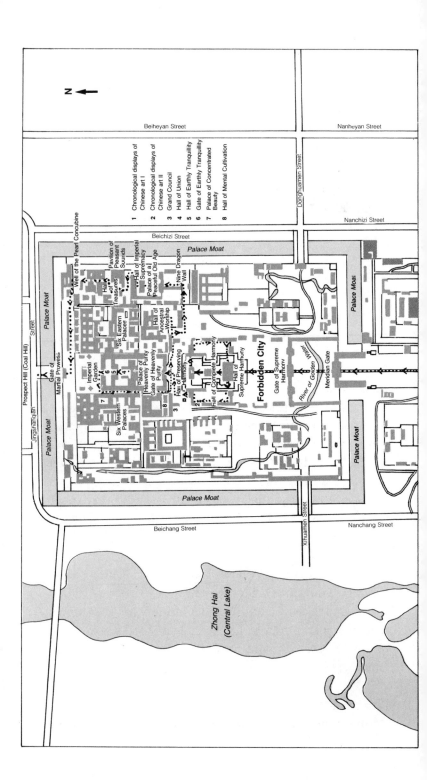

N ←

Beiheyan Street

Nanheyan Street

1 Chronological displays of Chinese art I
2 Chronological displays of Chinese art II
3 Grand Council
4 Hall of Union
5 Hall of Earthly Tranquillity
6 Gate of Earthly Tranquillity
7 Palace of Concentrated Beauty
8 Hall of Mental Cultivation

Donghuamen Street

Nanchizi Street

Beichizi Street

Palace Moat

Well of the Pearl Concubine

Pavilion of Pleasant Sounds

Hall of Imperial Supremacy

Hall of Treasures

Palace of a Peaceful Old Age

Nine Dragon Wall

Six Eastern Palaces

Hall of Ancestral Worship

Palace Moat

Gate of Martial Prowess

Imperial Garden

Palace of Heavenly Purity

Gate of Heavenly Purity

Hall of Preserving Harmony

Hall of Complete Harmony

Hall of Supreme Harmony

Forbidden City

Gate of Supreme Harmony

River of Golden Water

Meridian Gate

Palace Moat

Prospect Hill (Coal Hill)

Jingshanqian Street

Six Western Palaces

Palace Moat

Xihuamen Street

Palace Moat

Beichang Street

Nanchang Street

Zhong Hai (Central Lake)

Palace Moat

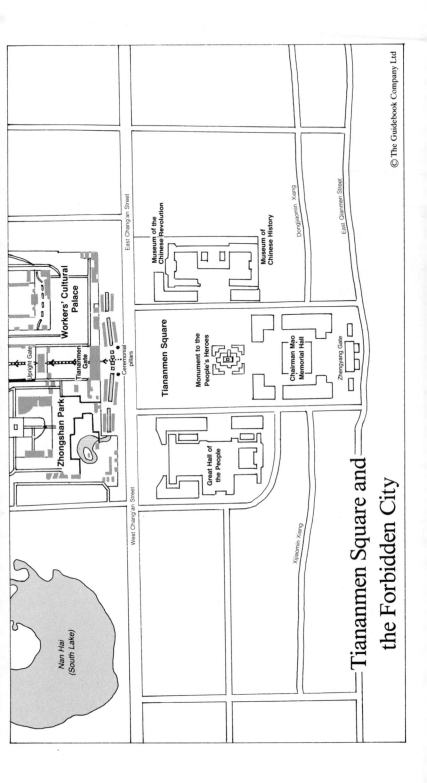

Tiananmen Square and
the Forbidden City

© The Guidebook Company Ltd

How to Get There
Bus routes 1, 2, 4, 5, 10, 20, 52 and 57 stop near the square.
If you take the Beijing underground, get off at Qianmen
Station.

How to Get Away
Bus routes 101, 103 and 109 stop at the rear (north) gate of
the Forbidden City.

Begin by making your way to the prominent **Monument to
the People's Heroes**, erected in 1958 in the centre of
Tiananmen Square. Six years of planning went into this
monolithic political statement, and more than 10,000
people throughout China, including peasants, soldiers and
factory workers were consulted to ensure that the edifica-
tory carved panels on the base of the monument would be
comprehensible to all. Climb the steps on the north side
and face Tiananmen Gate to the north.

First a bit of background. Here on the night of 4 April
1976, during the Qingming festival, a traditional holiday
when Chinese people sweep the graves of their dead
relatives, wreathes commemorating the recently-deceased
Premier Zhou Enlai were removed from the monument by
the police. The response to this act of official desecration
was a popular protest on 5 April that led to mass arrests and
the death of hundreds at the hands of armed troops over the
next few days. In the aftermath Deng Xiaoping was dismissed
from his posts in the Chinese Communist Party and government by the Gang of Four, a leftist junta headed by
Mao's widow Jiang Qing, who blamed Deng for the
breakdown of public order. The government's original
verdict that the Tiananmen Incident of 5 April was 'counter-
revolutionary' in nature was reversed in 1978 following the
fall of the Gang of Four, whereupon it can to be known as
'a completely revolutionary event.' Deng Xiaoping's subsequent rehabilitation and the legitimization of what came to
be called the April Fifth Movement prepared the ground for
the birth of the Chinese democracy movement in the late
1970s.

In China, history has a bad habit of repeating itself with a vengeance. On 4 May 1919, patriotic university students and intellectuals had gathered in front of Tiananmen Gate, the large edifice at the north end of the Square, to protest the Versailles Treaty and the occupation of Shandong Province by the Japanese. The May Fourth Movement that arose from this event, with its slogan 'Democracy and Science,' paved the way for the acceptance of Marxism in China and the birth of the Chinese Communist Party in 1921. Anti-imperialist and other public demonstrations of a patriotic nature were also held in Tiananmen Square in 1925, 1926, 1938 and 1947.

And then in the first days of June 1989, yet another generation of Chinese martyrs was created in the proximity of Tiananmen Square. A few hours before sunrise on 4 June 1989, the Chinese People's Liberation Army (P.L.A.) shot and/or crushed to death with tanks hundreds, if not thousands, of unarmed students and other citizens who had been demonstrating for democratic reforms in defiance of martial law that had been imposed in parts of Beijing in late April. As in several anti-government protests in Tibet since the mid-1980s, the P.L.A. had turned its weapons against the Chinese people. One tragic irony is that the massacre was ordered, or at least condoned, by Deng Xiaoping who ten years earlier had given the green light to post-Cultural Revolution reforms.

In June 4 there are additional parallels with the April Fifth Movement. The 1989 demonstrations began on the Qingming Festival with students mourning the sudden death of Hu Yaobang, who had earlier been dismissed from his post as Party Secretary for, among other things, refraining from cracking down on student protests. The 1989 demonstrations coincided with official celebrations of the 70th anniversary of the May Fourth Movement. After the 4 June massacre, Hu Yaobang's successor as Party Secretary, Zhao Ziyang, was dismissed from his official posts and blamed in part for the chaos, just as Deng had been in 1976. The government justified the use of military force by insisting that the demonstrations joined by millions of Chinese citizens throughout the country (and 1.5 million more in Hong Kong) had become a 'counter-revolutionary insurrection' that had to be suppressed to save China.

From your vantage point on the Monument to the People's Heroes you will be looking at a color portrait of Mao Zedong straight in the eye. On 1 October 1949, the real Mao stood a few feet above his air-brushed forehead with its receding hairline which hangs on **Tiananmen Gate**, the principal entrance to the Forbidden City, and declared, 'The Chinese people have stood up.' This is the same spot where the warlord Yuan Shikai made a public appearance in 1912 after being inaugurated the first President of the Republic of China. Now, for 30 *yuan*, foreigners can mount the gate and declare whatever they please; Chinese peasants, who pay 10 *yuan* for the same privilege, enjoy being photographed here from below with their arm raised in a dramatic gesture.

Mao's portrait, occupying what must be the primest bit of wall space in China, was not always a permanent fixture here. In the early 1950s the Beijing Mona Lisa was only put up on 1 October, China's National Day, and 1 May, International Labour Day. In the early years of the Republican Period (1911–49), the spot was occupied by a blue and white (the Kuomintang colors) portrait of Sun Yat-sen, and later by one of Chiang Kai-shek.

Tiananmen Square is reputed to be the largest urban plaza in the world, with a stated capacity of 500,000 people, each to his own chequerboard brick. Curiously, in the aftermath of the Tiananmen massacre in 1989, a Hong Kong magazine published a letter in which the writer took the Chinese government to task for having built a square so large that a huge mob might take it over and use it for anti-government protests.

But the creation of Tiananmen Square was part of a greater strategic urban plan. Thirty years earlier, in 1958, C.P. Fitzgerald had observed prophetically in his *Flood Tide in China*:

> The purpose of an imperial city was to
> enshrine the palace, which indeed occu-
> pied a very large part of the whole walled
> enclosure . . . Wide straight streets ran
> from north to south and east to west,
> streets far wider than the traffic of the age
> required, a fact which has fortunately saved
> Peking from the sad necessity of demolish-
> ing many ancient buildings to accommo-
> date the traffic of modern times. The
> purpose of this design was probably not so
> much a geomantic requirement as a meas-
> ure of military precaution. The wide streets
> giving unhindered access to all parts of the
> city enabled troops to move swiftly to any
> point threatened by riot or rebellion.[1]

The two top-heavy buildings flanking the square, the **Great Hall of the People** to the west (left), and the **Museum of Chinese History** and the **Museum of the Chinese Revolution** to the east (right), were completed in 1959 during the final days of China's ideological tryst with Russia, and exude the gruff charm of Stalinesque neo-classicism. The **Chairman Mao Mausoleum** behind you was completed in 1977, a year after Mao died in September 1976. Architecturally it represents an attempt to harmonize with the other buildings flanking the square, but it some-how gives an impression of being temporary. To tone down the deification of Mao, a Museum of Revolutionary Heroes devoted to the exploits of Zhou Enlai, Zhu De, Liu Shaoqi and Mao himself (the four worthies on the 100-*yuan* banknote, China's biggest) has been installed on one of the upper floors. The museum features such tricks of the trade as air-brushed photos of the Communist leadership and the toothbrush and towel Chairman Mao used in Yenan.

---

(1) C P Fitzgerald *Flood Tide in China*
     (London: The Cresset Press 1958), pp. 8–9.

Worthwhile stuff for revolution buffs, but not regularly open to the public.

If you wish to view Old Mao's embalmed remains, and are a foreigner or a 'compatriot' from Hong Kong, Macau or Taiwan, you can cut into the usually long queue by approaching the mausoleum entrance in the square from the west. No cameras or handbags are allowed inside. If you don't have a taxi or bus to put them in, there is a checkroom service on the east side of the mausoleum. Mao's body lies sequestered in a discreetly lit crystal coffin that is supposedly lowered into an underground fridge during off-duty hours. One curious rumour has it that Mao's left ear nearly fell off and had to be replaced because of shoddy workmanship by Vietnamese embalmers. In fact the lighting in the mortuary has become dimmer and dimmer over the years. The mausoleum is open every morning at 8:30 and most afternoons.

Now back to the monument. You, the megalith behind you and Mao's mausoleum further to the south are all standing on the semi-sacred north–south central axis of Old Peking. Before the Monument to the People's Heroes was built and Mao laid to rest, it was theoretically possible for the emperor seated upon his throne in the **Hall of Supreme Harmony** in the Forbidden City, to have an uninterrupted view of the south gate of the city, the **Gate of Eternal Stability** (*Yong ding men*), as all the gates on the axis were arranged in a perfectly straight lane.

The **Museum of Chinese History**, nearly as spacious as Tiananmen Square itself, is worthwhile for its extraordinary art collection and exhibits of early Chinese scientific achievements. Plan at least two hours. The **Great Hall of the People**, the venue for important Party and Government conferences and meetings between Chinese and foreign heads of state, is open to the public several days of the week and has a room dedicated to each province and autonomous region, including Taiwan and Tibet. It has facilities for serving 5,000 guests at State banquets and 10,000 at cocktail parties.

Before 1949, Tiananmen Square was a narrow corridor on the central axis of the city, which took the form of a T-square, with its top abutting on Tiananmen Gate and its bottom coinciding with the Zhonghua (central flowery) Gate that was demolished in the early 1950s. During the Qing dynasty, the T-shaped area was off limits to all but high-ranking officials, and was a major obstacle to east–west traffic. On the east and west sides of this corridor on the land now given over to by the square stood the civil and military ministries or boards, respectively, of the Ming and Qing dynasties. This pattern of east/military, west/civil segregation is repeated in the palace gates: only the emperor could use the central entranceway; military officials, the west entrance and civil officials, the east. Now everyone entering the Forbidden City passes through the central gate of Tiananmen.

It is an open secret that there is a network of underground tunnels beneath Tiananmen Square (and other parts of the city) that date from the late 1950s and 1960, when Sino-Soviet relations had deteriorated to a point where the Chinese leadership feared Moscow would drop an atomic bomb on Beijing. (Similarly it is said that Shanghai long remained underdeveloped because Mao feared a U.S. naval attack via Taiwan on the once-great port city.) The tunnels were dug by teams of local youth and peasants from the Beijing suburbs who worked for brief stints on small sections of the project in order to prevent anyone from gaining an understanding of the entire system. Many of the resulting fallout shelters have been turned into restaurants, shops and hotels. In June 1989, when soldiers of the People's Liberation Army attempted to gain access to Tiananmen Square through air vents connected to these shelters, they were foiled by the demonstrators.

Rumour has it that there is an automobile tunnel linking the Great Hall of the People with Zhongnanhai, where the top Chinese leaders live, work and play. Another tunnel supposedly connects Zhongnanhai with the east–west line of the Beijing underground metro, facilitating a

Beijing traffic policeman

quick getaway in a private subway car to the 'secret' military airport in the western suburbs.

The Forbidden City

Only about one third of the buildings in the Forbidden City are now open to the public, many fewer than in the 1930s. And as of 1 January 1989, only 30,000 tourists (20,000 Chinese and 10,000 foreigners) are permitted to visit the Forbidden City each day. This decision was based on the urgent need to preserve the steps, pathways, buildings and decorations that are gradually being worn away by millions of hands and feet every year. Entry is through the **Meridian Gate** (*Wu men*) in the south part of the complex, or the **Gate of Martial Virtue** (*Shen wu men*) in the north.

The Forbidden City served as both residence and court for 24 Ming and Qing emperors over the course of five centuries, from its grand opening in 1421 until 1924, when Puyi, the deposed last emperor who in 1912 had relinquished the throne, was rudely kicked out of his own home. Portions of the palace were converted into an art museum in 1914 to display a small selection of objects from the imperial collections, and the **Palace Museum** (*Gu gong bo* *wu yuan)*, which comprises both the palace and the art collections, formally opened in 1926.

On the eve of the Japanese occupation in 1937, the most valuable works of Chinese art were crated and transported to Nanjing and Shanghai for safekeeping. When these cities were on the verge of falling to the Japanese, the crates were shipped to the inland provinces of Sichuan and Guizhou. In the late 1940s they were returned to Peiping, as the city was then called, and in 1948 as Chiang Kai-Shek retreated from the mainland with the remnants of the Kuomintang troops, a total of 2,972 crates of the finest jades, bronzes and paintings were transported by military planes and ships to the island of Taiwan, where they now make up the bulk of the magnificent collection of the fortress-like Palace Museum, built into the side of a mountain in the suburbs of Taipei. In Chinese political parlance and echoing the promise made to Hong Kong, 'One country, two systems,' this situation can be called, 'One museum, two collections.'

Beginning in 1952, the People's Government, carried out a major palace-cleaning, during which 250,000 cubic meters of rubbish was discarded. During the Cultural Revolution (1966–76) Zhou Enlai is credited with having extended his personal protection to the Forbidden City when the Red Guards threatened to destroy it.

The Beijing Palace Museum still has one of the largest collections of Chinese art in the world, and has replenished its earlier depleted holdings with donations from China and overseas as well as through 'acquisitions' or acts of 'liberation' from 'reactionary' private collections during the Cultural Revolution. Thousands of items in the museum remain uncatalogued, among them some 150,000 paintings and tonnes of precious Qing-dynasty documents in Manchu, a language understood by only a small handful of scholars in China. The museum displays in the Forbidden City are minimally labelled and poorly lit: surly guards refuse to turn on the lights (after telling you there are none) out of fear of fire.

Pyrophobia is nothing new in the Forbidden City; large sections of the palace have gone up in flames in the Ming, Qing and Republican periods. The worst fire in modern times took place in 1923 and resulted in the loss of many valuable antiques. The former emperor, Puyi, had ordered his eunuchs to make an inventory of the works of art in the **Palace of Establishing Happiness** *(Jian fu gong)* in the northwest section of the palace. A number of these devious non-men who had been spiriting away priceless treasures from this palace over the years panicked when they received their orders and set the fire to destroy all evidence of their transgressions. The fire was extinguished by soldiers from the Italian legation guard only after extensive damage had been done. At the suggestion of Puyi's English tutor, Reginald Johnston, a tennis court was built in the freshly cleared rectangle. Henry (the English name Johnston conferred on Puyi) and his brother William (Pujie) also learned to ride a bicycle here, and had some of the original high thresholds in the Inner Court removed or provided with ramps to facilitate his movements.

In late 1986, in an impressive bit of muckraking, the Beijing *Guangming Daily* [2] listed 13 organizations (work units) that at the time were occupying one eighth of the building space (and close to one half of the floor space) of the Forbidden City:

1) Museum of the Chinese Revolution: woodwork and painting shop, warehouse
2) China Overseas Exhibition Company: offices and woodwork shop
3) International Friendship Building Planning Committee: occupies buildings and has built its own temporary structures
4) Cultural Relics Publishing House: paper storage, three temporary buildings
5) Cultural Relics Preservation Research Institute

---

(2) *Guangming Daily*, 9 October 1986; 14 November 1986.

6) Cultural Relics Publishing House; linotype work-shop (now closed), new typesetting workshop with 30 employees
7) China Antiques Store, headquarters
8) Xu Beihong Memorial Hall: offices and storage
9) Yuanmingyuan Association
10) Chinese Ancient Architecture Exhibition Company: storage
11) Museum of Chinese History: storage
12) First Historical Archives of China: four buildings
13) People's Liberation Army

In 1975, the P.L.A. built four large palace-style build-ings, complete with imperial-yellow glazed tile roofs near the west gate of the palace. One purpose of these offices was to block the line of vision that extends from the roof of the Beijing Hotel to Zhongnanhai. A closer glance reveals that these three buildings blend poorly with the rest of the palace, and are actually a tasteless eyesore, particularly when considering who built and continues to occupy them.

The situation is serious because the Palace Museum lacks storage space for its own collection; more than 100,000 items are in the Nanjing Museum. And as mentioned above, because visitors are confined to a relatively small area of the palace, certain pavements, columns and balus-trades are subjected to inordinate wear and tear.

Reduced to its basic components, the Forbidden City is a network of walled courtyards within walled courtyards. Once inside the palace, the only communication with the outside world is upwards, through the sky. As Harold Acton wrote, 'For once the sky was part of the architectural design.' [3] All distant views within the palace are severed by walls with the discipline of an insidious geometrythat breeds myopia, self-absorption, introspection, defensive-ness and by extension, xenophobia.

---

(3)   Harold Acton *Memoirs of an Aesthete* (London: Methuen 1948), p. 276.

The Forbidden City is the epitome of Chinese exclusiveness. It was designed both to keep strangers out and the emperor in. The English critic William Empson, who lived in Beijing for several years, described it as 'a biological device for ruling the world.' [4] Like Chairmen Mao and Deng, who occupied their own imperial quarters in the 'sea palaces' in Zhongnanhai, the Chinese emperors before them often grew restless from being constrained for so long in a brick and stone spider web and would head off to their summer palaces or visit the capital's red-light districts incognito.

At the centre of the Forbidden City sat the **Son of Heaven**, theoretically the possessor, quite literally, of All Under Heaven, the world—for heaven (sky) and the walls of the palace were all he could see from his limited perspective. Compare Versailles, with its endless views, joyful fountains and forests, and its vanishing perspectives. The vast ceremonial courtyards of the Forbidden City, flat and bare as a monk's shaven head, had no trees where a sniper might conceal himself; or perhaps trees would somehow diminish the grandeur of the buildings. The chilling courtyards of the Forbidden City are the drained swimming pools of Atlantis, an archaic expression of empire.

The grand rectangular maze of rectangles would have had an overwhelming effect on the visitor—most of whom were Chinese officials attending business at court—entering the palace from the south. As William Willets wrote:

> From the moment he crossed the outer
> moat he would have been forced into a sort
> of automatic dance, its rhythm set by the
> changing masses and spaces of each succes-
> sive stage over which he made his way . . .

---

(4) William Willetts *Chinese Art, 2 vols.*
     (Harmondsworth, Penguin Books, 1958) II, p. 679.

One can well imagine the growing bewilderment and disquiet of such a person as he passed through one blank wall and beneath one brooding gate-house after another, to find beyond it only a featureless avenue leading to yet another wall and gate. Reality was softening into a dream. His mind, so long attentive to a distant goal somewhere ahead in this labyrinth of straight lines, so long expecting a climax that never seemed to come, must at last have refused to record and memorize the minor differences in scale, proportion and decorative detail of the buildings that were the only landmarks of his progress. As he pressed forward into a world of emptiness and of deadening silence, dream must have intensified into a nightmare of *déjà vu*. Whatever self-possession he may have had at the outset must long since have drained away when, crossing Wu Men [Meridian Gate], he finally entered the precinct of the Forbidden City . . . And, however ineffectually it may have regulated its own internal affairs, there can be little doubt of its capacity to reduce outsiders to a state of supplicatory awe.[5]

An absolute form of male chauvinism was practised in the imperial palaces. With a few temporary exceptions the emperor was the only functional male of the species among thousands of court ladies, concubines, maids and eunuchs—the latter described by Harold Acton as 'a bustling and cackling intermediate sex with the disadvantages of both.'

---

(5) William Willetts *Chinese Art*, II. pp. 678 – 9.

There are records of eunuchs in the palace during the Han dynasty (206 B.C.–A.D. 220). Their numbers and baleful influence reached a peak in the Ming (20,000–30,000), but by the Qing the total was less than 10,000. The fabulously wealthy eunuch Li Lianying was the Empress Dowager Cixi's right hand 'man' in bringing about the decline and fall of the Qing dynasty in the late 19th century.

The general formula of palace design was set down in the Zhou dynasty (12th–first century B.C.): left, ancestors; right, earth; front, court; rear, marketplace. For the most part, the Yongle emperor followed this plan when he built the Forbidden City in the early 15th century. To the left (southeast) of the palace stood the Ancestral Temple of the emperors, now the **Worker's Cultural Palace**; to the right (southwest) was the **Altar of Land and Grain**, a site of imperial sacrifices, today **Zhongshan (Central) Park**. The southern half of the palace is devoted to court functions; but for some reason, the rule of the rear markets was not applied. The northern section of the palace contains the residential quarters of the emperor and his empress, consorts and concubines, with attached gardens and temples.

Construction: A Ming historian claimed that 100,000 artisans and one million unskilled coolies participated in

Procession for an Imperial wedding

The empress' sedan chairs and carriages passing through the marble bridge over the Golden River

Honour guards with lanterns at the head of the empress' sedan chair passing through Wu Men Gate; from the painting of Emperor Guang Xu's Grand Wedding

the construction of the palace. The principal building materials are wood, stone, brick and glazed tiles. In the Ming, timber was shipped to Peking from Sichuan, Yunnan, Guangdong and Guizhou provinces by the Yangtze River and the Grand Canal. Shipments from southwestern China would take as long as four years to reach the capital. During the Qing dynasty the forests in northeast China were the major source of the wood used for further extensions to the palace. The same Ming source quoted above says: 'For every thousand men that went into the mountains (to cut wood), only five hundred returned.'

The porcelain vents set into the burnt madder walls of buildings directly beneath bracket systems are there to prevent the wooden columns that support the building from rotting.

The white marble used for decorative and structural purposes in the palace was quarried in Fangshan, some 50 kilometers (32 miles) southwest of Beijing. The roof tiles and bricks paving the courtyards were fired locally and in Shandong Province and Suzhou. During the Ming dynasty glazed roof tiles were fired in Liulichang in south Peking.

The statistics concerning Beijing bricks are mind-boggling: 12 million bricks were laid in the wall surrounding the Forbidden City; 20 million in the courtyards and interior walls of the palace; 80 million in the Peking city walls. As these bricks weighed an average of 24 kilogrammes (almost 53 pounds) each, it has been estimated that, in the early Ming dynasty, 1.93 million metric tonnes of bricks were fired to build the new capital.

The broad defensive moat that surrounds the palace freezes in winter and is now used for recreational skating. In the old days sleds pulled by coolies provided local transportation around the circumference of the Forbidden City. The mud dredged to form the moat was piled up to the north of the Forbidden City to form Prospect Hill (*Jing Shan*), also known as Coal Hill. So fertile was this mud that beginning in the 17th century, a crop of lotus was planted here to supply the imperial kitchens with lotus root. In the 18th and 19th centuries, as much as one third of the area of the moat was profitably rented out for lotus cultivation.

The huge bronze and iron vats placed throughout the palace, some of them gilded, were kept filled with water, drawn from the **River of Golden Water** that flowed through the palace, as a fire prevention measure. In the winter, eunuchs would keep them wrapped in padded cotton cosies and set charcoal braziers underneath them (note the space left for these in the marble bases) to prevent the water from freezing up. Japanese troops removed and destroyed many of the vats during their occupation of Peking (1937–45).

The first electric lights in Peking shone for the Empress Dowager Cixi in 1888, when a foreign company installed a 5,000-watt generator in the palace. Otherwise oil lamps were used indoors, and standing oil lamps lit up the courtyards and exterior corridors at night.

Two methods were used to heat the palace. In some of the residential quarters, a system of underground flues warmed the floors and raised brick beds *(kang)* that were a common feature in north China homes; otherwise charcoal braziers were placed about the ceremonial and other residential halls. Rank determined the amount of charcoal allotted to each palace resident. Daily quotas in the Qianlong period, in catties (one catty equals about 500 grams or 1.1 pounds), reveal an interesting pecking order:

120 – Empress Dowager	30 – Princess
110 – Empress	20 – Prince
90 – Imperial Consort	10 – Imperial grandson
75 – Consort	

The charcoal used to heat the palaces and for cooking was of such high quality that it was entirely smokeless. This explains why there is not a single chimney or smokestack in the entire Forbidden City.

China's emperors had no designated place to go to the toilet. When the need arose, a eunuch would appear with the imperial potty, which was a simple platinum bowl with a cover set in a wooden frame with a horse-shoe shaped seat upholstered in yellow silk. The palace eunuchs and maidens used more conventional chamber pots. With such a dense population, did the Forbidden City stink like a latrine? Not at all. The super fine ash from the charcoal burnt in the palace was placed in every potty and night pot to absorb the noxious odors. Young eunuchs washed the chamber pots out after every use, and the accumulated waste was removed from the palace at regular times each day.

As usual, Cixi was a cut above the rest in this regard. Her personal potty was filled with the fine sawdust of fragrant wood, which emitted the same delicious scent both before and after it was used. A nice bit of panoply accompanied Cixi's evacuations. A specially designated eunuch would carry her carved sandalwood potty, covered with a cozy of yellow imperial silk, and a palace maiden set it down on a square of oil cloth next to the Old Buddha. Toilet paper was placed in the mouth of the carved wooden gecko that clung to the outside of the potty. When she was finished, this little ritual was repeated in reverse. Cixi probably suffered from hyperthyroid, and had a ravenous appetite. This made it difficult for her to control her bowel movements, and thus this little entr'acte was repeated many times each day.

In the early Ming (14th–15th centuries), large sheets of toilet paper were manufactured in the palace using tribute hemp from Sichuan, though the emperor had his own personal brand, in imperial yellow and squeezably soft, each piece measuring only 7 x 9 centimeters (2.7 x 3.5 inches). From the Ming Wanli period on, imperial toilet paper was imported from Hangzhou. Cixi's own brand of toilet paper had a high cotton content, and was folded neatly and ironed flat by her attendants.

Like toilets, there were no designated dining rooms in the palace. The Son of Heaven called for his meal whenever and wherever he pleased. But as he had to go through elaborate procedures with the Office of Household Affairs to arrange for his palace ladies to sup with him, he took most of his meals alone, attended by eunuch servers and tasters. Sharing a sea cucumber with a concubine was much more convenient in the summer palaces and gardens where the rules governing access to His Presence were less rigid.

Safety was a top priority in the emperor's diet. A silver plaque was inserted into each of the dozens of dishes served at each meal, as it was believed that silver would blacken if it came into contact with a poisonous substance. A eunuch taster sampled a mouthful of every dish placed before the emperor, providing a second level of security. Palace regulations also forbade the emperor to take more than two bites of any dish, lest his preferences provide a clue for a potential poisoner. A eunuch stood next to the emperor while he ate. His job was to warn the Son of Heaven sternly if his chopsticks hovered over the same plate for the third time. For the same reason, the emperor could not request any particular food, and his servants were not allowed to recommend any dish or ingredient, even a particular vegetable or fruit in season. And thus all the imperial menus were chosen by the imperial kitchen, where strict discipline also prevailed.

In the late Qing dynasty, one of the larger kitchens in the palace (*Shou shan fang*) had 100 stoves with three persons attending each of them; a chef, a food cutter and a helper. The stoves were numbered, and precise records were kept of the name of the person who washed, cut and fried each dish each day, in order to be able to trace the guilty party should something go amiss.

Palace records are similarly detailed in reference to the shipment of fresh lychees to North China from the South. Every Chinese high school pupil learns the story of how the Xuanzong emperor of the Tang dynasty had lychees brought to the capital of Chang'an (present day Xi'an) by means of the imperial pony express system to satisfy the cravings of his famed pudgy concubine Yang Guifei. In the Qing dynasty, advanced naval technology made it possible for entire lychee trees to be put on boats in the coastal province of Fujian and shipped by sea to Peking. Palace documents give the number of boats dispatched, the number of trees on each boat, and the number of lychees growing on each tree. The records also tell us how many lychees were consumed in the palace each day, as well as the number of lychees the emperor presented to each concubine and minister, all of whom are named.

Drinking water for the palace was drawn from a spring in **Jade Spring Mountain** (*Yu quan shan*) in the north-western suburbs (see page 239) and was transported to the palace daily. Water used for sanitation, fire prevention, and construction in the palace was supplied by the **River of Golden Water** (*Jin shui he*) that runs through the courtyard in front of the **Gate of Supreme Harmony** (*Tai he men*).

Notes on the Walk: The Forbidden City is an excellent place to get lost in, as its symmetrical layout facilitates a quick escape to the exits from wherever you may be. Our walk will take us from south to north, through the **Tiananmen**, **Duanmen** and **Wumen gates**, the **Three Harmony Halls**, the chronological art displays, and then the residential section in the north of the complex with its many small art collections. We conclude by climbing **Prospect Hill** at the north entrance to the palace, although only on clear days is the view from there worth the climb.

The Walk: From **Tiananmen Square** head north across Chang'an Boulevard, the city's major 12-lane east–west thoroughfare, and cross one of the seven white marble bridges over the stream to the south of **Tiananmen Gate**, the front entrance of the Imperial City. There are two pairs of elaborately carved marble **ceremonial pillars** (*hua biao*) here, one standing inside and the other outside the gate. As the story goes, the lions that face away from the palace have their mouths open because it is their job to inform the emperor of any wrongdoing committed by palace officials during his absence from the palace. The lions facing the palace have their mouths closed to remind whoever knows that the emperor has left the palace in mufti to remain silent about it. The emperors passed through Tiananmen Gate several times a year on their way to major sacrifices, imperial weddings and military campaigns.

Imperial trials for serious crimes were held in front of Tiananmen Gate, and when the death sentence was handed down, a red tick was penned by the guilty man's name on the official document, as it still is today on public execution notices. In the Qing dynasty imperial edicts were attached to the mouth of a carved golden phoenix that was lowered from the top of the gate onto a tray held by officials from the Board of Ceremonies. In the Ming, they were attached to a dragon's head suspended from the end of a pole by a colored cord.

Continuing north, pass though a long, narrow court-yard interrupted at its south end by the **Upright Gate** (*Duan men*), which served a defensive rather than ceremonial purpose and was never mounted by the emperor. Troops guarding the palace would gather here on summer nights to gamble and occasionally a high official would join them for a round. Continue north until you come to the next structure, the U-shaped **Meridian Gate** (*Wu men*), the considerably larger formal entrance of the Forbidden City. This gate can be thought of as a pair of dragon jaws ready to snatch up whoever comes near them and deliver them into the maw of the palace.

Tickets for foreigners (and other hard currency holders such as Hong Kong and Macao compatriots) are sold in a kiosk on the east side of the plaza in front of the Meridian Gate. These tickets provide access to some of the special-ized collections in the north section of the palace, such as the **Hall of Clocks**, **Hall of Treasures**, **Opera Theater**, and **Imperial Garden**. An admission ticket for foreigners costs FEC30, but the often obnoxious ticket-seller will try to rent you the optional recorded tour description, read by Peter Ustinov, that costs an additional FEC28. It is frequently necessary to argue with them that you *don't* want to listen to Peter, who relates the history and lore of the palace.

In the past, officials awaiting admission to an imperial audience in the palace would gather at the Meridian Gate at about 3 A.M. A number of snack sellers set up their stands near the gate to provide the early risers with a hot breakfast.

65

A desolate scene of Wu Men (Meridian Gate) Qing dynasty

Once every three years, the emperor would mount the Meridian Gate tower and announce the names of the successful candidates in the triennial palace examinations. As usual the central entrance in this gate was reserved for the emperor alone, but an exception was made for the three top-scoring candidates in the examinations, as well as for the emperor's fiancée, who was carried into the palace on a sedan chair. The structure over the central gate tower housed a throne; the side towers, a drum and a bell respectively. The bell was struck when the emperor passed through the gate, and the drum beaten when the sacrifice to the ancestors was held in the Ancestral Temple. In the Ming dynasty the emperors held banquets here for high officials, during which the Son of Heaven would compose poems along with his guests. In the Qing dynasty, the emperor would issue the new calendar prepared by his astrologers from here each year, and inspect freshly captured prisoners of war.

Passing through the gate, we come to the first broad courtyard of the palace with its five marble bridges spanning the **River of Golden Water** (*Jin shui he*). The river, fed from a sluice gate in the northwest corner of the Forbidden

City moat, follows the contours of a hunting bow symbolic of military prowess.

The gate before you, the **Gate of Supreme Harmony** *(Tai he men)*, is guarded by a pair of bronze lions and leads to the courtyard that contains the **Three Harmony Halls** (Supreme, Complete and Preserving Harmony). The Ming emperors held audiences in the tower of this gate, and when imperial audiences were moved into the Hall of Supreme Harmony, the gate continued to be used as a depot where the emperor changed from his palace palanquin to a larger sedan chair when setting off on sacrifices outside the palace. The Gate of Supreme Harmony burnt down in a huge fire in 1888 and was rebuilt the next year.

The fire was viewed as inauspicious. It was only one month away from the day selected for the wedding of the Guangxu emperor, and this gate was to play an important role in the ceremonies for the grand occasion. As it was impossible to change the date, something had to be done about restoring the Gate of Supreme Harmony.

The solution was to rebuild the gate in wood, with every detail, including the glazed tile roof, crafted to resemble the original structure. A contemporary document recorded that 'even people who had served in the Inner Court for years were unable to distinguish it from the original.' The present Gate of Supreme Harmony dates from 1889, one year after Guangxu's marriage.

The low buildings on the east side of the courtyard were in the Qing dynasty the offices of a department that tracked the progress of imperial orders, and of another office that handled official appointments and honorary titles. During the Ming, the buildings on the west were a school for the imperial princes. During the Qing, they became the offices of a Manchu-Chinese translation bureau, and of a secretariat that kept fastidious records of the emperor's movements and pronouncements.

Passing through the Gate of Supreme Harmony we come to a second huge and empty courtyard the largest in the palace. Fifteen layers of bricks, seven laid flat and eight placed upright, pave the ground here to prevent intruders from burrowing their way into the sacred precincts of the palace from the outside. The low buildings to the side were storage rooms for leather and furs, silk, armour, saddles, ceramics, gold and silver, tea and clothing. On ceremonial occasions this courtyard was filled with the vast panoply of officials, guards and eunuchs in gorgeous dress, as seen in the film, *The Last Emperor*.

The **Three Harmony Halls**, so called because the word 'harmony' appears in each of their names, stand on a three-tiered marble terrace over 7 meters (23 feet tall), surrounded by elaborately carved balustrades and a total of 1,142 dragon heads whose mouths function as drains when it rains. One art historian with an eye for the macabre wrote that the balustrades produce a very complicated and restless effect, which from certain viewpoints is not unlike a modern graveyard. [6] The 18 bronze incense burners on the steps of the terrace, cast in the Ming dynasty, represent the 18 provinces of the Qing empire, and served several functions. First, the burning sandalwood raised a smoke-screen of anonymity for the emperor, for on windless days the smoke would obscure the entire hall. Second, the incense neutralized the noxious odours of the eunuchs, whose sanitary habits were notorious. Foreigners in the 19th century complained that the poorly cured fur garments worn by Manchus in the winter smelled like dead animals. One also wonders if any voices could be heard over the din produced by the strident wind and percussion instruments played during the ceremonies.

The **Hall of Supreme Harmony** (*Tai he dian*), the first of the Three Harmony Halls, was first built in the early 15th century but was twice destroyed by fire in the Ming dynasty (1420 and 1557) and once again in the Qing dynasty. The present hall, one of the largest of its type in China, dates from 1695, although it has been refurbished several times.

---

(6)   D.G. Mirams *A Brief History of Chinese Architecture* (Shanghai: Kelly & Walsh 1940), p. 79.

Here the emperor would take part in lavish ceremonies on the first day of the lunar year (the Chinese New Year), at the winter solstice and on his birthday. Other rites included the announcement of a new reign period, interviews with the top candidates in the imperial examinations, and the commissioning of high-ranking military officials who were about to set out on major campaigns. During the Ming and early Qing dynasties, the 'finals' in the imperial examination system were administered here. The following description of the panoply in this hall is from the 1860s:

> . . .[The Emperor] sits on a high throne in the centre of the vast and gloomy hall, facing the south, while about fifty attendants of high rank [chiefly Manchus] stand on each side. These constitute the Emperor's suite, and they enter the temple by side-paths and side-doors—the Emperor himself entering by a central raised path, several feet higher than that by which his attendants enter. In front of the hall, south of the front balustrades, is the space appropriated to the nobility and officers who come to perform the act of prostration. They are arranged in eighteen double rows; the civil officers are on the east side, and the military on the west. Nearest to the hall steps, and upon them, are the princes of first and second degree; with the [two] Manchu ranks. . ; followed by the five orders, of Chinese nobility. . . These make in all nine. Then come the mandarins of nine grades. Stones are fixed in the pavement to mark their positions, and over these stones are placed copper covers shaped like mountains. Here they perform the immemorial ceremony of the nine prostrations before the unseen emperor,

who, deep in the recesses of the hall, is
concealed still more completely by a cloud
of incense.[7]

The objects now displayed on the south terrace are a
sundial and a bronze grain measure, the latter a symbol of
the emperor's fairness and incorruptibility. What resembles a swastika on its base is actually an inside-out swastika,
an ancient Indian Buddhist symbol of good fortune that
means 'ten thousand' in Chinese. The much-rubbed crane
and tortoise incense burners are traditional symbols of
longevity. When the Xuantong emperor, Puyi, was placed
on the throne here in 1908 at the age of three, he is reported
to have cried throughout the ceremony. The throne on view
today is a reproduction dating from the 1950s. In 1915, the
president of the Republic of China, Yuan Shikai removed
Qianlong's actual throne and replaced it with a Western-
style chair better suited to his bandy legs. The present
throne was reconstructed recently based on a 1900 photo-
graph. It was assembled using bits and pieces of an
undateable throne found in a palace warehouse.

The large elegantly named 'golden bricks' paving the
interior as well as in most of the other ceremonial and
residential halls were for the most part made in Suzhou.
After being fired for 130 days, they were soaked in tung oil
and polished until they glistened.

The next hall on the north–south axis is the square **Hall
of Complete Harmony** (or **Middle Harmony**, *Zhong he
dian*). The smallest of the Three Harmony Halls, this is
where the emperor would prepare for important rituals to
be performed in the Hall of Supreme Harmony, or inspect
the seeds and farm implements to be used in the important
sacrifice at the Temple of Agriculture. Here also the emperor
would confer titles of honour upon the empress, and

---

(7) Joseph Edkins *Peking*; in Alexander Williamson, *Journeys in
North China, Manchuria, and Eastern Mongolia; with Some Account
of Corea* (London: Smith, Elder & Co 1870), p. 325.

compile the imperial family tree. The two sedan chairs placed inside are of Qing vintage and were carried by eight bearers. Like the other two harmony halls, the Hall of Complete Harmony also contains a throne.

In the **Hall of Preserving Harmony** (*Bao he dian*), the next building on the axis, the Ming emperors would change their robes before and after attending ceremonies elsewhere in the palace, and occasionally hold banquets for high officials. Here also the emperors feted the Mongol nobility and delegations from tributary states. Beginning in the Qianlong period and up to the first years of the 20th century, the palace examinations were held here every three years. The emperor would preside over ceremonies held at the start and completion of the exams. In 1795, a Dutch mission was invited to a banquet here. The diarist Van Braam recorded that they were served enough mutton to 'disgust a man with (it) for the rest of his life.'

This is a convenient point to make a detour to see the two extensive **Chronological Displays of Chinese Art**, which begin with the Shang and Zhou jades and bronzes in the long narrow side halls to the east of the Hall of Preserving Harmony. This is a comprehensive though poorly lit (depending on the time of day) survey that includes many masterpieces and a number of superb copies. As you backtrack south you will progress through the Qin, Han, Tang, Five Dynasties, Song and Yuan periods. Then cross the courtyard to the other side of the terrace and work your way back north through the Ming and Qing, including memorable examples of Qing kitsch some of which originated in the palace workshop.

Emerging into the sunlight from the cabinets of Qing baubles, make your way north into the large courtyard to the rear of the Hall of Preserving Harmony, and examine the large stairway that leads down from the centre of the terrace. The largest of the three slabs of carved marble set in the middle of the two staircases is 15.2 meters (50 feet) long, 3.3 meters (11 feet) wide and weighs 200 tonnes. It was installed here around 1420, when the palace was first built, but some of the carving on its surface dates from the Qianlong period more than 300 years later. The stone, quarried in Fangshan near Beijing, was transported to the palace in winter by harnessing to it over 1,000 horses and mules that hauled it over a sheet of ice formed by spreading water on the road from wells dug along the way. Only recently was it suggested that this huge slab is actually two pieces of marble that dovetail perfectly in a joint hidden under the curved contours of the cloud whorls.

In imperial times the large rectangular courtyard we are now standing in was off limits to all but the highest ranking officials and those having special appointments with the emperor, who lived with his empresses and concubines in the apartments immediately to the north. Underlings accompanying officials on business were forbidden from going within 50 meters (164 feet) of the side gates.

In the northwest corner of this courtyard—in recent times the location of a fast-food venue—stood the office of the **Grand Council** (*Jun ji chu*). Founded in 1729 as a command centre for military campaigns being waged at the time in northwest China, it evolved into the office responsible for issuing imperial decrees. The peace of this precinct was shattered one day in 1813, when a band of bold peasants broke in and got as far as the Hall of Mental Cultivation, to courtyards to the north of here. The Jiaqing emperor was away from the palace at the time, and though the trespassers were swiftly arrested, the emperor was so terrified that he cancelled his birthday celebration that year.

The low gate on the central axis, the **Gate of Heavenly Purity** (*Qian qing men*), serves as the main entrance to the north section of the palace, known as the **Inner Court**. The buildings in the first large rectangular courtyard inside the gate stand on a raised marble terrace, and in terms of overall layout resemble the Three Harmony Halls in miniature. In the early years of the Qing dynasty, the emperor would hold regular audiences seated in a throne situated immediately inside this gate, with his subordinates arranged on the stairs before him.

The **Palace of Heavenly Purity**, the first building in this complex, was the emperor's living quarters during the Ming and early Qing dynasties. It was here in 1542 that one of the Jiajing emperor's concubines led a contingent of more than a dozen palace women in an attempt to strangle the emperor in his sleep, but the knot in the noose they had brought along slipped. For their pains, the gang was executed in public à la Peking duck, by having their throats cut and the flesh of their limbs sliced off. Following this incident, the Jiajing emperor spent 20 years 'cultivating his mind' in solitude in a palace in what is now Zhongnanhai, only returning to the Hall of Heavenly Purity one day before his death. The Ming Wanli emperor passed away in the small room on the west side of the Hall of Heavenly Purity, and his son the Taichang emperor only remained in the throne for a month before he died in the hall itself after taking a double dose of a mysterious medicine.

The Qing dynasty emperors also slept and attended daily affairs in the Palace of Heavenly Purity, though after the death of Kangxi most official business was transacted in the **Hall of Mental Cultivation** *(Yang xin dian)*, in the courtyard to the north of the Grand Council. From that time on, the Palace of Heavenly Purity was used for court

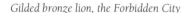

Gilded bronze lion, the Forbidden City

rituals, banquets, and meetings with foreign missions and high officials. It was here that on several occasions Kangxi and Qianlong invited men aged 60 or over to lavish feasts to celebrate their own longevity; one such feast was attended by 3,000 venerables. During the Qing dynasty this hall was also used as the first resting place of the emperors upon their demise, regardless of where they had died. The emperors' remains were then removed to a hall behind **Prospect Hill** (also called **Coal Hill**, to the north of the Forbidden City), and then interred in the **Eastern** or **Western Qing Tombs**. The Tongzhi emperor died of smallpox in the Palace of Heavenly Purity in 1874.

The plaque inscribed by the first Qing emperor, Shunzhi, that hangs over the throne in the hall reads 'Upright, Great, Brilliant, and Lucid,' enumerating with modesty the qualities an ideal Son of Heaven should possess. Beginning in the Qianlong reign, the name of the successor to the throne was not announced publicly, as it had been previously, but was written on two pieces of paper, one kept on the emperor's person throughout his reign, and the other placed in a small strongbox that was stored behind this plaque. The box was opened when the emperor 'mounted the dragon' or caught the last palanquin to heaven.

The buildings that line the east and west sides of the courtyard of this complex contained at various times a Confucian shrine, a Qianlong–period clepsydra (water clock), stores of incense and imperial stationery, a wardrobe full of the emperor's gowns and other accessories, the office of the Hanlin secretariat, a study where the emperor reviewed documents, and of four literary men who advised the emperor on poetry, and the office of eunuch affairs.

To the north of the **Palace of Heavenly Purity** is the **Hall of Union** (*Jiao tai dian*), the living quarters of the empress in the Ming and the place where Qing empresses would receive obeisance from the high-ranking civil and military officials on their birthdays. From Qianlong times, this hall was used to store a collection of imperial seals, the oldest of which was said to belong to Qin shi huang di First Emperor of the Qin dynasty (third century B.C.).

Behind the **Hall of Union** is the **Palace of Earthly Tranquillity** (*Kun ning gong*), a **yin** (earthly, feminine) counterpart of the **yang** (heavenly, masculine) **Palace of Heavenly Purity**. In the Ming, this hall was the sleeping quarters of the empresses. It continued to bear this name during the Qing, though in fact the empresses did not stay here. In the Qing dynasty, the Palace of Earthly Tranquillity was rebuilt so that its entrance stood at the east end of the south side of the hall rather than in the centre, as was the general rule in the Forbidden City. This feature, and the presence of heated beds (**kang**) inside, can be explained by the fact that during the Qing dynasty the palace was used as a shrine for secret Manchu shamanistic practices. There was a daily ritual sacrifice to some 15 gods, including Sakyamuni Buddha and a number of Mongol deities. Four pigs were offered in sacrifice each day, while at major rituals in the spring and autumn personally attended by the emperor and empress, 39 pigs went up in smoke. Several of the Qing emperors and empresses lodged in the east 'heated chamber' attached to this hall on their three-day honeymoon. The buildings behind the hall to the north were the imperial clinic and pharmacy.

In the northeastern corner of the courtyard, behind the Palace of Earthly Tranquillity is a small display of European and Chinese toys from the 18th and 19th centuries. It should not be missed.

Passing north through the **Gate of Earthly Tranquillity** (*kun ning men*) we come to the **Imperial Garden** (*Yu hua yuan*), parts of which date back to the Ming. This garden was only one of the many retreats the emperors had at their disposal in Peking, but in spite of its proximity they tended to spend less time here than in the garden palaces at Zhongnanhai, the western suburbs (in the Yuanmingyuan, Yi he yuan and Yuquan shan) and Jehol (present-day Chengde). In this palace garden a vast array of disparate architectural elements is crowded into a small space, yet it still gives the impression of spaciousness. The paths are decorated with charming mosaic designs of auspicious plants and animals. The rockery hill in the north part of the garden dates from the Ming Wanli period. The emperor and his consorts would climb to the top of this manmade mountain on several occasions during the year: when the paths of the stars called the **Herding Boy** and **Weaving Girl** crossed in the heavens for an annual assignation; on the Mid-autumn Festival to view the full moon; and on the ninth day of the ninth month, the **Double-Ninth Festival** when it was customary to climb to a high place. These occasions were also celebrated by the general populace. Reginald Johnston, Puyi's English-language teacher, lived for a time in an apartment in the south section of this garden.

The maze-like traffic pattern of the Forbidden City makes it necessary for us to backtrack a bit here. Or use this opportunity to break up your visit by leaving the Forbidden City through the **Gate of Martial Prowess** (*Shen wu men*) which stands immediately to the north of the Imperial Garden. If you divide the visit into two sessions, you can enter the Forbidden City from this rear gate on your second session.

Marble balustrade alongside the River of Golden Water

Heading south from the Imperial Garden, we return to the open courtyard that separates the Inner and Outer Courts via either of two routes:

1) by following the corridor to the east of the **Palace of Heavenly Purity** complex to the specialized collections of bronzes, ceramics and arts and crafts in the contiguous courtyards known as the **Six Eastern Palaces**, all former residences.

2) by taking the corridor to the west to the **Six Western Palaces**, residences of the Qing emperors and empresses. It was here that Cixi (when she was not in the Summer Palace or Zhongnanhai) lived during the bulk of her career, from 1865 to her death in 1908.

In order to see both the east and west palaces it will be necessary to make a circle, as one cannot cross through the Palace of Heavenly Purity.

We will proceed down the west corridor. In was in the north chamber of the **Palace of Concentrated Beauty** (*Chu xiu gong*), that Cixi gave birth to the boy (Zai Chun) who was to become the Tongzhi emperor. The interior of this hall has been restored to the way it looked on the Empress Dowager Cixi's 50th birthday in 1885, according to a description found in the imperial archives, and at best what is here is frowzy kitsch. Some of the gates in these courtyards, as well as those in the Six Eastern Palaces, have names appropriate for the hatchery of the imperial brood, such as One Hundred Sons and One Thousand Infants, for this is where the concubines favoured by the imperial presence lived. But apparently the names worked: Qianlong sired 35 sons by his various consorts, though only 17 grew to maturity. For the most part the interiors here have been restored to the style of the early 19th century.

The **Palace of Eternal Spring** (*Chang chun gong*) to the southwest on the next north–south axis contains a small theatre, one of several in the palace where the Empress

Yellow glazed roof tiles, the Forbidden City

Dowager watched performances of Chinese opera. It was in this palace that she celebrated her 50th birthday with long hours of opera-going. It is now closed to the public.

The most important building in the Western Palaces area is the **Hall of Mental Cultivation** *(Yang xin dian)*, the living quarters of the Qing sovereigns beginning with Yongzheng in the 1730s. Yongzheng moved here from the Palace of Heavenly Purity after the death of his father, Kangxi, who had lived in the latter for 60 years. From the early 18th century to the end of the Qing dynasty the emperors handled the most important affairs of state in the Hall of Mental Cultivation. This is also where Puyi, the last emperor, abdicated the throne in February 1912.

This courtyard, like the Forbidden City itself, is divided into two sections, the ceremonial in front (or south) and the living quarters in the rear. In the east 'heated chamber' of the front section, the Empress Dowager Cixi ruled China 'from behind a curtain' seated on the larger of the two thrones while the young Tongzhi and Guangxu emperors held court here; the latter died in this hall in 1908.

The residential chambers have an intimate charm not found in the rest of the palace. The east 'heated chamber' was the emperor's bedroom; the west 'heated chamber' served as a Buddhist chapel. In the room in the northeast corner the emperor would disport with his highest-ranking concubine. The northwest-corner chamber served as the duty room for lesser concubines waiting on the emperor. Eunuchs carried the concubines into the imperial boudoir wrapped up in a rug, and were never more than a few steps away from the emperor, even when he was in bed. The Son of Heaven's most intimate retainers would stand on the other side of a screen while he made love to his palace ladies, and shout warnings such as 'Preserve your Imperial body, Sire!' during the course of the night. Court astrologers determind the optium hours for the emperor to be intimate with his ladies, based on calendrical cycles of *yin* and *yang*. If the timing was right, they figured, their union would result in the birth of a dragon boy who would inherit the throne. The fact that most of the emperors had dozens of sons and daughters makes the contribution to the astrologers seem like so much hocus pocus.

South of the **Hall of Mental Cultivation** is the former site of the **Imperial Kitchen**. The Qing emperors usually took two main meals a day, breakfast at around 6.30 A.M. and lunch at 12.30 P.M., with lighter repasts in the afternoon and evening. Each formal meal consisted of as many as 108 dishes and was served on plates of gold, silver, jade, enamel and porcelain (some of which is on display in the Hall of Jewellery, see page 90) set on several dozen tables, many well out of the emperor's reach, as well as out of sight. As a result, many were not replaced at every meal and within a few days grew quite stale. Several restaurants near the Forbidden City did a vigorous trade in palace leftovers spirited out of the palace by the men who worked in the kitchen, not all of whom were eunuchs. While no rooms were specifically designated as dining rooms in the Forbidden City, as mentioned above, most imperial repasts were served in the familiar surroundings of the Palace of Heavenly Purity and the Hall of Mental Cultivation.

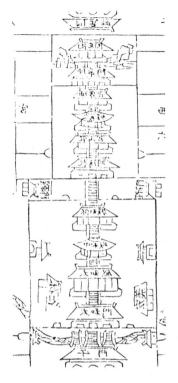

Gates and palaces of the Forbidden City, Qing dynasty gazetteer

This would be the time to see the specialized collections of jade, porcelain and bronzes displayed in the halls off the north–south alley directly east of the Palace of Heavenly Purity.

To continue the walk: leaving the courtyard that separates the ceremonial and residential quarters, walk east through the raised gate, go down the incline and bear left into the courtyard where the hall contains a wonderful collection of Chinese and European clocks, some of the cherished playthings of the Qing emperors. This is the **Hall of Ancestral Worship** (*Feng xian dian*), where the spirit tablets of the deceased Qing emperors and empresses were kept.

From here we visit the large group of buildings in the northeast corner of the Forbidden City, the **Palace of a Peaceful Old Age** (*Ning shou gong*) which now houses extraordinary collections of paintings, ancient stone rubbings, and 'jewellery', as the signs in English say—actually a selection of the household effects and personal sacred objects belonging to the Qing rulers. This part of the palace was originally built to accommodate the emperor's parents, as well as the empress and the highest-ranking concubines.

The Palace of a Peaceful Old Age is a near replica in terms of layout of the Palace of Heavenly Purity. Here Kangxi refurbished a number of Ming halls and named the palace in honour of his mother's 60th birthday.

In the 37th year of his reign, Qianlong began to convert these buildings into a retirement home that he planned to move into upon completing 60 years of rule, a full 23 years away. He chose the number 60 out of respect for his grandfather Kangxi, who had ruled China for 61 years. The palaces and the garden in the east half of the compound were completed in four years, but according to some sources, Qianlong never lived in them. When he was 85, Qianlong held a grand banquet for old men here, with a guest list of over 5,000 venerables. Cixi later chose the Palace of Peaceful Old Age as her own place of 'retirement' when the Guangxu emperor attained his majority in 1889.

The vestibular courtyard to the south of the palace contains a **Nine Dragon Wall**, one of two in Beijing (the other is in Beihai Park. The dragon symbolizes the celestial potency of the emperor, as well as controls wind and rain. The number nine is the most auspicious *yang* (male, active) number. As there are nine types of dragons in the world, this wall represents all the dragons in the world, and hence functions as a sort of insurance policy for the inhabitants of the palace.

Heading north through the gate opposite the Dragon Wall, we come to a large courtyard empty except for some grand old cypress trees, the occasional vintage crow, and a pair of bronze lions. Beyond the second gate is the **Hall of Imperial Supremacy** (*Huang ji dian*), a near replica of the Palace of Heavenly Purity. Here Cixi held her final audience before fleeing Peking for Xi'an following the Boxer Uprising in the summer of 1900. Her coffin was also stored here for a year before burial. Today the corridors lining this court-yard house exhibitions of paintings, calligraphy (west side) and rubbings of ancient stone inscriptions (east side), while the hall itself houses one section of the newly-renovated and well-lit **Hall of Treasures or 'Jewellery'** (*Zhen bao guan*), with its lavish collection of practical, ceremonial and religious *objets d'art* . There are mountain dioramas of carved jade, solid gold dishes, a large mat woven of ivory splinters, imperial robes, Lamaist reliquaries and other objects characteristic of the extravagant taste of the Manchu emperors. The state-of-the-art displays here are always packed with visitors, but it is worth nudging and waiting to get a glimpse of extraordinary objects on display.

In a courtyard to the north–east of the Palace of Peaceful Old Age is a tall three-tiered opera stage, the **Pavilion of Pleasant Sounds** (*Chang yin ge*), complete with stage traps and hand-operated pumps for on-stage fountains. The pavilion is a clone of the **Garden of Harmonious Virtue** (*De he yuan*) in the Summer Palace, where Cixi frequently held command performances, particularly on her birthday. The building to the north that faces the stage, where the court denizens would sit during performances, contains an interesting collection of Peking-opera costumes and props.

Emerging from the Pavilion of Pleasant Sounds, cross the courtyard to the **Garden of the Palace of a Peaceful Old Age** (*Ning shou gong hua yuan*), also known as the **Qianlong Garden**. This lovely secluded corner of the palace contains many of the elements found in traditional gardens in Suzhou: Lake Taihu stones piled up to form screen walls, a huge maze set around a building; man-made hills; pavilions in different styles; and winding paths that direct the visitor to a series of everchanging views. The layout produces claustrophobia and seems appropriate for an old emperor with myopia.

The **Pavilion for Seeking Pleasure** (*Xi shang ting*) near the southern entrance of the garden has in its floor a winding channel approximately 10 centimeters (four inches) deep called the 'Cup Floating Channel.' The original idea for this amusing design is drawn from a famous essay, the 'Preface to the Orchid Pavilion,' by the fourth-century writer, Wang Xizhi. In the pavilion, scholars and palace ladies floated their wine cups on the surface of the miniature stream which was supplied with water from a large urn placed nearby. While the cups bobbled along the channel, they would challenge each other to improvise poems before a cup reached the end. The punishment for procrastinating was to drink the wine in the cup.

Passing out of the northern section of the Qianlong garden, you find yourself in a courtyard that three halls now being used to display a large collection of Ming and Qing household furniture. From south to north, the three halls are named the **Hall of Nourishing Heavenly Nature** (Yang *xing dian*), where Qianlong lived upon his retirement; the **Hall for Joy in Old Age** (*Le shou tang*), formerly a library; and the **Pavilion of Peace and Harmony In Old Age** (*Yi he xuan*), where Qianlong came to read and relax in his later years.

The courtyards to the northwest of here that you will pass through on your way out of the palace have a charmingly run-down and authentic look about them, and one fears that if they were repaired and painted, they would lose their character.

Finally, don't forget to pay your last respects at the **Well of the Pearl Concubine**, located in a narrow corridor in the very northeast corner of the palace behind the Hall of Treasures. The sad demise of this young woman, Guangxu's favourite, took place the very same day Cixi fled Peking in the aftermath of the Boxer Uprising in 1899. There are at least two versions of this bleak tragedy. According to the first, Cixi had the girl thrown down the well after she had begged the Empress Dowager to leave Guangxu behind in Peking to help resolve the political crisis that had befallen the dynasty. The second version, based on the account of a eunuch who claimed to have witnessed it, tells how Cixi had ordered the concubine to commit suicide, but when she voiced her protest, Cixi ordered another eunuch to force her down the well.

To exit from the Forbidden City, walk west to the **Gate of Martial Prowess** (*Shen wu men*), the principle north gate of the Forbidden City, where you can get a bus or taxi. The gate tower houses an excellent exhibition of traditional Chinese architecture with blueprints and tools used in the building of the Forbidden City. Though, all the labels are in Chinese, the huge gate tower, the view from it and the objects on display make a visit worthwhile (extra ticket required). If you still have the energy, it is recommended to climb **Prospect Hill** (*Jing shan*), also popularly known as **Coal Hill** (*Mei shan*). The five pavilions on the hill, each (once upon a time) sheltering its own bronze Buddha, date from the time of Qianlong.

To get to Prospect Hill cross the road (**Jing shan qian jie**) and buy a ticket in the kiosk. This road is a modern imposition upon former imperial property, and dates from the 1920s.

The customary route up Prospect Hill is via the east slope. At the foot of the hill you will pass a scholar-tree (also called a locust or sophora) with a sign commemorating the

A collection of opera hats worn by actors and actresses

spot where the last emperor of the Ming dynasty supposedly hung himself as the capital fell to the invading Manchus.
The chain that had been attached to the tree—to remind
passersby of the emperor's heroic unwillingness to be
captured by the enemy—is said to have been removed by
the Allied Armies in 1900. The original scholar-tree, called
the Guilty Scholar-tree, was deracinated by Red Guards in
the Cultural Revolution. A substitute tree was planted in
1981, but it is unlikely that it has much of a conscience.

The buildings on the north side of the hill, once a
temple complex containing a collection of portraits of the
deceased Qing emperors, and the place where the remains
of the empresses and empress dowagers rested before being
buried in the suburban mausoleums, are now used as a
Children's Palace.

Walk · 2

The Former Legation Quarter, Dazhalan, Liulichang

Former Legation Quarter

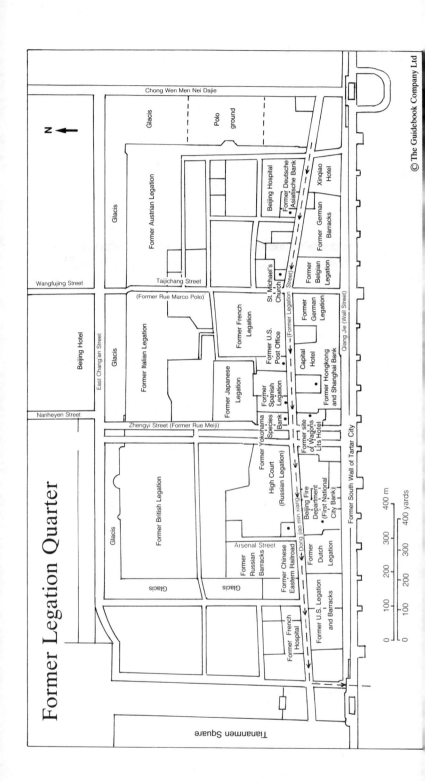

© The Guidebook Company Ltd

Duration
Approximately three hours.

Description
Begin with a stroll through the **Former Legation Quarter**, a Chinese version of a European ghost town, continue through some of the bustling, winding hutongs of the old Chinese City in the **Da zha lan district** and conclude in **Liu li chang Street**, a recently renovated Qing-dynasty shopping area that has been a marketplace for Chinese books and antiques for more than 300 years.

Starting Point
The Xinqiao Hotel in Dong jiao min xiang.

How to Get There
Buses 3, 9, 32, 44, 103, 104, 111 to **Chong wen men**. Or take the Beijing underground train to **Chongwenmen station**, walk one block to the north and turn left.

How to Get Away

Buses 14, 15, 25 and 45 stop on **South Xinhua Street** near Liulichang. By walking north a few minutes, you can get on the Beijing underground (metro) at **Hepingmen Station**, immediately next to the world's largest Peking duck restaurant (sometimes called the **Wall Street Duck**, as one of the Peking city walls once ran east–west in front of it).

History of the Legation Quarter

The street known today as **Dong jiao min xiang** ('Eastern lane where the peoples mingle') was formerly called **Dong jiang mi xiang** ('Eastern glutinous-rice lane'), and from 1900 through the 1940s in English as Legation Street. This was the location of most of China's foreign embassies and consulates. Today it is a somewhat depressing hodgepodge of crumbling, rehabilitated and new buildings, barely breathing its last as a historical site. Yet it offers the visitor sufficient vignettes of the Peking past and some pleasant surprises to make it worthwhile visiting.

In the late 13th century, the Grand Canal was connected to the urban waterway system of the Yuan dynasty capital of Dadu, making it possible for rice and textile shipments from the South to travel by water without transhipment to the imperial granaries. A rice market grew up in the vicinity of present-day Dongjiaomin xiang, the main thoroughfare of which was named *Jiang mi xing*, or the 'Lane of Glutinous Rice from the South.' This name stuck throughout the ensuing Ming and most of the Qing dynasty, although by the Ming sea transport was sufficently developed so that the canal ceased to be used for grain transport. The name *Dong jiao min xiang*, Eastern Lane Where the Peoples Mingle, dates from the later part of the Qing dynasty, and for many decades the two nearly homonymous names were used alternatively. Dongjiaomin xiang still refers to the entire former Legation Quarter as well as the street itself.

During the Ming and early Qing dynasties, the large rectangular area southeast of the Forbidden City was the location of the Six Boards, or ministries, of the imperial government. The first embassy of a 'foreign' nation in China, as opposed to tributary states like Burma, Annam, Korea and Mongolia who also established their missions here, was that of Russia, which was built on the future site of Legation Street in 1727. More than a century passed before France and Great Britain became the first European countries to establish their diplomatic presence here, after their troops destroyed the Yuanmingyuan (the old Summer Palace) in 1861.

The next major lurch in the evolution of this quarter can be credited to Empress Dowager Cixi, who in 1900 succeeded in unleashing the furore of the peasant secret society, known as the Boxers or 'Righteous and Harmonious Fists,' against foreigners and Chinese Christians in Peking.

The Empress Dowager had personally witnessed a demonstration of the Boxers' magical invulnerability to bullets and ordered her court attendants and palace ladies to practise the martial arts. In early 1900, the Boxers, with the support of the court, began to destroy rail and telegraph lines in north China as a symbolic attack on foreign influence in China. It was with rifles and torches rather than fists that they, reinforced by regular troops, attacked the Legation Quarter on a sweltering mid-June day that year, and held some 900 foreigners from 12 countries and 2,300 Chinese Christians under siege for 55 days. The miraculous survival of the majority of the besieged was due to the fact that the Manchu Rong-lu, who was in charge of the Beiyang (Northern Warlord) army, was not sympathetic to the Boxers, and only attacked the legations in form. The harsh retaliation of the 18,000-strong relief forces composed of soldiers from Britain, the U.S.A., Japan, Russia and France eventually led to the signing of the Peace Protocol of 1901, which gave foreign governments the right to establish legations in Peking. A wall was built around the quarter, and an open area (the *glacis*) outside the walls was provided for foreign troops to perform military exercises and play polo. As most of the buildings in the area had been burnt to the ground by the Boxers, the few remaining early structures here date from the first decade of this century.

In the immediate aftermath of this humiliating blow to imperial prestige, Cixi, the emperor and the court chose the most expedient path to safety: they fled Peking for two years, travelling as far west as Xi'an. Upon her return to Peking in 1902 Cixi discovered to her great dismay that those in power during her absence had granted the right of extraterritoriality to the eight countries whose armies had retaliated against the Boxer punch. Unlike the Shanghai international settlements, wrested from China by the terms of the unequal treaties from 1842 to 1860, Chinese people were not permitted to live in the Peking Legation Quarter.

When Chiang Kai-shek moved the capital of the Republic of China from Peking to Nanking (now spelled Nanjing) in 1928 (Nanking had briefly been the Ming capital in the mid-14th century) the foreign embassies followed suit, after which the 'Peiping' legations continued to maintain *de facto* extraterritoriality until they were taken over by the People's Government in 1949. In 1948 the eastern section of the legation quarter, part-glacis, part-polo-ground, was converted into an emergency airfield by general Fu Zuoyi, but it was little used. Today this area is Dongdan Park and Dongdan Stadium.

In the early 1950s, most Western countries withdrew their embassies from Beijing and set up shop in Taiwan, only to return to the mainland in the 1970s. In the interim the buildings in Legation Street were assigned to countries friendly to China: Bulgaria, Hungary, Burma, East Germany and India. In the 1950s the Soviets moved their legation to the spacious grounds of the early Russian Church mission in the northeast corner of the old city, where today it still lolls in the shadows of the Sino-Soviet falling out of 1960. In the 1980s foreign residents in Beijing were regularly invited here to enjoy champagne and caviar served by conspicuously muscular young Russians at Friday night film showings. All you had to do was phone the embassy and advise them your nationality, local address and status in China (tourist, diplomat, businessman, 'foreign expert,' or journalist), and the number of people coming in your car or taxi—they never asked your name.

No Beijing map available to the public today identifies the numerous government organizations now located in the former Legation Quarter, which include the High Court, Fire Department, Beijing City Government and Municipal Party Committee, Beijing Public Security Bureau, and the Association for Friendship with Foreign Countries. In the northern part of the Quarter, east of the Museum of Chinese History, are the ministries of Public Security and State Security. Some of these 'work units' have signs on their doors. Buildings without signs in China are assumed to belong to either the army or the police.

The Walk Nagels' *Guide* describes the quarter in the 1960s, with a *soupçon* of French disdain:

> It has nothing Chinese about it. The
> European houses combine all the styles in
> fashion at the beginning of the 20th cen-
> tury: mock gothic, mock baroque, mock
> Empire, modern style, with all the bad
> taste of the European nations and America
> put together.[1]

Sadly there is less and less to mock here, as the long–neglected buildings are being torn down one by one and replaced by new office blocks and hotels. And while the former Legation Quarter extends north as far as East Chang'an Street, few of the buildings in the northern section retain their original aspect or are concealed by walls impenetrable by mortal tourists. Thus we have confined our walk to Dongjiaomin xiang.

---

(1)   *Nagel's Encyclopedia Guide to China*
      (Geneva: Nagels Verlag, 1980), p. 531.

M. Henri Borel, 'Official Chinese Interpreter in the Dutch East Indies,' visited Peking around 1909 and recorded the following opinion of the quarter:

> What I, as an artist, cannot forgive my white brethren is that they have made this European Ghetto in Peking so ugly and commonplace. . . The entire Gesandschafts-Viertel [Legation Quarter] in Peking is a wretched crowd of dull buildings trying to look fine, all scrolls and bays and trivialities, all in that vile conventional modern style which causes the new portions of all European capitals to look exactly like each other. A dull, crude common-place city of barbarians, shapeless, colourless, lacking in distinction, huddled in the midst of the exquisite old Chinese architecture which makes Peking a magnificent dream.[2]

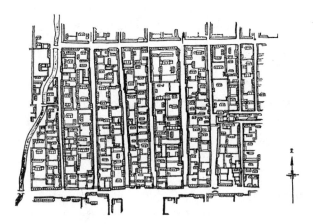

Street plan in the Qianlong era

---

(2) Henri Borel *The New China: A Traveller's Impressions* (London: T. Fisher Unwin, 1912), p. 42.

Start your walk at the **Xinqiao Hotel**, located at the east end of Dong jiao min xiang where it meets Chong wen men nei da jie. The Xinqiao (New bridge) dates back to the 1950s when friendship bridged the ideological gap between the Chinese and Soviet peoples, but in recent years most of the residents have been Japanese businessmen. On the north side of the street at the first corner is the former Deutsche Asiatische Bank. To the north of this once stood the German hospital, now swallowed up by Beijing Hospital.

At the next crossing, where Dongjiaominxiang meets Tai ji chang, the church on the north side of the street, **St. Michael's**, was built by the French Vincentians in 1902 and once housed an excellent organ which is no longer to be seen. It has recently been restored in a shabby, economical fashion and is open for masses as the Dong jiao min xiang Catholic Church. The impressive red building on the south side of the street was the Belgian Embassy, modelled after a villa in Brussels that belonged to King Leopold II (1835–1909). After 1949 it became the Burmese Embassy. Today, it is one of the several buildings making up the Ruijin Hotel, which is run by the State Council.

Cross Taijichang, formerly Rue Marco Polo (one of the many pre-1949 foreign street names that might be restored, since Marco has contributed more free propaganda for China over the centuries than any other foreign devil, despite the fact he may have never been here). The large, walled and guarded compound with its impressive fortress-like gate on the north side of the street **#15**, the former site of the French legation, is now a state guesthouse where Prince Sihanouk stays on his visits to Beijing. This compound, like that of the former British legation or ('fu'), was a Manchu prince's mansion in the 1860s before financial troubles forced its owners to rent it out. The buildings in the compound were nearly totally destroyed during the Boxer catastrophe. Next to the former French legation is a Chinese bank and post office that took over the premises of the U.S. post office in the 1920s.

Heading west, the large new hotel on the south side of the street, the **Capital Hotel**, is run by the State Council, and stands on the site of the German legation. Next door to it is the Hongdu Tailors, reputedly one of the best in Beijing. Jardine Matheson, the Hong Kong traders, once had an office in this block. Somewhat beyond it, on the second-to-last plot on this block, there once stood a general store called Keirulf's, the first shop for foreigners in Peking, and similar to today's Friendship Stores in several respects. An essential 1930s guidebook, *In Search of Old Peking,* informs us that:

> The Chinese strongly opposed [Keirulf's]
> opening in the early nineties on the ground
> that Peking was not a Treaty Port and
> therefore foreign trade forbidden, but
> finally gave way to the argument that the
> members of the Legations required a shop
> where they could buy the necessities of
> life. . . As a matter of fact, it was not the
> Diplomatic Body. . .that made the fortune
> of Kierulf's store, but the Manchu and
> Mongol princes who right up to the time of
> the 1911 Revolution could be seen almost
> any day wandering through the shop,
> accompanied by a bevy of concubines and
> their retainers, selecting every and any
> kind of foreign toy that happened to strike
> their fancy.[3]

On the right at the intersection of **Zheng yi Road** (formerly Rue Meiji), the well preserved building on the corner is the former Yokohama Species Bank, now a

---

(3)   L.C. Arlington and William Lewisohn *In Search of Old Peking* (Peking: Henry Vetch 1935; reprinted by Oxford University Press, 1987), p. 10.

Chinese finance corporation. The building next to it was the Spanish legation. The south corner was the site of one of Old Peking's best-known hotels, the Grand Hotel des Wagons-Lits. Borel stayed there briefly and described his room:

> A trim English bed with silk eiderdowns, lace curtains, a large wardrobe with mirror, electric light bulbs, a lavatory with taps for hot and cold water, a little lamp with red silk shade on a small table by the bed, a comfortable easy-chair—everything in the best modern style. Did I come to Peking for this? . . . I expected to reach to China's mysterious capital, and I find myself landed in a Parisian hotel.[4] The hotel's clinetele, 'high, low and middle-class . . . mixed into a social hotch-potch' soon got on his nerves: I found it impossible to collect my thoughts in the clamour and rushing to and fro of all these noisy, showy wanderers. Behind the assumed airs of luxury and distinction I perceived too much of the snobbishness and vulgarity of Monte Carlo and such places. And I moved into a small, second-rate hotel outside the walls of the Legation Quarter, in the Tartar City, opposite the Italian Glacis on the Viale d'Italia, the Hotel de Pekin.[5]

This of course is the central section of the now–famous Beijing Hotel on East Chang'an Boulevard, which in those days.

---

(4) Henri Borel *The New China: A Traveller's Impressions*, p. 32.
(5) Henri Borel *The New China: A Traveller's Impressions*, p. 79.

> . . . was furnished as poorly as possible
> with ramshackle beds, worn-out mat-
> tresses, sheets full of holes, and ordinary
> iron garden chairs. On entering such a
> room one feels a sensation of being down
> on his luck, of having seen better days . . .
> The rooms are comfortless, decay stares at
> one from broken tables and dilapidated
> ash-trays that seem to be advertisements
> for whisky. . . Yet. . . from this miserable
> little hotel I learned to understand Peking.
> **(6)**

The pleasant park in the middle of **Zhengyi Road** was created in 1925 when the canal that conveyed water from Zhongnanhai and served as a receptacle for rubbish from the neighbourhood was filled in. The wide east–west road to the south, Qian men dong Street, was the location of the southern wall of the **Tartar City** until the wall was demolished in the 1960s. To the south of this wall lay the **Chinese City**. The street immediately inside the wall that ran parallel to it was called Wall Street. Where the canal passed through the wall there was a sluice gate, through which the British Indian troops made their way into the Legation Quarter to relieve the prisoners during the Boxer siege in 1900: it was known as the Water Gate.

In the middle of the next block the former site of the Russian legation on the north is now occupied by several buildings belonging to **China's High Court**. The modest wooden door to the west of the main gate is where Chinese citizens or organizations enter complaints against state organizations or their employees. The squat building with grey Roman columns on the south side of the street directly across from the High Court, now the headquarters of the Beijing Fire Department, was the National City Bank of New York, and before that, the Russia Asiatic Bank. The

---

(6)   Henri Borel *The New China: A Traveller's Impressions,* p.83.

emblem in the shield crowning the columns appears to read N.C.B.. In the low building further down the street, belonging to the Beijing Public Security Bureau, Chinese citizens apply for passports to go abroad. The yellow-tiled building on the corner of the north side of the street was the office of the Chinese Eastern Railway, and somewhat beyond this quiet alley running north off the street that until recently had an old sign embedded in its wall that read U.S.S.R. Embassy Compound Lane. The Russian barracks once lay to the east of this wall. A bit further back on Legation Street, the bricked-up gate used to be the entrance to the Dutch legation, which managed to please the usually bilious Dutchman Borel, who described it as possessing. . .

> . . . something of aristocratic simplicity. It has the stately distinction of the finest old mansions and castle of the Netherlands. It is solid yet characteristic, sumptuous yet sober, and has a genuine Dutch stamp.[7]

***

(7)   Henri Borel *The New China: A Traveller's Impressions,* p. 43.

The next building on the south side of the street is the former American legation, rebuilt in 1901 after the Boxer catastrophe, and now belonging to the People's Court. The building on the north side of the street, a bit further down, was the French Hospital. This takes us to the end of Legation Street.

Here you will find a staircase that descends to **Tiananmen Square**, which is treated in Walk 1. Head south and cross the broad street where the city wall once stood, now Qian men dong Street, but as mentioned above once called Wall Street. The large brick building on the corner is the **Railroad Workers' Club**, formerly the old Peking Railway Station, the terminus of the line from Tianjin. The present Beijing Railway Station which is worth a visit just to watch the people waiting for their trains now lies about one mile to the east of here.

Immediately to the west are two large city gates which were at one time part of the south wall of the Tartar City. The southernmost structure is the **Arrow Tower** (*Jian lou*), which burnt down in 1900 and was reconstructed in 1903 following the design of a German architect, who added the European-style eyebrows over the windows. The city wall itself extended east and west from the **Gate Facing the Sun** (*Zheng yang men*), the structure to the north with its single opening. Until around 1915 a semi-circular *enceinte* wall linked the Arrow Tower to the gate, providing shelter for two temples and a number of stalls that conducted their trade inside. By looking at the **Gate Facing the Sun** from the side, you can get an idea of the impressive height and thickness of the dearly departed city walls.

Debates about preserving the old walled city of Peking raged for decades. During the Japanese occupation (1937–45), Japanese planners supported the idea of building a modern **New Capital** (*Xing jing*) in the western suburbs outside the old walled city, and arguments in favour of this plan continued to be raised in the early 1950s, notably by the American-trained architectural historian Liang Sicheng. The Liang camp advocated leaving the old city walls intact and preserving untouched most of what stood inside them. But a directive from Chairman Mao himself sealed the fate of the walls, and now the western suburbs remain relatively undeveloped except for military bases, high officials' *dachas* and a 'secret' military airport, the Xi Yuan.

As the construction of public housing could not keep up with population growth (thanks to Mao's having urged the masses in the 1950s to procreate vigorously as a national defense tactic), nearly all of the tens of thousands of traditional courtyard houses in Beijing were converted into **da za yuan**, literally 'big heterogeneous courtyards.' This meant that residences formerly occupied by a single family were subdivided and as many as four or five families were moved in. And during the Cultural Revolution (1966–76), most of the space in the courtyards was filled up with jerry-built kitchens, bedrooms, and storage rooms to accommodate the offspring of the post-Liberation baby boom. In the 1950s a few privileged Red-blooded families were assigned spacious traditional courtyard houses (with servants)—the finest of them consisting of three or more contiguous courtyards on a north–south axis—complete with gardens, rockeries and ponds, not to mention modern plumbing, hot water, and central heating. One method the Chinese Government used to obtain these properties during the first decade of the People's Republic was to first accuse the original owners of these homes of being 'bourgeois landlords' and confiscate their 'surplus' property. Then the government would drive the landlords out of their own homes by raising property taxes to the point where they could no longer afford to pay them, having already been deprived of their main source of income.

Dazhalan (Dashalar)

From the **Railroad Workers Club**, continue southwest along the semi-circular street crowded with hawkers and shops, and cross the large north–south street, **Qian men Street** (*Qian men da jie*). If for some reason you feel you need some Kentucky Fried Chicken to bolster you at this

Dazhalan

N

Chairman Mao Memorial Hall
TIANANMEN SQUARE
High Court
Gate Facing the Sun
Arrow Tower
Railroad Workers Club

Dongjiaomin Xiang
Xinqiao Hotel
Taijichang
Capital Hotel
Zhengyi Road
Dongjiaomin Xiang
East Qianmen Street

West Qianmen Street

Langfang Tou Tiao
Langfang Er Tiao
Qudeng Hutong
Saolu Hutong
Yanshou Street
Liulichang

Dazhalan Street
Zhubaoshi Jie
Qianmen Dajie
West Dazhalan Street
Meishi Jie
Shaanxi Lane
Zhushikou Xi Dajie

Chongwenmen Wai Dajie
Dong Dajie
Zhushikou
Zhu Shi Kou

© The Guidebook Company Ltd

point, it is available at a large and successful joint-venture outlet a few minutes to the west of the intersection. If you choose not to patronize the Colonel, then turn left into the next north–south street, **Zhu bao shi jie** (Jewellery Street). Several doors down on the second floor of a commercial building is the traditional style **Lao She Teahouse**, named after the famous Beijing author of Richshaw Boy, who committed suicide during the Cultural Revolution. Performances by old time ballad singers, conjurors and stand up comedians are held here in the afternoon and evening.

The area we are in now is popularly called **Da sha lar**, Pekinese dialect for Da zha lan, literally 'big stockades.' Stockades of wood or iron were used here in Ming times to close off the streets during the evening curfew. Dashalar and its environs were the most important commercial and entertainment districts during the Ming and Qing dynasties. One reason for this is its location immediately outside of the Imperial City, where certain classes of establishments were prohibited, notably theatres, shops, restaurants and brothels. Here in the relatively free atmosphere of the Chinese City, Manchu officials would let down their queues, and emperors would come in mufti to taste the pleasures of the common man.

The street life in this part of town was described by a traveller in 1888:

> . . . all manner of cheap, useful things, and
> stores of food are also outspread upon the
> ground, and became more and more
> thickly coated with dust [the dust of
> Peking!] as the ceaseless traffic of the day
> moves on. The strange market seemed to
> extend for nearly a mile, and oh! the noise,
> and oh! the extraordinary variety of smells,
> all evil, which assailed us as we passed the
> busy crowd of much-chattering buyers and
> sellers.

On all sides were merchants shouting out descriptions of their wares; blind musicians wandering about in companies, making horrible discords; jugglers exhibiting strange feats to the delight of the crowd; barbers plying their razors on shaven crowns and faces, and carefully plaiting the long black tresses; while quack doctors and mountebanks of all sorts each added their share to the general din. Dentists and chiropodists both shout their invitations to suffering mankind to enter the booths, where, in presence of all who care to gaze, they carry on their work. The chiropodists are said to be exceedingly skilful.[8]

Preparing snacks

(8)   C.F. Gordon Cumming *Wanderings in China* (Edinburgh and London: William Blackwood and Sons, 1888), p. 448.

The world's oldest profession has a long history in China, the world's oldest continual civilization, and the Eight Big Hutongs, a district southwest of Dashalar, was where the action was. Like their counterparts in Japan, high-class courtesans were sought out as much for their companionship or for their literary and musical talents, as for their physical charms. Brothels with dreamy names like The Cassia and Lotus Garden, or The Fragrant Clouds provided a range of services to their male customers. If you were dining out in a restaurant, you could send a boy with a chit to a brothel and your favourite would be delivered to your side by rickshaw in a matter of minutes. Chinese guidebooks to Peking published in the Republican period placed the houses in three classes and listed the girls' 'flower names,' described the appointments of the rooms (some even had electric fans), quoted prices and outlined brothel protocol. For example, new customers paid cash, while regulars could sign and settled their accounts three times a year. Good customers also enjoyed discounts. In early 1920s there were 78 first-class houses, 85 second-class houses and 57 third-class houses in Peking, in addition to Japanese–brothels where the Chinese customers might go and brothels for foreigners where Chinese were not welcome. Though morally reprehensible to some, the profession was practised with the approval of the government, which licensed the brothels and the girls, and carried out regular health inspections. Courtesans and concubines have always had their place in Chinese society, and there were as many dire tragedies as glamorous success stories. Lao She's story, *Crescent Moon* [9] chronicles the career of a Peking prostitute in a memorably moving way.

The Dazhalan district remains refreshingly seedy today and for the most part the buildings have not been torn down or modernized, although they have suffered seriously because of a lack of maintanance. Some of the first-

---

(9)   Lao She *Crescent Moon and Other Stories*
      (Beijing: Panda Books, 1985), pp. 191–231.

class brothels occupied the solidly built two-storey buildings that still line the streets. Prostitution is of course, illegal in China today, but the profession has seen a revival since the late 1970s when China opened to the West in more ways than one.

Continue south along Zhu bao shi jie and turn into the second street on your right, **Lang fang er tiao**, in the old days known in English as Jade Street. For the sake of orientations on the northwest corner of the street there is a pale green two-storey ornate building. Note the appropriateness of these small *hutongs* for travel by rickshaw and pedicab.

As you stroll down the *hutong*, notice the carved and painted wooden decorative panels on houses **#10, 12** and **14**. These were once fairly common on both shops and private homes. At **#56**, you will be able to see women in white hospital gowns wrapping squares of dough 'skin' or dough pockets around a ground pork filling to make *jiaozi* dumplings and *baozi* steamed buns, favourite northern Chinese snacks. Most of the tiny restaurants you will pass by here are privately run. At **#80**, a two-storeyed building, the old sign carved in brick set into the wall reads Ruiwenzhai Jade Shop. The large building on the left at **#102** was a bank before 1949. The second crossing, where there is an outdoor vegetable market, is called **Mei shi jie** (Coal Market Street), a street once famous for its restaurants.

Cross Mei shi jie, bear left (or south) and enter **Qu deng hutong** (Matches Alley). At **#8**, there is a nearly obliterated Chinese character for 'felicity' on the lintel above the door. Note the old door handles on **#11** and the carved stones at the base of the door. There are two beams in the lintel at **#13**. Beams of this sort appear above the front doors of 'better' homes and palaces in Beijing, always in twos and fours depending on the statue of the inhabitants. The double doors at **#17** are peppered with a nailhead design to protect them from being kicked to pieces. **#19** with its four beams was the home of a noted Qing-dynasty scholar, who was awarded this property by the emperor. Incidentally, before military ranks were restored in 1988, you could determine the rank of a soldier in the People's Liberation Army by counting his pockets; two meant an enlisted man, four an officer. Officers are further distinguished by the quality of the cloth and tailoring of their uniforms.

An auspicious couplet is carved on the door of **#21**. Note the decorative stones, functioning as door gods and dismounting stones, at **#23**.

Bear right at the next intersection, go past the shop on the corner, and bear left and enter **Sao fu** (broom) *hutong*. On the first door on the left, note how here again, the Chinese character *fu* 'felicity' on the lintel has been nearly wiped out. During the Cultural Revolution, auspicious inscriptions like *fu* and *shou* 'longevity' (look for the huge black *shou* in the hand of the Empress Dowager in the Palace of Benevolence and Longevity in the Summer Palace) were obliterated as part of the campaign to blot out remnants of the feudal past, and its accompanying felicity.

You can inspect a typical big heterogeneous courtyard (*da za yuan*) at **#31**, where one of the inhabitants runs a public telephone service. At present, one out of about 50 families in Beijing have their own telephones at home. It costs ten *fen* to make a call here. For incoming calls, if the proprietors have to go out into the *hutong* and get you, it costs 20 or 30 *fen*, and in bad weather the price may be negotiable. While your fingers are wandering around the dial you may observe the life going on around you. There is generally greater activity before lunch and dinner, and less during the Chinese post-prandial siesta hour, which runs from noon to two, or from noon to three in the summer.

Continue to the end of this *hutong*, turn left and continue on for about 50 meters (165 feet). You will run into a busy food market. This is **Yan shou** (increasing longevity) **Street**, marked by a sign on the wall above an abandoned millstone. Another minute's walk brings us to the east end of Liulichang, our final destination on this walk.

Please note: the route just taken is a simple one and should not constrain you from exploring further afield.

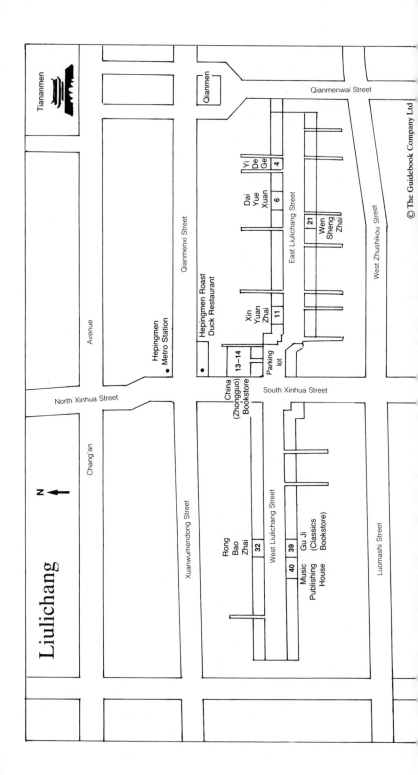

Liulichang

N

Tiananmen

Chang'an   Avenue

North Xinhua Street

Xuanwumendong Street

Qianmenxi Street

Qianmen

Qianmenwai Street

Hepingmen
Metro Station

Hepingmen Roast
Duck Restaurant

Xin
Yuan
Zhai

11

13–14

China
(Zhongguo)
Bookstore

Parking
lot

South Xinhua Street

Dai
Yue
Xuan

6

Yi
De
Ge

4

East Liulichang Street

21
Wen
Sheng
Zhai

West Zhushikou Street

Rong
Bao
Zhai

32

West Liulichang Street

40   39

Music
Publishing
House

Gu Ji
(Classics
Bookstore)

Luomashi Street

© The Guidebook Company Ltd

There are traces of Old Peking to be found in every *hutong* in this part of town, and a morning or afternoon spent walking or riding a bicycle here will inevitably be rewarding.

Liulichang

The history of Luilichang, literally 'glazed tile factory,' as a centre of cultural activity in Peking dates back to the first half of the 17th century. During the early Ming, this street was the site of one of the five kilns in the vicinity that produced bricks and glazed tiles especially for the palaces and halls being built in Yongle's new capital. Canals linked the kiln with sources of clay and other raw materials in the western suburbs, and the former presence of bridges spanning these canals is attested to by contemporary street names containing the word 'bridge.'

During the Qing dynasty, the district gradually became a popular residential neighbourhood for Chinese officials serving in the Manchu government who were not permitted to live in the Tartar City. The area was also a popular locale for guesthouses run by provincial and prefectural benevolent associations where native sons visiting the capital on business or sitting for the imperial examinations could stay. This all-male cadre of officials, merchants and young scholars whiled away their leisure moments in the brothels and restaurants of nearby Dashalar. But they also patronized the many local stalls and shops dealing in scholarly books, brushes, ink, paper, paintings, calligraphy, rubbings, antiques, curios and such scholarly affectations as spectacles and tobacco pipes that had opened here to meet their needs. Another historical factor in the development of Liulichang was Qianlong's late-18th-century project to compile a vast *Encyclopedia of All Knowledge Under Heaven*, for which the court needed to acquire a huge corpus of old and rare books.

After the fall of the Qing dynasty in 1911, Liulichang became an outlet for Manchus recently deprived of their hereditary stipends, to dispose of their private libraries and antiques as a means of survival. Many of the rare Chinese books and works of art that are now in the collections of Western libraries and museums were acquired at this time.

Regarding the present antiques trade in and around Liulichang, Juliet Bredon's warning written 60 years ago in 1932 still holds true:

> Alas, the days of marvellous finds and
> bargains . . . are over. Do not imagine that
> if by chance a good piece comes on the
> market, any stranger will pick it up for a
> song. . . . Approach all curios, and most
> dealers, with caution.[10]

There are two types of shops in Liulichang today, government and private. In the state stores prices are fixed, and, particularly on less expensive items, it is futile to attempt to practise the fine Oriental art of bargaining. But you would be foolish *not* to bargain in the privately run shops here, and elsewhere throughout Beijing. Other antique markets can be found at Hongqiao, near the Temple of Heaven; at the **Chaonei Market** near the embassy area; and at the somewhat isolated **Old Goods Market** (*Jiu huo shichang*) about two kilometers south of Jinsong. Bredon teaches us precisely how to do it:

> . . . it is usual for most dealers to ask from
> a quarter to two-thirds more than they
> hope to receive—sometimes as much as
> they dare, or believe the customer can be
> induced to pay . . . Offer, as a rule, a little
> more than half what is asked, then, as the
> merchant gradually comes down in his
> price, increase very gradually until neutral
> ground is reached. Finally, split the

---

(10) Juliet Bredon *Peking* (Shanghai: 1931; reprinted by Oxford University Press 1982), p. 448–51.

Itinerant Restaurateur, Qing dynasty

difference, and the bargain is yours. If one is in a hurry or shows any enthusiasm for the article in question, it is impossible to make a cheap purchase. Point out the defects in the piece under discussion . . . A good plan is to leave the shop when the owner, afraid of losing a customer, runs after you with a last offer—the lowest price, or nearly—that he is prepared to accept.[11]

As for the shops themselves, Juliet Bredon is an astute judge:

. . . Some have facades of gilded wood so elaborately carved that we feel they should be put under glass as a protection against the dust, but none have show windows.

---

(11) Juliet Bredon *Peking,* p. 473.

> Indeed, few have windows at all, and the
> dark, low doorways give little promise of
> the treasures to be found within. It is fatal
> to judge, as we would at home, by appear-
> ances . . . The biggest, and the cleanest
> shops in Peking may not have the best
> things. Often a merchant hidden away in a
> blind alley has the rarest treasures . . . [12]

In the mid-1980s, Liulichang was transformed from the ground up into a spick-and-span idealization of its former, more homely seediness. The street is divided into two sections, east and west, by South Nan xin hua Street. The east section contains dozens of antiques shops; the west, mostly shops selling books and paintings. We enter Liulichang from the east end, and pass a number of privately owned curio shops. Despite the warnings above, these shops are worth pottering around in, if only to train and test your eye. They occasionally have museum-quality pieces for sale, but unless you know your way around antiques, it is unwise to spend large sums in them.

For many centuries and as recently as the early 1950s, Liulichang was the site of an outdoor bazaar held every year during the first two weeks of the Chinese new year, the so-called Spring Festival. This event, known as the Changdian (Tile-factory district) Fair, took place in both East and West Liulichang, in the **Temple to the God of Fire** (*Huo shen miao*) on East Liulichang Street (now a neighbourhood cultural 'palace'), and all along Nanxinhua Street. H.Y. Lowe was a habitué of the fair, and gives this colourful description of what was on sale here in his charming book on Peking, *The Adventures of Wu*:

> . . . here is a full representation of Peking's
> own and imported toycraft, from the

---

(12) Juliet Bredon *Peking*, p. 444.

cheap native jack-in-the-box made of
paper and mud to the expensive clock-
work toy train or toy airplanes, papier-
mâché theatre masks complete with beards
of white or black horse hair, life size
wooden replicas of ancient war weapons
familiarly seen in the hands of the military
heroes of the Chinese stage, little motor-
boats with oil burners that spin about in a
face basin filled with water, and midget
movies shaped by the clever hands of the
makers from the tinsmith's castaway pieces
of tin and from pieces of old films cut into
'stills'. Paper butterflies operated by a
rubber band propeller that actually soar
into the sky are sold after demonstration
and trial. The toy-balloon sellers bring
their chemical laboratories with them
including little pieces of galvanized iron
with the indispensable zinc coating and
bottles of sulphuric acid, with which in a
flask hydrogen is 'brewed'and balloons
filled right under the eyes of the watchful
and waiting customers.[13]

Other handicrafts included pinwheels,
paper lanterns (especially for the Lantern
Festival on the 15th day of the first month),
painted kites, diabolos, shuttlecocks, rice-
flour dough figurines, tiny monkey puppets,
birds and butterflies made of dried mud,
miniature buildings crafted of coloured straw
for use in bonsai landscapes, pocket cross-

---

(13) H.Y. Lowe, *The Adventures of Wu: The Life Cycle of a Peking Man*
(Peking: The Peking Chronicle Press, 1940–1; reprinted by
Princeton University Press, 1983), II, p. 174.

bows, and the famous 'pupu deng, the gourd-shaped sounding bottle of blown glass in a vicious colour of dark red with the bottom end not much thicker than the film on your teeth which Pepsodent toothpaste destroys and which are played by alternatingly blowing and inhaling to produce the characteristic sound from which their name is derived.' [14]

So-called Canton goods-dealers sold 'old pieces of cut-glass vases and plates from Hamburg or brass samovars from Tomsk, hardwood boxes and trays with inlay work of mother-of-pearl.' [15]

In the Temple of the God of Fire one could find the stalls and booths of the jewellery traders, who kept their electric lights burning during the day, quite an extravagance in those times. Here the ladies would haggle genteelly for precious and semi-precious and not-so-precious stones.

Old books, paintings and calligraphy were displayed along Xinhua Street. The books ranged from rare editions of the Chinese classics to such Western works as 'bulky volumes of some old export catalogues of railway locomotives and plumbing or electric fixtures, or even some hoary, old editions of commercial directories of London or Antwerp, older than the booksellers themselves.' [16]

The book fair has been revived in a way and takes place during the first two weeks of the Spring Festival in the

---

(14) H.Y. Lowe *The Adventures of Wu*, II, p. 175.
(15) H.Y. Lowe *The Adventures of Wu*, II, p. 176.
(16) H.Y. Lowe *The Adventures of Wu*, II, p. 178.

courtyard of the **China Book Store** (*Zhong guo shu dian*), the former **Ocean King Village** (*Hai wang cun*). The name derives from a merchant in the Liao dynasty (*c.* A.D. 1000) who monopolized the local grain barge business when this was a district of canals. Elsewhere in Beijing, a number of 'temple fairs' are held during the Spring Festival, with traditional *pupu deng* among the goods being offered.

No fair could be complete without its food stalls, and Changdian had its own specialities: sour bean juice; sweet black peas cooked into porridge; spherical dumplings of glutinous rice filled with sweetened walnuts; sesame seeds preserved fruit or date butter; cotton candy; and candied crab apples on a stick.

A number of speciality shops that operate in Liulichang today have venerable histories. Short descriptions will follow the street number, beginning from the east. None of the antiques stores will be mentioned here, as they have mostly lost their character. But they too are worth a visit as a way of observing the official approach to antique dealing.

#4—Yi De Ge has been manufacturing Chinese India ink since 1865. Before the middle of the 19th century, all ink used by calligraphers and painters in China came in the form of dry sticks that had to be rubbed with water on an inkstone. This long, tedious process might have offered leisured poets and scholars an opportunity to meditate on the act of creation while they exercised their elbows, but candidates sitting for the imperial examinations had little time or patience for such practices, so a clever scholar named Xie—who had failed in the examinations himself— came up with the idea of making ink in liquid form and selling it to the examinees before they were sealed up in their cubicles. His venture was an immediate success.

At first Xie used a rather primitive method to make his ink. He combined lamp black scraped off metal plates suspended over oil lamps, tar from burnt rosin collected in chimneys, bone glue and water. Today modern machinery is used and the ingredients are a bit simpler: Sichuan carbon black scented with musk, camphor and borneol. The factory produces about ten million bottles of ink per year.

#6—Dai Yue Xuan has been selling brushes for Chinese painting and calligraphy since 1916. Great precision is required in trimming the animal hairs that make up the tip and securing it in the bamboo handle. The brushes are classified into four types, according to the sort of hair used: goat, fox, rabbit and various combinations of the three.

#11—Xin Yuan Zhai is famous for its sour plum juice, a beverage made from the dried pulp of plums picked before they are ripe, mixed with ground cassia buds, according to a recipe from the Qing-dynasty palace kitchen. The shop was founded over 200 years ago.

#21—Wen Sheng Zhai has specialized in manufacturing decorative lanterns and fans since the 18th century. It made its name by supplying 'palace lanterns' to the Qing palace and mansions of the Manchu princes, and the shop's lanterns are still hung on Tiananmen Gate during the Chinese new year.

#32—Rong Bao Zhai Studio is the largest and most famous shop in Liulichang. It deals in the 'Four Treasures of the Studio'—ink, brushes, paper and inkstones; Chinese scroll paintings and calligraphy; and most notably coloured woodblock reproductions of paintings. Rongbaozhai was founded in the 17th century, but not until 1894 did it adopt its present name, a shortened form of the adage 'an honourable name is a priceless jewel'.

The basic techniques used in woodblock printing date back over 1,000 years to the Tang dynasty, but the Rongbaozhai workshop has devised ways to produce such fine reproductions of brush paintings that noted painters like Qi Baishi have mistaken them for their own originals!

Scholarly books, new and used, in Chinese and Western languages, are sold in the China Book Store on the north side of the parking lot east of South Xinhua Street, and in several shops on the south side of West Liulichang Street. The China Book Store also has a large selection of used books in Japanese and Western languages, as well as rare books published in China. Some of the stock is drawn from pre-1949 libraries, embassies churches and private collections. This is a fascinating hodgepodge for bibliophiles, with many surprises. Prices range from reasonable to high. A much smaller collection of this type can be found on West Liulichang Street at **#39**, the Bu Ji (Classic) Bookstore. Many of the better art books have English abstracts. **#40** specializes in Chinese and Western musical instruments, some of which are wonderful handicrafts. From here you could walk back to Dashalar via a different route, or end the day with a Peking duck dinner at the nearby Quanjude restaurant at Hepingmen.

Walk · 3

Beihai Park and the Three Rear Lakes— Shi Cha Hai

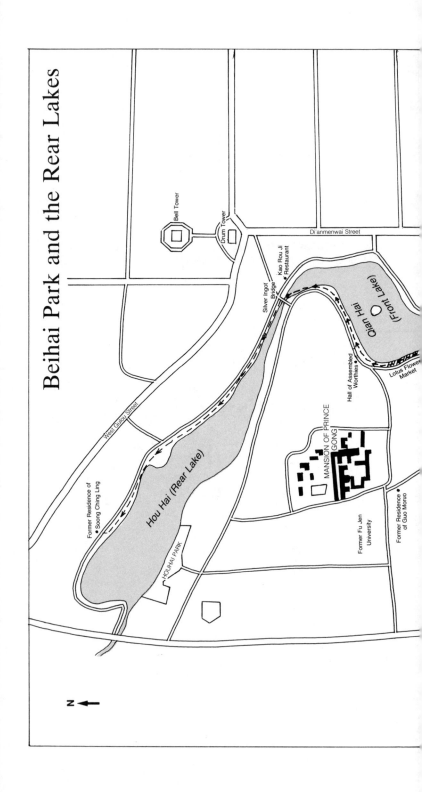

Beihai Park and the Rear Lakes

N

Bell Tower

Drum Tower

Di'anmenwai Street

West Gulou Street

Kao Rou Ji Restaurant

Silver Ingot Bridge

Former Residence of Soong Ching Ling

Hou Hai (Rear Lake)

Qian Hai (Front Lake)

Hall of Assembled Worthies

Lotus Flower Market

MANSION OF PRINCE GONG

HOUHAI PARK

Former Fu Jen University

Former Residence of Guo Moruo

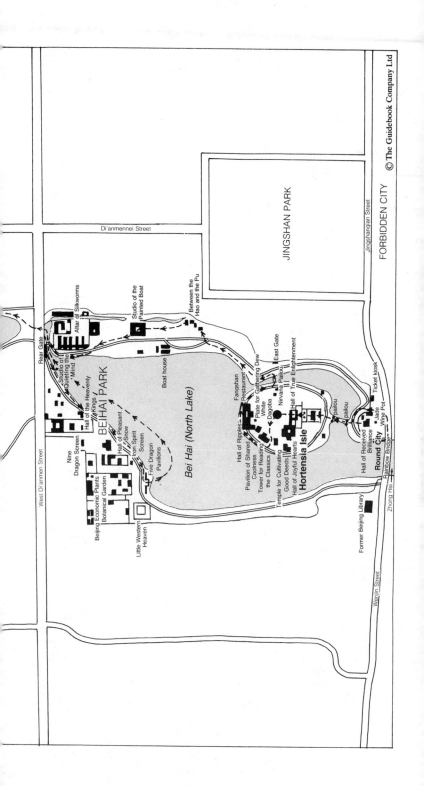

BEIHAI PARK

Bei Hai (North Lake)

JINGSHAN PARK

Di'anmennei Street

Jingshanqian Street

West Di'anmen Street

Wenjin Street

Zhong Hai

Rear Gate

Studio of Quieting the Mind

Hall of the Heavenly Kings

Altar of Silkworms

Studio of the Painted Boat

Between the Hao and the Pu

Boat house

Nine Dragon Screen

Hall of Pleasant Snow

Iron Spirit Screen

Five Dragon Pavilions

Beijing Economic Plants Botanical Garden

Little Western Heaven

Hall of Ripples

Fangshan Restaurant

East Gate

Plate for Gathering Dew

White Dagoba

Nirvana Pailou

Hall of True Enlightenment

Pavilion of Shared Coolness

Tower for Reading the Classics

Temple for Cultivating Good Deeds

Hall of Joyful Hearts

Hortensia Isle

pailou

pailou

Hall of Received Brilliance

Round City

Jade Wine Pot

Ticket kiosk

Rainbow Bridge

Former Beijing Library

FORBIDDEN CITY

© The Guidebook Company Ltd

Duration

Approximately five hours.

Description

Visit imperial parks that fit 13th-century descriptions by Marco Polo. Stroll along the shores of man-made lakes once reserved for the imperial family. **Beihai Park** is open from 7 A.M. to 7.30 P.M. in the winter and from 5.30 A.M. to 9.30 P.M. in the summer. The **Rear Lakes**, known popularly as **Shi cha hai** ('Sea of Ten Buddhist Temples') have no opening and closing times. It is suggested that you begin in Beihai Park in mid-morning, eat traditional snacks for lunch at the stalls in **Lotus Flower Market** (*He hua shi chang*) on the western shore of **Front Lake** (*Qianhai*) and watch the sun set through the willows on the shores of **Rear Lake** (*Hou hai*) in the early evening.

Starting Point

Rainbow Bridge that divides Beihai from Zhonghai.

How to Get There
Buses 5, 101, 103, 107, 109, 111 stop at Beihai.

How to Get Away
From the **Drum Tower** (*Gu lou*), take buses 5, 8, 18, 107, 204, 305 or the Beijing underground (metro) at *Gu lou da jie*, about a ten-minute walk north from the tower. From the rear gate of Beihai (*Bei hai hou men*) take buses 13, 42, 107, 111, 118, 204.

A string of six contiguous lakes runs north–south through the centre of Beijing, fed by a stream that has its source in the northwest suburbs. Practically speaking the six lakes are divided into three areas: the three lakes of Shi cha hai in the north, which are now part of a park; **Beihai** (North 'sea') in the middle, also a park; and **Zhongnanhai** (Central and South 'seas') in the south, which are part of the walled compound of the same name, now the headquarters of the Central Committee of the Communist Party of China, a sanctum sanctorum where China's top leaders live, work and play.

The history of imperial lakes goes back more than 2,000 years. In the third century B.C., the megalomaniac First Emperor of the Qin dynasty (who resided at Xianyang, near present-day Xi'an in central China) dispatched one of his officials and a boat full of children on a quest for the elixir of immortality. They sailed eastward over the sea, so the legend goes, in search of the fabled Isles of the Blessed, where they hoped to trade the children for the youth-giving drug. Needless to say, they never returned.

One century later, the **Han Martial Emperor** (reigned 140–86 B.C.), taking a hint from his less than illustrious predecessor, had a pool dug on his palace grounds in Chang'an (now Xi'an) and piled up the sludge into three hills, thus creating his own backyard isles of the blessed. He called this body of water the **Pool of Great Secretion** (*Tai ye chi*; also rendered as the **Pool of Great Fertilizing Spume**, or the **Great Saliva Pool**; the esoteric liquid referred to here is the result of the metaphysical confluence of *yin* and *yang* and does not refer to the stuff spittoons are filled with).

Every dynasty that has made Peking its capital has had a pleasure park, complete with pool and peaks, in the vicinity of present-day Beihai Park. The nomenclature is rather complex. As early as the Tang dynasty (618–906), there was a park of this nature in Youzhou, as the regional capital of that dynasty was called. When the Liao dynasty (907–1125) made Youzhou its summer capital, they rebuilt the gardens here. The emperors of the Jin dynasty (1115–1234) constructed an artificial hill in the middle of the lake that they had expanded, and transported Lake Taihu stones from the Song-dynasty palace at Bianliang (now Kaifeng) in the south to decorate it. The present name of the island in Beihai Park, **Hortensia Isle** (*Qiong hua dao*) dates from this period. In the 13th century after the founding of the Yuan dynasty, this part of the city became an imperial garden in the Mongol palace, and in the early 15th century Emperor Yongle of the Ming dynasty created Nanhai, the southernmost of the six lakes that resembles a curled-up appendix. Throughout the Ming and Qing dynasties, the three southern lakes (Beihai, Zhonghai and Nanhai) formed part of the private gardens of the emperors. Zhonghai and Nanhai were the liquid entrepieces of the **Western Garden** (*Xi yuan*), so named because of its location due west of the Forbidden City.

After the fall of the Qing dynasty in 1911, the new Republican government established its Presidential Palace on the shores of Nanhai but only made use of it until 1925. After the founding of the People's Republic in 1949, Mao Zedong followed suit and chose Zhongnanhai to be the epicentre of communist state power. Many of the Qing-dynasty structures in the compound were removed to other places, torn down or fortified, as one Chinese source puts it laconically, 'for practical reasons.' Office buildings for the State Council, military barracks, a helicopter pad, subterranean residences, strategic command centres and escape tunnels were installed as part of the apparatus of modern empire.

At present, heads of state are the only foreigners who may enter Zhongnanhai with impunity. They are usually photographed with the current Chinese leadership in the *Zi guang ge*, the **Palace of Purple Effulgence** (also known as the **Hall of Mongol Princes**), the illustrious front parlour of the three governments that have ruled China since 1644. At other times, selected Chinese citizens (such as relatives of the soldiers who were killed in June 1989 during the Tiananmen incident), groups of school children and a quota of Chinese tourists are allowed to visit a limited section of the grounds on Saturdays and Sundays and take a peek at Chairman Mao's spartan study.

Marco Polo's 13th-century travelogue contains perhaps the most famous description of a Chinese garden ever written. But remarkably, no contemporary Chinese source mentions Marco Polo or anyone vaguely resembling him, and there is increasing doubt among scholars that he ever set foot in China. Still the following passage seems like a reasonable account of the imperial palace garden in the Yuan capital of Khanbaligh ('city of the Khan'), and tallies with contemporary Chinese reports:

> Moreover on the north side of the Palace, about a bow-shot off, there is a hill which has been made by art; it is a good hundred paces in height and a mile in compass. This hill is entirely covered with trees that never lose their leaves, but remain ever green. And I assure you that wherever a beautiful tree may exist, and the Emperor gets news of it, he sends for it and has it transported bodily with all its roots and the earth attached to them, and planted on that hill of his. . . And he has also caused the whole hill to be covered with the ore of azure, which is very green. And thus not only are the trees all green, but the

hill itself is all green likewise; and there is nothing to be seen on it that is not green . . .

On the top of the hill again there is a fine big palace which is all green inside and out; and thus the hill, and the trees, and the palace together form a startling spectacle; and it is marvellous to see their uniformity of colour! Everyone who sees them is delighted. And the Great Kaan [Kublai] had caused this beautiful prospect to be formed for the comfort and solace and delectation of his heart.[1]

Ser Marco was likely describing the protuberance that is now **Hortensia Isle** (*Qiong hua dao*), where palace buildings stood during the Yuan. He may also have been referring to the **Round City** (or **Round Castle**, *Tuan cheng*), which at the time was an island in the lake linked by wooden suspension bridges to Hortensia Isle to the north, and to the shores of the lake on the east and west. One section of one of the bridges stood on piles set in two boats, which could be moved to allow grain transport ships to pass through.

In the early 15th century, a strip of water to the east of the Round City was reclaimed in order to facilitate the transport of bricks, tiles, rocks and timber being used in the construction of the new Ming walls and palaces of Peking. The present brick wall that surrounds the Round City dates from 1745.

The Manchus' first major construction project in these parts, after the founding of the Qing dynasty in 1644, was the huge Tibetan-style White Dagoba that crowns Hortensia Isle (1651). For a full three decades (1741–71) during the Qianlong reign, work continued on the park; the exquisite garden within a garden on the north shore of the lake (see below), the **Studio of the Mirror of Clarity** (*Jing qing zhai*),

---

(1) Sir Henry Yule *The Book of Ser Marco Polo*, 3 vols. (London: 1921), pp. 365 – 6.

after 1913 known as the **Studio of Quieting the Mind** *(Jing xin zhai),* and the **Studio of the Painted Boat** *(Hua fang zhai)* on the eastern shore of the lake, both date from this period. For the most part the present layout of Beihai Park follows Qianlong's design.

The Empress Dowager Cixi, a garden fancier whose lavish late 19th-century embellishments set the tone for all subsequent restoration work, diverted funds originally designated for the Chinese navy and carried out major restoration work at Beihai Park and the Summer Palace from 1885 to 1888. One interesting 1888 addition was a miniature railway line (with an engine built by the French company Decauville) that ran for about a mile from Zhongnanhai to a small terminus in front of the Studio of the Mirror of Clarity. Though this was not the first railway in China (Englishmen had built a 500-meter [550–yard] line in 1865), the Zhonghai–Beihai Express was instrumental in convincing Cixi that it was necessary to build railways on a large scale in China. One unsubstantiated legend tells that after the Decauville engine exploded (the line was maintained by eunuchs), the Empress Dowager had the train hauled along the tracks by her eunuchs with a golden rope. But she tired of this imported toy and had the tracks removed soon after this accident.

In 1900, following the siege of the legations by the Boxers, troops of the Eight Allied Armies occupied a number of buildings in Beihai Park and plundered many of the relics. Traces of their visit remain in the form of bullet holes in some of the older buildings.

Immediately after the fall of the Qing dynasty in 1911, sections of the park were occupied by the troops of Chinese warlords, although the grounds officially remained the property of the deposed emperor. Beihai Park opened to the public in 1925, shortly after Puyi had been removed from the Forbidden City.

During the Cultural Revolution, Mao's spouse Jiang Qing (a latter-day Cixi in politics but who, in matters of taste, was decidedly inferior to the Manchu dowager) lived

Old view of the bridge separating Zhonghai and Beihai Lakes

for a time in the Studio of the Painted Boat on the east shore of the lake.

Note: On this walk be sure to wear running shoes or hiking boots, as the distances are long and you will be climbing about some ancient rocks.

The Walk takes you from the Round City to Hortensia Isle, along the east shore of the lake to the north section of the park, out the rear gate, and along the shores of the **Shi cha hai**.

Begin at the **Rainbow Bridge** that divides **Zhonghai** (Middle Sea) from **Beihai** (North Sea). This elegant Ming-dynasty marble bridge was widened and reinforced in the 1950s to accommodate modern traffic, and the two *pailous* that stood at each end, inscribed 'Golden Turtle' and 'Jade Butterfly' respectively, were removed at this time. To the south of the bridge lies Zhongnanhai, home and offices of China's ruling elite. The folks you see boating on the lake in nice weather are the staff of the State Council and the soldiers who guard them.

Buy your ticket in the kiosk near the parking lot, enter the park, bear left and climb up into the mini-fortress known as the Round City (*Tuan cheng*), which doesn't open until 7 A.M. and requires a separate admission ticket.

In the Yuan dynasty, the Round City was the site of palace buildings and the barracks of the palace guard. The main structure in this round enclosure, shaped like an elaborate Maltese cross, is the **Hall of Received Brilliance** (*Cheng guang dian*), where the Qing emperors occasionally changed their clothing and drank tea while they stopped here to rest on their journeys from the Forbidden City to the suburban gardens. The present building dates from the Qianlong period, though literary evidence suggests that an earlier building on this spot was round. The hall now houses a large and somewhat chunky **Jade Buddha** that bears a strong resemblance to the image in the Jade Buddha Temple in Shanghai. There are two explanations of its origins. The first is that it was a tribute gift to the Chinese emperor from Tibet. The second, compiled from several sources, is more intriguing.

In 1893, a Peking–based Buddhist monk travelling in Burma claimed that he was on a religious mission for the Empress Dowager Cixi. Suitably impressed, Burmese monks presented him with one large and two small jade Buddhas when he left to return to China. When he arrived in Peking, he put the images on display in his temple. But they caused such a sensation that an investigation was carried out, as a result of which the monk's ruse was exposed. The monk had little choice but to give the large jade Buddha to Cixi, who instead of punishing him for his presumptuousness, rewarded him generously. Incidentally, before setting out on his trip to Burma, this venerable bonze had sold the contents of his temple to Li Lianying, the fabulously wealthy eunuch who was the Empress Dowager's favourite. The left arm of the serene figure (In her *Peking*, Juliet Bredon states that the figure is made of Italian alabaster, and was a gift to Qianlong from the king of Cambodia) bears a scratch on its left arm that has been attributed to the foreign allied armies in 1900.

Another important jade relic in the **Round City** is the **Jade Wine Pot**, resting in its own pavilion that stands in front of the **Hall of Received Brilliance**. This huge vessel is believed to date from the Yuan dynasty, when Kublai Khan used it to decorate his Broad Cold Palace on **Hortensia Isle**. The palace collapsed in 1579, during the Ming dynasty, and it was removed to a Taoist temple. When it was rediscovered in the early Qing dynasty, the Taoist priests were using it to pickle cabbage. Qianlong paid a hefty sum for it when he purchased it from the monks in 1745, and had it installed in its present pavilion after inscribing a wine-drinking song on its interior wall. If this tale is true, then the pot is the oldest cultural relic in Beihai Park.

In 1915 Yuan Shikai held a series of preparatory meetings in the Hall of Received Brilliance before crowning himself emperor, a dream that lasted only 83 days. In 1924 the last president of the Republic, Cao Kun, was incarcerated in the Round City for two years by the warlord Feng Yuxiang. He was subsequently released by Zhang Zuolin, another warlord.

Today several of the buildings of lesser importance have been converted into shops and offices; one tenant is a distributor of videotapes.

Return to Beihai Park through the north gate of the Round City. Continuing north across the fine marble bridge flanked at each end by *pailous* (with the names 'Accumulated Jasper' and 'Heaped Clouds'), you come to **Hortensia Isle** (*Qiong hua dao*). Until the late 1980s, there were a number of large earthenware vats at the base of the mountain to the west of the bridge containing the famous collection of goldfish genetically engineered for grotesqueness that go back around a century. As a testimonial to their memory, we cannot resist quoting at length Peter Quennell's paean to these creatures written in the early 1930s:

> . . .As large very often as a clenched hand,
> gross and torpid, softly coloured and slow
> swimming, each of them was an Elagabalus
> of the fish world, a puffy boneless sybaritic
> freak, accompanied when it moved by its
> own draperies, a tail and fins considerably
> longer than itself, which eddied, rippled
> and drooped like a gauzy train.

> . . .Imagine a group of opulent French
> bourgeoises, inconsolable yet voluptuous
> in widow's weeds. They suggested the
> catafalque or the crime passionel, the
> husband slayer sobbing in the dock or the
> Niobe-like relict of a great man oozing
> between the arms of her supporters . . .
> Many centuries of cultivation lay behind
> them, the Bourbons and Hapsburgs of their
> breed, a queer comment on nature's
> elasticity and the Chinese passion for
> stretching it to the full and squeezing a
> strange beauty from horror and ugliness.[2]

You are now standing on **Hortensia Isle**, named after a plant reputed to have immortality-conferring properties, and built up from mud dredged out of the lake, the same technique used to create Prospect Hill to the north of the Forbidden City and Longevity Mountain in the Summer Palace.

As you begin your ascent of the hill directly in front of the bridge, the first building you will encounter is the **Temple of Eternal Peace** (*Yong an si*), the descendent of a Lamaist temple erected here by Shunzhi, the first emperor of the Qing dynasty, in the mid-17th century. The stone lions guarding this temple are resting with their heads facing the temple, rather than facing away from it, the orientation adopted by all the other stone and bronze lions in China. Actually these lions belonged to another no longer extant temple that stood with its façade directly opposite the Temple of Eternal Peace, where they had been performing their guard duties properly. Inside the court-yard there are typical drum and bell towers.

The next structure on the axis is the **Hall of the Wheel of the Law** (*Fa lun dian*). To the north of it there is a

---

(2) Peter Quennell *A Superficial Journey through Tokyo and Peking* (London: 1932; reprinted by Oxford University Press, 1986), pp. 178 – 9.

courtyard planted with a thorny bamboo grove and the two stone stele, each in its own pavilion. The inscriptions on the stele record the history of **White Dagoba Mountain** (*Bai ta shan*), as the man-made hill is called.

Climbing up the stairs to the ***pailou***, inscribed 'the purple effulgence of the dragon light' you come to a mid-level plateau which is supposedly strewn with some of the actual Lake Taihu stones that were transported here from the Song capital of Bianliang by order of a Jin-dynasty emperor in the 12th century. This lovely park-within-a-park, with its fine south-facing view, is part-wilderness, part manicured garden, and attracts practitioners of ***taiji*** and martial arts exercises in the early morning, a fine time to visit Beihai Park.

To continue your ascent to the Hall of Universal Peace (*Pu an dian*) and the **Hall of True Enlightenment** (*Zheng jue dian*), a sort of duplex temple, you can choose either of the two interior staircases that begin in the easternmost and westernmost of the six man-made caves. You will emerge into the light again at the base of an observation tower.

On this level, to the west, is the **Hall of Joyful Hearts** (*Yue xin dian*), where the emperors during the latter part of the Qing dynasty held meetings with their high officials. In the courtyard attached to the hall are two special rooms, one formerly used for making tea and the other for making pastries for the imperial breakfast buffet.

Originally one could climb up to the Dagoba on the terrifyingly steep staircase directly to its south, with its white marble balustrade decorated with cloud finials and dragon-head rain drains, but it is now wisely closed to traffic for safety reasons. Today the only way up is via the paths to the side of the dagoba.

The **White Dagoba** (*Bai ta*), a **Tibetan reliquary** (in Tibetan, *chorten*, a tomb for the remains of a Lama Buddhist monk or layman) was in Republican days known irreverently as the 'peppermint bottle' by foreigners. The first emperor of the Qing dynasty had this dagoba built on the ruins of a Ming palace in 1651 to commemorate the visit of the first Dalai Lama to the capital. It is made of brick, stone

Dragon boat race in Longtan Park

and wood. The dagoba was damaged twice in earthquakes during the 17th and 18th centuries, and large cracks appeared in it during the Tangshan earthquake in 1976, after which it was restored completely. During the restoration, archaelogists discovered a repository in the base of the dagoba containing altar tables, Tibetan Buddhist sutras, niches for Buddha images, miniature boat hulls worn around the waist in folk dances, and other ritual paraphernalia. In the interior of the dagoba there is a column approximately 30 meters (100 feet) tall. Beneath the decorative hardware at the top the restorers found a golden reliquary containing two sacred bone fragments, most likely belonging to eminent lamas.

The small sealed-up temple decorated with glazed-tile Buddhas on the south side of the dagoba is the **Temple for Cultivating Good Deeds** (*Shan yin si*), which once held a gilded bronze image of Yamantaka, a Lamaist deity with a terrifying aspect: 36 arms, 36 eyes, 7 heads and 16 feet. Yamantaka take was slain during the Cultural Revolution. There is a chauvinist Chinese saying: 'Only a horrible-looking god like Yamantaka can pacify such wild people as the Mongols (who believe in Lamaism).'

The Qing emperors held shamanistic rituals on this peak, and its strategic location in the city made it an ideal signal tower: five coloured flags were hoisted to convey military messages during the day, and coloured lanterns were lit at night. On a clear day there is an excellent view of the city.

To climb down, we will take a circuitous, but rewarding route. If you follow the instructions below to the letter, you should have no problem reaching our desired destination on the shore of the lake. If you get lost, simply do as water does, and seek the lowest level. . .

1. Go through the round moon gate in the wall behind (north) of the dagoba.
2. Weave in and out of the cave.
3. Walk through a rectangular pavilion, which offers you a view of a rock garden wall.
4. Go down through the gate, turn left through a bottle-shaped opening in the wall.
5. Bear right at the fork and follow the path down the hill, backtracking slightly while hugging the undulating wall. In a matter of minutes you will be on the shore of the lake.

(**WARNING**: don't be tempted to enter the red gate in the wall unless you wish to attempt some precarious climbing)

Find your bearings by locating the **Tower for Reading the Classics** (*Yue gu lou*), with its crescent-shaped walls, about 50 meters (165 feet) ahead on the path. The Tower contains a collection of stone tablets, dating back to the sixth or seventh centuries, that are inscribed with calligraphy by some of China's greatest masters. These stele are not meant to be admired in this form, but rather are used for taking rubbings of their inscriptions, one of the earliest forms of printing.

Heading north you will soon find yourself beneath the eaves of the two-storey veranda that begins at the tower called the **Pavilion of Shared Coolness** (*Fen liang ge*) and snakes along the north shore of the island. Qianlong had this long corridor built in imitation of a similar structure in a temple in the southern town of Jinshan.

A short way up the north face of the hill, but hard to see up close unless you climb back up among the twisting paths and Lake Taihu stones, is a terrace with a tall column supporting a cast bronze figure of a man holding a brass container over his head. This is the **Plate for Gathering Dew** (*Cheng lu pan*), the origin of which can be traced back to a Han-dynasty emperor who ordered his underlings to stand outside at night with containers to catch the dew. The emperor believed that dew consumed together with powdered jade could make him immortal. Qianlong contributed this gewgaw to the garden, as he wrote in an essay, purely for the sake of decoration, and not because he believed in the medicinal properties of jade and dew. The buildings that lie within the crescent embrace of the two-storey veranda are the private and public dining rooms of the **Fangshan Restaurant**, an excellent place for banquets (reservations recommended, but beware of imperial prices. When Fangshan, literally 'imitating imperial cuisine' opened in 1926 on the north shore of the lake where the Beihai Restaurant now stands, it was staffed by chefs who had worked in the palace kitchens up to 1924, when Puyi and company were booted out of the Forbidden City. Fangshan reopened in its present location in 1959.

In addition to imperial cuisine and the 108-dish Manchu–Chinese feast that is consumed over the course of three days, Fangshan is noted for a number of inexpensive pastries associated through legends with the Empress Dowager Cixi:

1. Baked wheat biscuits stuffed with spiced ground pork, which Cixi supposedly dreamed about one night and 'miraculously' was served for breakfast the next morning;
2. Sweetened pea starch pudding cut into cubes the size of dice;
3. Rolled up kidney-bean cakes, which Cixi first sampled when she invited a common street vendor, whom she heard calling his wares, into the palace; and
4. Thimble-sized cones of sweetened cornmeal. While fleeing Peking in 1900, Cixi got so hungry that she ate the heavy steamed corn bread, shaped like a cone the size of a fist, that served as a staple food for northern Chinese peasants. When she asked for it upon her return to the capital, her pastry chef reproduced them in miniature and sweetened them.

The entrance to Fangshan is located at the northern tip of Hortensia Isle, where you may board a dragon boat for the five-minute ride to the Five Dragon Pavilions on the north bank of the lake. Fangshan itself occupies a group of structures with an elegant name, the **Hall of Ripples** (*Yi lan tang*). In warm weather, the Qing emperors and Cixi would board their boats here (they were stored in the boathouse on the eastern shore of the lake) and in the winter observe ice skating displays performed by a specially trained army. As many as 1,600 ice fighters would join in these demonstrations on the frozen lake. Our walk will take us to the Five Dragon Pavilions by a less direct route along the eastern shore of Beihai lake.

From Fangshan, continue east around the northern shore of the island and through the gate tower that stands at the end of the veranda, the **Tower that Leans Towards the Light** (*Yi qing lou*). On the right you will pass a large commemorative stele inscribed by Qianlong that details some of the wondrous things to be seen in the park. In particular he commends a Song-dynasty official who brought the Lake Taihu rocks from southern China and arranged them in such a way that they resemble dragon scales. Further on is the **Nirvana *pailou***, in its fine setting, which directly faces the bridge. Crossing the bridge you come to the east entrance of the park, and by turning left (north) and walking along the path approximately 120 meters (400 feet) you come to the first group of buildings on your right. Between the **Hao** and the **Pu** (*Hao Pu jian*).

This complex, dating from 1757, is one of several gardens-within-a-garden in Beihai Park. Qianlong borrowed the name of this garden from a Liang-dynasty emperor who around A.D. 550 had named a garden after two rivers mentioned in the works of the early Taoist philosopher Zhuangzi—whose fish tale we told in the chapter 2 on the Summer Palace. The Hao was the stream in which those happy fish were swimming, while the Pu was the scene of another famous incident:

> Zhuangzi was fishing in the Pu River one day, when the King of Chu sent two ministers to see him: 'We have come to entrust you with the affairs of the state,' they said.
>
> Zhuangzi, continuing to fish without turning his head to look at them, replied: 'I have heard that in Chu there is a mystical tortoise which died 3,000 years ago, and that your king keeps it wrapped up in a box in his palace. Tell me, would this tortoise prefer to be dead and to have its remains revered as something rare and precious, or would it rather be alive, wagging its tail in the mud?'
>
> The ministers said, 'Naturally it would rather be alive, wagging its tail in the mud.'

'Scram!' Zhuangzi retorted, 'I prefer to
wag my tail in the mud.'

Decorative corridors climb up and down the rockeries here, but the highlight is the small pond with its lovely pavilion and seven-segment bridge. The water that fills the pond is not drawn from Beihai lake but rather from a stream that is fed by the **Front Lake** (*Qian hai*) to the north of Beihai Park and flows along the eastern wall of the park.

Cixi would come here to listen to performances of ballads after the Summer Palace was sacked in 1860. Heading north from the Between the Hao and the Pu the large barns built over the water are boathouses, which in their original incarnation date back to the Ming dynasty. The height of the present boathouses, dating from the late Qing, suggests the impressive dimensions of the pleasure craft used by the imperial family.

Qianlong created the next building along the shore of the lake, **Studio of the Painted Boat** (*Hua fang zhai*) at the same time as Between the Hao and the Pu. Here, outside the main entrance, the emperor would observe an annual archery contest participated in by Manchu princes, court officials and imperial retainers. The distinguishing feature of the studio is its large square stone-lined pool surrounded by narrow corridors. Cixi is said to have smoked opium in the rooms in the northwest corner of the complex, and in 1900 the French army made its headquarters here. During the Cultural Revolution, Jiang Qing stayed in the secluded northeast courtyard on several occasions, in the very place where Cixi had kept the Guangxu emperor under house arrest. In 1979, the Studio was the venue for the first exhibition of dissident art held in post-1949 China, organized by the group called the Stars. Though open to the public for several years in the late 1980s, this beautiful complex has been taken over by the 'China International Friendship Liaison Society,' and now friendly international tourists are not permitted to liaise with the past on the premises.

Further to the north beyond the amusement park is the **Altar of Silkworms** (*Can tan*), which was converted into a teahouse during the Republican period once the ancient rituals ceased, and now a nursery for the offspring of high officials (off limits to the curious). The altar was formerly the site of a quaint ceremony (testifying to an early division of labour in China by sex) carried out by the empress in honour of the Goddess of Silkworms, the originator of sericulture, who is the wife of the mythical Yellow Emperor. One can imagine the Empress Dowager, confronted by a crowd of peasant women in tattered cotton gowns, saying 'Let them wear silk.' As Juliet Bredon described the ritual:

> A picturesque note was added by certain details, such as the Empress and her attendants plucking a few leaves from the sacred mulberry-grove near the altar with little sickles, the handing of these leaves to ladies in charge of the precious insects, the inspection at later periods [mostly through delegates] of their growth, of the washing of the cocoons in the sacred moat existing for this purpose, finally of the making of the silk which was used on occasions of Imperial worship, on the same principle as the grain raised by His Majesty's hand at the Temple of Agriculture.[3]

The agricultural ritual was performed in the third lunar month (late April–early May) by the emperor with the assistance of his underlings and a brigade of 100 aged peasants selected from the capital region. With these worthies at his side, the Son of Heaven would guide a golden plough drawn by a pedigree ox with no blemishes on its coat and till six furrows in a ritual field. Similarly—

---

(3) Juliet Bredon and Igor Mitrophanow *The Moon Year* (Shanghai: 1927; reprinted by Oxford University Press, 1982) pp. 66 – 7.

ironically, perhaps—in the 1980s, Deng Xiaoping ventured into the fields in the third lunar month with his own high officials (some of whom *were* peasants) at his side and personally planted a symbolic tree to kick off the annual nationwide greenification campaign.

Continuing north past the Altar of Silkworms, cross the bridge that leads to the rear gate of Beihai Park, and veer left. Our first destination, the **Studio of Quieting the Mind** (*Jing xin zhai*) — extra ticket required — is an exquisite private garden built by Qianlong in 1758 and was first named the **Studio of the Mirror of Clarity** (*Jing qing zhai*) by him. It was later renovated by Cixi, who often came here for lunch and used it for storing the imperial seals. During the Qing dynasty, the studio served as a schoolroom for Manchu princes. In 1900 it was occupied briefly by the Japanese army, and in 1913 Yuan Shikai gave it to the Foreign Ministry to use for meetings with foreign guests. Later it was taken over by the Institute of History and Philology of the Academia Sinica, and from 1949 to 1981 it was similarly occupied by a literary research organization and the State Council. Puyi, the last emperor of China, wrote his memoirs, *From Emperor to Citizen,* here. In 1982 it was restored, fitted out with a potpourri of antiques and curios and opened to the public. Fortunately, it is rarely crowded.

Each of the halls in the Studio has its own pool of water in front of it, with the exception of the **Chamber of Piled Emeralds** (*Die cui lou*), which stands at the highest point in the Studio in the northwest corner. This building was the Empress Dowager's 1885 contribution to the complex, when she carried out a major building campaign on many of the imperial properties which she paid for with naval funds. Like the **Hall for Distant Views** that sits up against the north wall of the Summer Palace, the north windows of the Chamber of Piled Emeralds offered the secluded denizens of the imperial palaces a glance at the outside world, should they choose to look.

There is a vast Taihu-stone rockery in the second, rear courtyard, where a concealed waterfall beneath the rectan-

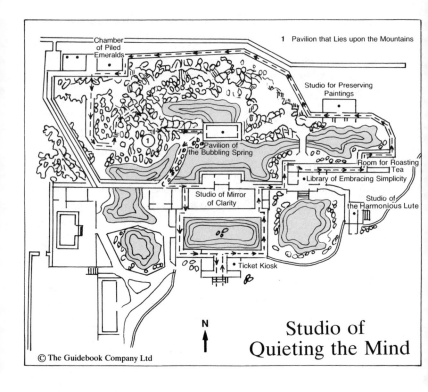

Studio of
Quieting the Mind

© The Guidebook Company Ltd

gular pavilion on the water adds a tranquillizing touch to this small and almost confining space. The other structures are the **Room for Roasting Tea** (*Bei cha wu*), a tiny room in the east corner, originally used by Qianlong for that purpose but now a shop where tea is sold by the cup; the **Studio of the Harmonious Lute** (*Yun qin zhai*), which is not a music room at all—the name describes the trickle of an artificial waterfall in the tiny courtyard.

Water is an indispensable element in all Chinese gardens, and garden builders display remarkable skill in its disposition. One Western theory of Chinese history posits that the stability of the Chinese state depended on the maintenance of countless hydrology projects throughout the empire, from the tall Yellow River dykes to the capillary-like canals that irrigate the vast fertile Yangtze delta. In this garden, water conservancy in miniature is put to aesthetic ends. The finest view in the Studio of Quieting the Mind is obtained from the easternmost point in the large, rear courtyard next to the Room for Roasting Tea.

The circular route indicated on the map takes you to all the main buildings of the studio: the **Studio of the Mirror of Clarity** (*Jing qing zhai*); the **Library of Embracing Simplicity** (*Bao su shu wu*); the **Studio of the Harmonious Lute** (*Yun qin zhai*); the **Room for Roasting Tea** (*Bei cha wu*); the **Studio for Preserving Paintings** (*Yan hua xuan*) where there is a painting of peonies by the Empress Dowager; the **Chamber of Piled Emeralds** (*Die cui lou);* the **Pavilion that Lies upon the Mountains** (*Zhen luan ting*); and the **Pavilion of the Bubbling Spring** (*Mi quan lang*). Put these elegant names together and you almost have a poem.

Leaving the studio, turn right and head southwest along the willow-lined shore (Cixi would have ridden her French train) to the next major complex of buildings with a large *pailou* in front of it, the **Hall of the Heavenly Kings** (*Tian wang dian*), which in the Ming was a workshop for the translation and printing (with woodblocks) of Buddhist scriptures. It was rebuilt by Qianlong in 1759. In 1945, a pair of gilded pagodas in one of the temples here was dismantled by some Japanese 'imperialists' who were about to ship them to Japan. The crates got as far as Tanggu, the port of Tianjin (Tientsin), when Japan surrendered. They were eventually shipped back to Peking, but by then the pagodas were too badly damaged to be restored. The rear courtyards contain a Qianlong-period pagoda and a two-storey glazed-tile hall that closely resembles the Temple for Cultivating Good Deeds that is perched immediately south of the dagoba on Hortensia Isle.

Further to the northeast, behind the Beihai Restaurant, stands one of China's three **Nine Dragon Screens** (*Jiu long bi*; the others are in the Forbidden City and in the city of Datong). Why nine? The dragon, a mythical beast supposedly modelled after the water snake, the gecko or the alligator, had nine sons, but none of them grew up to be a full-fledged dragon since they each were preoccupied with a specific task:

Son #1	curls up on the tops of bells and gongs
Son #2	hangs around the pegs of string instruments
Son #3	rests on top of stone steles
Son #4	supports stone steles on his back
Son #5	balances on the roofs of temples
Son #6	lives on the beams of bridges
Son #7	rests on the Buddha's throne
Son #8	is attached to sword hilts
Son #9	guards the gates of prisons

The Beihai dragon wall is unique among the three in that it is free-standing and is decorated on both sides with six-colour glazed-tile dragons swimming in the waves. Qianlong built this wall as a 'spirit screen' to deter the God of Fire from destroying one of the buildings attached to the workshop for the translation and printing of Lamaist scriptures he had built in honour of his mother. The wall performed this function faithfully until 1919 when the workshop building went up in flames. It is now conferring its protection upon the Beihai Gymnasium, which stands on the site of the former workshop. Scholars claim that there are altogether 635 dragons on this wall, counting the tiny ones in the eaves.

The **Hall of Pleasant Snow** (*Kuai xue tang*), and the **Hall of Crystal Waters** (*Cheng guan tang*) which comprise the complex of buildings to the east of Beihai Restaurant (now a mediocre place for a meal, but when the fashionable Fangshan Restaurant was located here in the 1920s and 1930s one of Empress Dowager Cixi's former chefs earned himself an excellent reputation with his dumplings), was an imperial residence in the Qing dynasty where Qianlong once kept a famous collection of inscribed stone tablets. It was rebuilt twice in the 19th century and in 1900 became the headquarters of the foreign allied armies, who left it in ruins. Cixi did up the place again in 1901, and between 1913 and 1915 it was the home of Cai E (also known as Cai Songpo), who led the movement to prevent Yuan Shikai from realizing his imperial ambitions. After Cao's death the building became the Songpo library and Cai Songpo shrine.

In front of the Hall of Pleasant Snow near the boat dock stands another interesting relic, the **Iron Spirit Screen** (*Tie ying bi*), actually a slab of dark igneous rock and not

Artist in Beihai Park

made of iron at all. This Yuan-dynasty stone was installed here in 1947, when a patriotic Chinese bought it from a 'foreigner' who was about to ship it home. Before this it had stood in front of a Buddhist convent in the northern part of the city which had been a bell foundry during the Ming dynasty. But the legend that the stone acquired its metallic appearance by absorbing the smoke pouring out of the foundry has no basis in fact. The image carved with remarkable vigour carved on both sides is a mythological scaly beast with a fiery tail.

Proceeding along the shore, the decorative structures jutting into the lake 'in the shape of a writhing dragon,' are the **Five Dragon Pavilions** (*Wu long ting*), which were first built on this spot in the Ming dynasty. Their name arises from the resemblance of the stone balustrades that link them together and the peninsula they stand on to a curling dragon. An anecdote calculated to inspire filial piety tells how the Qing emperor Kangxi settled his mother and grandmother in one of the pavilions, hopped into a boat on the lake, paddled up to where they were sitting, and politely served them snacks. Qianlong used the pavilions for fishing. He would angle from the central pavilion while his retinue would fish from the pavilions to the side. One doubts his ministers even dared to bait their hooks out of fear of pulling in a bigger fish than the emperor's.

The large complex of buildings to the north of the Five Dragon Pavilions is the **Beijing Economic Plants Botanical Garden**, most frequently visited by school pupils on field trips with their teachers.

This was formerly the site of the **Temple of Happy Meditation** (*Chan fu si*), first built by the Ming-dynasty emperors to provide their empresses and high-ranking concubines with a place to spend the hot summers. In the 18th century, Qianlong converted this resort into a temple which, like the Altar of Silkworms described above, was used for the ritual worship of silkworms, and later installed a large Buddha with One Thousand Hands and One Thousand Eyes. The Eight Allied Armies plundered the temple in 1900 and made away with the jewels encrusting the image. In 1919, a warlord army occupied the temple, and shortly afterwads it was destroyed by a fire and never rebuilt.

The most worthy object here, sitting in the neglected northwest corner of the Botanical Garden, is an octagonal pagoda containing 16 portraits carved in stone, of *lohans*, or Buddhist immortals. The original artist was a Tang-dynasty monk who was also a gifted painter, although these lively images of eccentric holy men were carved in the Qing. This part of the garden also contains something extraordinarily rare in Beijing—grass lawns.

The next pleasant surprise on the itinerary is the huge square pagoda, perhaps the largest of its kind in China, called **Little Western Heaven** (*Xiao xi tian*), originally built in 1770 as a shrine to Guanyin, the Goddess of Mercy. Surrounded by a moat, four guard towers and four *pailous*, this huge square building once housed a tall mountain made of clay, crowned with an image of the Goddess of Mercy and festooned with 800 smaller *lohans*, or Buddhist worthies, as well as temples and trees. It was modelled after Mt Putuo, a sacred island located in one corner of the Buddhist paradise. The original mountain was restored by Cao Kun, President of the Republic in 1923–4, as an act of devotion. But in 1953 a committee of scholars and experts decided that Cao had done a tasteless job of it and had the mountain dismantled. This left the building structurally unsound, so it was later taken apart and rebuilt. It was dazzlingly restored and repainted in the late 1980s. Note especially the splendid ceiling. In the winters, huge carved ice sculptures are displayed here, including a Buddha or two.

The Rear Lakes

We now leave Beihai Park and the former imperial city and enter the southernmost part of the former Tartar, or Manchu city. The Rear Lakes have undergone great changes in the last 1,000 years, yet judging from early descriptions, they still retain something of their original rural character. There are records of lakes here, and poems in praise of their beauty, dating from as early as the third century A.D.. Today, as of yore, the large private homes of the Chinese leadership dot the south shore of Shichahai Rear Lake. As H.Y. Lowe wrote in the late 1930s,

> With few exceptions all the [Manchu] princes had their mansions in that neighbourhood, a quiet and picturesque district conveniently near to their 'jobs' at the Forbidden City—like Beverly Hills is to the movie studios of Hollywood.[4]

The historical nomenclature of the lakes is complex and at the end of the day it may all seem quite irrelevant. However, there are three lakes (literally 'seas') in this district today, **Front** (*Qianhai*), **Rear** (*Houhai*), and the **West** (*Xihai*, also called *Ji shui tan*, **Reservoir Pool**, is not on our walk).

As early as the Wei dynasty (*c.* 250) conservancy projects carried out in the western suburbs of the city provided a steady flow of water to this district, where a lake was formed. Nearly one millennium later, the 12th-century Jin rulers built their pleasure palaces on its shores. When the Mongols established their capital, Khanbaligh (in Chinese, *Dadu*) upon the ruins of the Jin capital Zhongdu, the lake was incorporated into the new walled city. Later an east–west road was built that cut the lake in two; the southern part of the lake was incorporated into the palace grounds and became the **Pool of Great Secretion**, the forerunner of Beihai lake, while the northern part remained outside the city limits. By channelling additional water from the springs in the western hills, the lakes were enlarged and deepened.

---

(4) H.Y. Lowe *The Adventures of Wu: The Life Cycle of a Peking Man* (Peking: 1940 – 1; reprinted by Princeton University Press, 1983), I, p. 162.

The Mongols called them *haizi,* the Chinese word for 'small seas'; in Mongolian the meaning of the word expands to mean 'garden' or 'park.'

Following the dredging of the Tonghui Canal, which linked the city of Khanbaligh to nearby Tongxian, the northern terminus of the Grand Canal, these lakes became the major inland receiving port for rice shipments from South China. Early texts from this period describe how during the summer months, the splendid lotus blossoms that filled the lake drew crowds of viewers here, establishing a Peking custom that is still popular today. The lakes in the Yuan were many times larger and deeper than the decorative ponds are today, and could accommodate the hefty grain barges that supplied rice from the south to the capital.

When the Chinese Ming conquered the Mongol Yuan and shifted the north wall of the capital approximately three kilometers (two miles) to the south, the Pool of Great Secretion was again sliced in two leaving a good portion of it outside the city limits. The enlargement of the moat around the city walls drained off much of the water that had supplied the lake, and consequently its importance as a grain port declined. The construction of another north–south road resulted in the lake being further split into the **Ji shui tan** (Reservoir Pond) to the west, and the articulated **Shichahai** (Sea of Ten Buddhist Temples) to the east. At the time there were numerous temples on the shores of the lake. During the Ming dynasty, the horses in the imperial stables were washed in the lake in an annual ritual that took place on the 12th day of the sixth moon. Horses that had been ridden by the emperor were draped with imperial yellow silk horse blankets, embroidered with dragons, and were led into the water before all the others. Sledging on the ice in winter and boating amidst the lotuses were other popular pastimes in the Ming dynasty.

Another form of 'recreation' took place here during the seventh lunar month. Monks and lay Buddhists gathered along the shores of the West Lake (the northernmost of the three Rear Lakes), burnt paper boats, floated lanterns on the water and recited scriptures to exorcise the ghosts of those unfortunate souls who had committed suicide by jumping into the lake.

In order to surround himself with souvenirs of the temperate climate of the land of his youth, the Ming Yongle emperor, a southerner by birth, imported rice farmers to work the paddies on the shores of Shichahai and supply the imperial pantry with rice. Buddhist temples, convents and private gardens sprung up around the lake at this time, and in several places fine bridges spanned the lake.

In the 17th century the Qing court designated the lake as an imperial garden and forbade all commoners from drawing its water. As a result the convents, monasteries and private gardens that had used water from the lake for ornamental purposes were forced to fill in their ponds and streams with soil. During this period, some of these buildings were replaced by Manchu princes' mansions, a few of which can be visited today .

The Qing-dynasty emperors came to the lakes once a year in winter to review Manchu army skating battalions playing war games on the ice, as they did in Beihai. An observation pavilion in one of the lakes built especially for this purpose was demolished by the allied armies in 1900.

In the Republican period a combination of official neglect and increased rice cultivation caused the lake to shrink and eventually it turned stagnant. After 1949 the lake beds were dredged, four large swimming pools were installed, roads were built over some of the old streams, and buildings erected over areas of the lakes that had been filled in with landfill and rubble. With the destruction of the city walls near Deshengmen gate, the narrow body of water outside the gate was turned into a concrete-lined open conduit. The Shichahai district is now undergoing rede-velopment with an end to preserving its heritage and creating cultural and recreational facilities such as the Lotus Flower Market.

Today in winter, when the Shichahai Front Lake freezes over, the scene is something out of a painting by Brueghel:

Dragon head spout, Beihai Park

two-year-olds strutting about in four layers of clothing, women hauling old bamboo baby carriages, youngsters pulling each other in circles on tiny sleds, couples sharing a single pair of ice skates. The sunlight in Beijing at this time of year, filtered by coal smoke and dust, somehow takes on a waxen Flemish quality.

Along with Tianqiao in the former Chinese city, Shichahai was one of the most popular recreation spots for people of modest means in Old Peking. The bustling summer scene at Shichahai some 60 years ago is described wonderfully in *The Adventures of Wu*:

> . . . Enterprising businessmen stake out
> plots along the wide walk which serves also

as a separating dyke and erect matshed
teashops of a de luxe type with elevated
floors for better views of everything
around. Little variety shows and stalls
where popular if rustic kinds of foods are
sold, side by side with fruit stalls and those
of a number of unexpected businesses
which seem to be there more for the fun
than for the profits. . .

For here is another world, a little
Peitaho (Bei dai he) Beach, a Bermuda, nay,
a Coney Island in the Chinese standard of
judgement. Peking people in every walk of
life make excursions here, a few make it
their summer resort. . . . [5]

While watching the magicians, comedians, jugglers
and ballad singers, you could enjoy such famous snacks as
sour bean juice, buckwheat cakes, cold starch-jelly, fried
sausage, sour plum juice with essence of cassia, baby corn
on the cob, fresh water caltrops, lotus seeds, almonds,
walnuts, and lotus seed porridge, to mention but a few.

The Walk is a simple one, and mainly atmospheric. From
the **Little Western Heaven** (*Xiao xi tian*) on the north shore
of the lake in Beihai Park, retrace your steps eastward until
you come to the rear gate of Beihai Park. Cross **West
Di'anmen Street** (*Di an men da jie*) and make your way to
the entrance of the **Lotus Flower Market** (*He hua shi chang*),
where the stalls sell some of the snacks mentioned above
and more.

The **Lotus Flower Market** was revived here in the
summer of 1990 after several decades of dormancy, and
borrows its name from a market that operated in this area
in early Republican days.

---

(5) H.Y. Lowe *The Adventures of Wu*, I, p. 161 – 2.

This is a fun place for an inexpensive lunch. As the dishes vary with the season, the following sample fall 'menu' hardly exhausts the entire range of offerings: fried spring rolls, barbecued mutton, steamed bread, wontons (*hun tun* in the local dialect), steamed and boiled dumplings (*baozi* and *jiaozi*), hand-stretched noodles, roasted chestnuts, lung and intestine soup, doughnuts, glutinous rice sweets, hot puddings flavoured with sesame, cassia, and almond, and various beancurd preparations favoured by vegetarians. All prices are marked, so all you need to do is point.

There is also a teahouse among the stalls where balladeers perform in the afternoons, and near the entrance of the market occasional wrestling demonstrations are put on by old-time buskers. In good weather, Peking opera amateurs also gather here to croon the oldies but goodies to each other.

Continue the walk by following along the shore of the lake until the market ends. When you leave the 'rear entrance' of the market, turn right onto the narrow road that skirts the lake. The two-storey building in front of you is the former **Hall of Assembled Worthies** (*Hui xian tang*), a restaurant and meeting place that was popular during the Republican period. When wedding banquets were held here, it was common to invite famous opera singers to perform a number or two. Mei Lanfang, who lived in a courtyard house nearby, was one of those great male divas who came here to sing—men played the leading female roles in Chinese opera.

Somewhat further on, the well-kept façade to the left of a hole-in-the-wall sweet shop is a large traditional multi-courtyard house occupied by a former chief of one of the Chinese ministries.

A few minutes' more strolling brings us to the **Silver Ingot Bridge** (*Yin ding qiao*) that divides **Front Lake** (*Qian hai*) from **Rear Lake** (*Hou hai*). Along with the lotus blossoms in the lakes, the view from this bridge of the Western Hills is one of eight cherished Peking look-sees canonised by the Qianlong emperor in the 18th century. Tradition has it that the bridge is at its best at sunrise, sunset, after rain or when it is snowing. The present incarnation of the bridge which takes its name from its resemblance to a Chinese 'shoe' ingot, an ancient form of currency, was carved out of white marble by stone one masons from Hebei Province in 1984.

Across the bridge and to the right is the restaurant called **Kao rou ji** (Ji's Roast Mutton), where Mr Ji and his descendants have been serving roast mutton for over 140 years. The grandsons of the founder built the restaurant here in 1927, before which they had been selling from a stall on the lake. The building was refurbished in 1955 and 1986. The mutton, sliced from the leg according to the desired degree of leanness or fattiness, is barbecued over wood after being marinated in a mixture of shrimp sauce, soy sauce, rice wine, vinegar, sesame oil, chili oil, leeks, coriander, ginger and sugar. Sliced cucumbers, sliced tomatoes, sweet pickled garlic cloves and raw leeks harmonise well with the strong-tasting meat. Like mutton hotpot, the barbecued mutton here is particularly satisfying in winter.

The comfortable-looking house next to the restaurant belongs to an overseas Chinese. From here you can see the **Drum Tower** (*Gu lou*) rising up in the distance.

You can end the walk on this poetic note or continue on past the bridge along the north shore of Rear Lake.

A former temple, the **Temple of Great Religious Transformation** (*Guang hua si*), you will pass shortly on your right is now a nursery school. In a few minutes you will come to the impressive front gate of Prince Chun's mansion, the residential portion of which has been occupied by the Ministry of Health for decades. This was the birthplace of the last emperor Xuantong, better known as Puyi, and his younger brother Pujie. The tall gate a bit further on belongs to the **Former Residence of Soong Ching Ling**, a European-style home built in the extensive garden of the Prince's mansion. Madame Soong (whose status as Honorary

Chairman of the People's Republic of China permits her to spell her name in this idiosyncratic manner), the Soong sister who was Mrs Sun Yat-sen, outlived her husband, the Father of the Chinese Republic, by about half a century. After 1949, Soong Ching Ling pursued a career as an often frustrated figurehead in the Chinese government. She died in Beijing in 1981. Her solid and spacious home, with its many bedrooms and double windows that filter out the noise and dust, offers a striking contrast to the average Beijing apartment, and candidly suggests the lavishness of the private residences of the Chinese leadership. It can be visited for a modest fee.

From here you might make a turn around and visit the recently restored **Mansion of Prince Gong** (*Gong wang fu*) that had served as the living quarters of the officials and families of the Ministry of Public Security, the former campus of **Fu Jen University**, formerly run by the Catholic Church, and the **Former Residence of Guo Moruo**, a writer who faithfully served Chairman Mao.

To get to the Drum Tower, return to the **Silver Ingot Bridge** and head northwest in the narrow *hutong*.

Walk · 4

Temple of Heaven, Temple of Sky

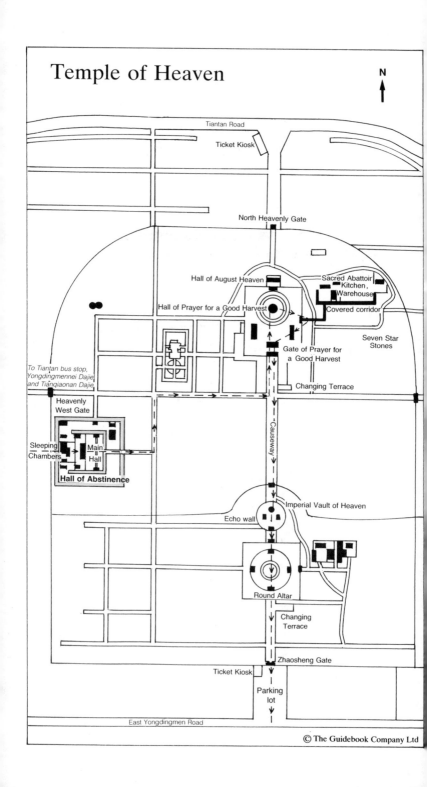

Temple of Heaven

N

Tiantan Road

Ticket Kiosk

North Heavenly Gate

Hall of August Heaven

Sacred Abattoir
Kitchen,
Warehouse

Hall of Prayer for a Good Harvest

Covered corridor

Seven Star
Stones

Gate of Prayer for
a Good Harvest

To Tiantan bus stop,
Yongdingmennei Dajie
and Tiánqiaonan Dajie

Changing Terrace

Heavenly
West Gate

Causeway

Sleeping
Chambers

Main
Hall

Hall of Abstinence

Imperial Vault of Heaven

Echo wall

Round Altar

Changing
Terrace

Zhaosheng Gate

Ticket Kiosk

Parking
lot

East Yongdingmen Road

© The Guidebook Company Ltd

Duration

Approximately three hours

Explore the ritual altars and round blue-roofed buildings where the emperors of China communicated through sacrifice with Shangdi, the Pearly Emperor Supreme Ruler in the Sky. This is the least physically demanding walk in this book: total walking distance is less than a mile. The designation **Temple of Heaven** does not apply to any particular building here, but is rather the name of the entire complex, which is now called **Tian tan Park**. In other words, there is no 'Temple of Heaven' per se. The imperial rituals were carried out at three main sites on a north–south axis: the triple-roofed **Hall of Prayer for a Good Harvest** (the building mistakenly referred to as the Temple of Heaven), the smaller **Imperial Vault of Sky**; and the starkly exquisite Round Altar. The park is open from 7 A.M. to 7.30 P.M. in the winter and from 5 A.M. to 9.30 P.M. in the summer.

The best time to take this walk is the very early morning. The light of the rising sun casts an ethereal glow on the halls and altar and the park is filled with people practising a dozen forms of early-morning exercise, from *qigong* breath energy posturing (the air is best at this time of day) and martial-arts inspired sword dancing, to opera singing, geriatric disco and last polkas in Peking. Visitors are always welcome to join in.

Starting Point
The west gate of **Tiantan Park** on **Yong ding men nei da jie/Tian qiao nan da jie**.

How to Get There
Buses 2, 17, 20, 36, 203.

How to Get Away
Bus 116 takes you north to the centre of the city from the south gate of Tiantan Park.

> The Temple of Heaven is stunning in its simplicity, rife with symbols and implications. Here for over 500 years the emperors of China carried out rituals to ensure the survival of Chinese civilization—the entire world as they knew it. As one British art historian wrote: 'I know of nothing in European architecture capable of producing the same impression of abstract beauty, of a peculiarly concentrated, almost nervous, tension.' [1]

The worship of Heaven, or Sky (which we will use here to avoid associations with Western theology) began as early as the Zhou dynasty, some 3,000 years ago. Sky was at that time conceived of as a deity that represented whatever happens with regularity, and thus was responsible for maintaining the cycle of the seasons and the social order,

---

(1)   William Willets *Chinese Art*, 2 vols.
      (Harmondsworth: Penguin Books, 1958) p. 677.

both of which were perceived as natural phenomena. The Chinese emperor was the Son of Sky, and thus the ritual worship of Sky was for him the fulfilment of filial obligations to his progenitor, who by extension was the ultimate ancestor of the Chinese people. The cult of ancestor worship performed in its most sublime form here was practised on a smaller scale in homes by individual families, who formed the lowest rung of a hierarchical system that was a perfect metaphor of social unity.

As the living representative of Sky on earth, the emperor reported regularly to his superior and, also submitted appeals for good weather and plentiful harvests, the basic requirements for a peaceful state. Confucius' pragmatic statement, 'To the people, food is heaven,' is simply a truncated version of the Sky–earth–man reality sandwich.

Early Western writers about China discovered in the imperial worship of Sky an expression of the universal original religion. One 19th-century cleric cited

> 'the probability that [the rituals performed
> at the Temple of Heaven] are all survivals
> of the religious ceremonies observed by the
> common ancestors of the races before the
> dispersion of mankind from the Tower of
> Babel.'

In *Peking*, Juliet Bredon wrote,

> 'It [the Temple of Heaven] is one of the few
> remaining relics of the original Chinese
> monotheistic faith—the old, old belief that
> God is everywhere, invisible and all-seeing,
> dwelling in a house not made with
> hands—held in Asia before the gods were
> personified and their images enshrined in
> temples.' [2]

---

(2) Juliet Bredon *Peking* (Shanghai: Kelly and Walsh, 1931; reprinted by Oxford University Press, 1982), p. 157.

She described the emperor's participation in the ritual as a worship which,

> '. . . recognizing as sole-divinity the spirit
> of the great blue dome overhead, dis-
> carded, for the occasion, all the idolatrous
> and superstitious practices of an essentially
> pantheistic race.' [3]

Another missionary writer was impressed by the pomp and panoply of the imperial rituals:

> 'In position, in attitude, in attitudinising,
> enrobing, incensing, and the rest, the
> Chinese have nothing to learn from the
> West.' [4]

And the Dutchman Borel, who was prone to having religious experiences in all the major tourist sites in Peking, saw the oft-repeated pattern of three found in roofs, platforms, gates and the stones paving the floors of the halls and altar, as an obvious manifestation of the Christian trinity.[5] Finally, an anecdote recorded by the American missionary W.A.P. Martin in 1897: 'Dr. Legge [British translator of the Chinese classics], the eminent missionary, before climbing the steps of this [round] altar heard a still, small voice, saying: 'Put off thy shoes; for the placewhereon thou standest is holy ground.'[6] It is recorded elsewhere that Dr. Legge walked barefoot when he was first admitted to the Round Altar.

---

(3) Juliet Bredon *Peking*, p. 161.
(4) John Ross *The Original Religion of China*
     (New York: Eaton and Mains, no date), p. 312.
(5) Henri Borel, *The New China: A Traveller's Impressions*
     (London: T Fisher Unwin, 1912), pp. 245– 60.
(6) W.A.P. Martin *A Cycle of Cathay, or China, South and North*
     (New York: 1897), p. 243.

Diagram of the Round Altar

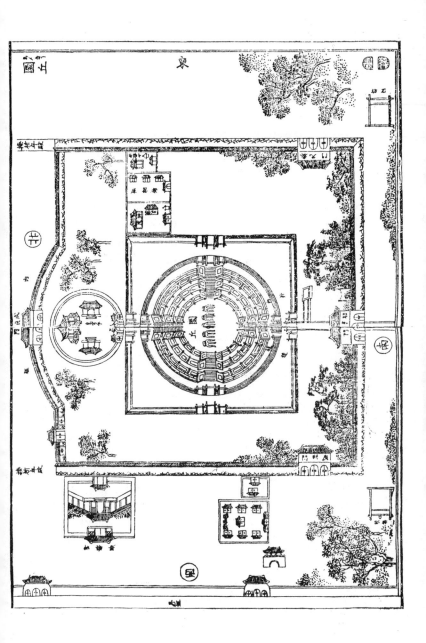

The **Temple of Heaven** is one of several worship sites in the capital where the emperors offered sacrifices. Its location in the southern part of the city derives from the notion that *yang*, the male vital principle, is located in the south; and as Sky is *yang*, it must be worshipped in the southern suburbs of the capital. Peking also had altars (*tan*) to the Earth (north of the city), Sun (east), Moon (west), Silkworms (in Beihai Park), Agriculture (to the west of the Temple of Heaven), and the Gods of the Soil and Harvest (in the centre of the city in what is now Zhongshan Park). Nearly all of these former places of worship were turned into parks when they ceased functioning in their original capacity in the early years of the Republic. Curiously enough, the **Altar of Silkworms in Beihai Park** is a nursery school for the pupae of bigwigs in the party and government.

In the 1950s the grounds of **Temple of Heaven Park** (*Tian tan gong yuan*) were reduced to approximately two-thirds of their dimensions during the Qing dynasty, when the surrounding wall was 5.6 kilometers (3.5 miles) long. The now-missing slice of land, on the west flank, is occupied by the **Museum of Natural History**, **Tiantan Dental Hospital**, **Tiantan Hospital**, a hotel and housing blocks. Observed from the south on a map or from the air, **Tiantan Park** takes the form of a squat rectangle topped by a semi-circle: an apple sitting in a box. Everything here is charged with symbolism. In traditional Chinese thought, Sky is round, Earth is square. The rounded north section functions like the semi-circular spirit wall around a traditional Chinese grave, diverting the evil influences originating in the north from the temple complex.

Though, in principle, access to the grounds of the ritual temple was as 'forbidden' to the common man as the Forbidden City itself, during the latter part of the Qing dynasty, entrance could be gained by anyone willing to hand the gatekeeper a small tip . A 1904 guidebook to Peking remarked:

> As a rule visitors have now to pay a small
> trifle for admission. On quitting each of

> these temples [in the Temple of Heaven] a
> little civility over and above this to the
> guardians of the Temples will generally
> elicit civility in return and greatly enhance
> the pleasure of the visit. Chinese value
> courtesy highly. [7]

In fact, the sacrificial altars were in use, and thus off limits to outsiders, less than ten days every year. After the Boxer Uprising in 1900, the park became the headquarters for the Bengal Cavalry under the British General Gaselee, whose troops staged theatricals on the altars in their leisure hours. There are also reports from around this time of impious foreigners dancing on the **Round Altar** under the moonlight. The **Hall of Abstinence**, the only formal residence on the premises, became the British officers' mess for a short time. Imperial cattle bred especially for the sacrifices that had become infected with the plague, were burnt on the Round Altar by the British. In the decades before the Temple of Heaven was opened as a public park, the grounds surrounding the ritual precincts were used as a polo ground, and after 1911, the government gave a plot of land and the buildings formerly occupied by the **Office of Sacred Music** to the **Forestry Bureau** which converted them into an experimental farm. At the same time a radio station was set up in the southwest corner of the grounds. In 1917, the troops of the warlord Zhang Xun camped in the Temple of Heaven, and a small battle broke out between them and the Republican army when Zhang and Yuan Shikai attempted to re-establish the monarchy by restoring Puyi to the throne.

The construction of the oldest building on the Temple of Heaven ritual grounds was completed around 1421, just as the Ming emperor Yongle was putting the finishing touches on the rest of his new capital. At first, the worship of Sky and Earth was conducted simultaneously here and

---

(7) Mrs Archibald Little *Guide to Peking*
      (Tientsin: Tientsin Press, 1904), p. 22.

at a corresponding temple in Nanjing. In 1530 the Ming dynasty reverted to the older practice of worshipping Sky and Earth at separate altars, and constructed the **Round Altar** for the worship of Sky at its present site, while a **Temple of Earth** (*Di tan*) was built in the north of the city. The round **Hall of Prayer for a Good Harvest** was first built in 1545, replacing an earlier square hall. During the Ming and early Qing, the tiles on the triple-tiered roof of this building were in three colours: the uppermost roof was blue, symbolizing heaven; the middle roof was yellow, representing the emperor; and the lower roof was green, representing the common people.

For about a century, from the early Qing until the time of Qianlong (reigned 1736–96), the rituals continued to be carried out in the old manner. But the growing prosperity and self-confidence the empire was enjoying in the mid-18th century and a series of successful military campaigns in the northwest, gave Qianlong building pains. The Round Altar was enlarged to nearly double its original size, and the triple roof of the Hall of Prayer for a Good Harvest was tiled in a uniform cobalt blue. Annual ritual worship continued uninterrupted until the 20th century; however it stopped for a few years around the turn of the century when the Empress Dowager Cixi placed the Guangxu emperor under house arrest.

A fire started by lightning destroyed the Hall of Prayer for a Good Harvest in 1889. Legend has it that the fire began when a centipede climbed to the golden knob at the summit of the roof and was struck by lightning as punishment for its boldness. In any case, 30 officials 'responsible' for the fire were executed. It took seven years to rebuild the hall due to a scarcity of timber and a lack of blueprints. The four giant columns that bear most of the weight of the roof are hewn of Oregon pine and were imported to China in the 1890s by the American lumber dealer and shipping magnate, Robert Dollar.

The ritual at the Round Altar was performed by a member of the imperial clan for the last time in 1910, when

Taking the birds for a walk

Prince Chun stood in for the Xuantong emperor (Puyi), who was then only four years old. On 10 October 1912, the first anniversary of the founding of the Chinese Republic, the Temple of Heaven was opened to the public. To celebrate the occasion, the age-old sacrifice was carried out, with significant modifications of a republican nature, by a civil official acting on behalf of the president, Yuan Shikai. On 23 December 1914, Yuan himself donned imperial robes and performed the winter solstice ritual for the very last time in Chinese history. The ceremony was filmed for posterity, and stills of it remind one of a Cecil B. de Mille spectacular. In 1918, the Temple of Heaven was formally opened as a park.

In 1948 some of the old cypress trees on the grounds were felled in preparation for the construction of an airfield that was never completed. Before this, the K.M.T. airforce had made do with an emergency airstrip closer to the city centre, in present-day Dongdan Park. The American scholar Derk Bodde, who went to Peking in 1948 as one of the first Fulbright fellows, reported on the scene on the Temple of Heaven grounds in the fall of that year:

> . . . all the buildings are filled with hun-
> dreds of young men . . . They are wartime
> student refugees from Shansi, some of

whom seem hardly older than 12 or 13. Most of the stone terraces outside, as well as the floors of the temple itself, are covered with their sleeping pads and meager possessions . . . The marble balustrades of the Altar of Heaven [the Round Altar] are festooned with bedding drying in the sun. The columns of the great temple and adjoining buildings, much faded from their former brilliant red, are covered with ugly written notices, and dust and debris lie everywhere on the once gleaming marble . . . the mental condition of these boys is far worse than that of the poorest coolies . . . Portions of the courtyard, and even of the lower tiers of the Altar of Heaven itself, are littered with their half-dried excrement. [8]

The Walk: Most tourists enter the **Temple of Heaven** through the north gate of **Tiantan Park** and visit the **Hall of Prayer for a Good Harvest** first. But we will do as the emperors did, and commence our visit at the **Hall of Abstinence** (*Zhai gong*). Purchase your ticket at the **West Gate of Temple of Heaven** (Tiantan) Park, and walk east among the groups (in the early morning) engaged in various forms of spiritual and physical self-cultivation until you get to the **Hall of Abstinence** (extra ticket required).

Here the emperor would spend a night readying himself spiritually and physically for the solemn ceremonies to be held the following morning. Three days previously, the **Son of Heaven** would begin his fast in the Forbidden City. This entailed refraining from eating meat, wine, pungent vegetables such as onions, garlic or scallions (though he

---

(8)   Derk Bodde *Peking Diary: 1948–1949, A Year of Revolution* (New York: Abelard-Schuman, 1950; reprinted by Fawcett World Library, 1967), pp. 31–2.

was permitted tea, snacks and blander vegetarian dishes, to stave off his hunger), and avoiding pleasurable liaisons with his empress or concubines. Nor was he allowed to discuss criminal cases, visit the infirm, listen to music or visit the tombs of his ancestors during this period of self-purification. Finally, on the eve of the sacrifice, the emperor took a ritual bath.

The Hall of Abstinence is a well-defended miniature citadel, surrounded on all sides by a broad moat, with a second U-shaped moat inside. In the covered corridors which run around the outside of the walled complex, eunuch sentinels would patrol during the emperor's residence. We learn from history books that during the Ming dynasty, the eunuchs on duty were expressly forbidden to eat meat, drink wine or expectorate while the emperor was in residence.

The Hall of Abstinence differs in two respects from other imperial habitations: first, it faces east rather than south; and secondly, the roof tiles are green, a colour that stands for the common people, rather than the usual imperial yellow. These features can be interpreted as symbolic gestures of humility in the presence of Sky. In other words, in the presence of Sky, even the emperor is a commoner.

As very little is known about the original furnishings of the Hall of Abstinence, the display in the Main Hall and the disposition of furniture in the Imperial Sleeping Chambers are educated guesswork on the part of the curators, based on similar quarters in the Forbidden City and Summer Palace.

In the central room of the **Main Hall**, constructed without rafters or beams, the emperor would confer with the officials in charge of the rituals. The side rooms served as waiting rooms for attendants.

The small white marble altar on the south corner of the patio in front of the hall held a series of removable plaques indicating the hour of the day, one way of reminding the emperor that he should practise self-cultivation and meditation in a 'timely' manner. The square-roofed pavilion on the patio held a bronze statue of the semi-legendary Leng Qian, an official of the Music Bureau, and an inscribed ivory plaque. The figure's closed mouth was a hint to the emperor that he should remain silent during his night of abstinence.

There are two bedrooms in the Sleeping Chambers behind the Main Hall. The emperor occupied the south chamber at the summer sacrifices, and the north bedroom on the eve of the sacrifices that took place at the winter solstice and in early spring. The north bedroom is equipped with a *kang* bed warmed by a system of underground flues. In 1807 a fire broke out in this old-fashioned heating plant and consumed the entire building. It was rebuilt shortly afterwards.

In the early 1980s the Hall of Abstinence fell prey to the Four Modernizations Programme and became for a   while the Marco Polo Shop, featuring Pierre Cardin fashions manufactured in China. The building has since been restored as a museum.

Exit the Hall of Abstinence through the east entrance, head north to the main east–west road that leads by the neat rows of cypress trees, to the raised **causeway** *(Dan bi qiao)* in Chinese 'the bridge of cinnabar steps.' The causeway is 360 meters (1,170 feet long) and is higher at its north end than at its south end. Head north on the causeway, which functions as a sort of camino real during the rituals, until you get to the gate that leads to the courtyard enclosing the **Hall of Prayer for a Good Harvest**. Here you must purchase a ticket valid for entrance to the three main structures. On the balustraded **Changing Platform** jutting out from the causeway to the east, a round yellow tent was erected where the emperor would change his clothing in preparation for the rituals. During the Ming dynasty, the emperors followed the Hindu custom of removing their shoes here before proceeding with the sacrifice in the Hall of Prayer for a Good Harvest. During the sacrifices, the causeway was covered with a coir mat to protect the imperial toes and soles.

The Gate of Prayer for a Good Harvest (*Qi nian men*) is the only Ming building in the temple complex (though its roof was replaced during the Qing). North of this gate lies the famous **Hall of Prayer for a Good Harvest** (*Qi nian dian*), with its three-tiered roof and tall three-tiered terrace of white marble, which is known as the **Altar of Prayer for Grain** (*Qi gu tan*), arguably the best known building in China.

The triple roof—symbolizing heaven, earth and man—of the Hall of Prayer for a good Harvest is as blue as Sky. Its three circular roofs are supported by three sets of columns; the lower two roofs by two sets of 12 columns each, one set representing the 12 months of the year, and the other the 12 two-hour periods of the day, while the uppermost roof rests upon the four Oregon tree trunks (previously mentioned) that represent the form seasons. There are 28 columns altogether, just as there are 28 constellations in the Chinese heavens. The hall is nine *zhang* (a traditional measure equal to about three metres or ten feet) tall; nine is the ultimate *yang* number, virile, creative, solar. The uppermost roof is 30 *zhang* in circumference; there are 30 days in a lunar month.

The hall offers particularly fine examples of the decorative and functional systems of bracketing that appear in every traditional wooden building in China. The entire weight of the roof is distributed through the brackets and supported by the columns; the walls are merely screens and support none of the weight. The result is a highly stable and attractive structure that is flexible to withstand strong earthquakes.

On the floor in the centre of the hall is a round stone with a 'found' picture of a dragon and phoenix. If you have difficulty distinguishing these two imaginary celestial creatures, it is because the heat of the fire of 1889 supposedly distorted the pattern beyond recognition. The dragon had originally resided in the cupola in the ceiling and descended to join the phoenix who for years had occupied the circular stone all by herself. The interior cupola here with its resident dragon is rivalled in splendour only by a similar installation in the **Hall of Supreme Harmony in the Forbidden City**. The three marble balustrades on the altar complete with dragon-head rain spouts are also of the same genre as those framing the Three Great Harmony Halls. They appear yet again at the Round Altar.

The rituals practised in this hall were quite straightforward. On the 15th day of the first lunar month (around February or March) the emperor made a sacrificial offering before the spirit tablets of Sky and the deceased emperors of the dynasty to obtain their blessing for the year and to ensure the proper natural conditions for a good grain harvest. Replicas of the spirit tables, inscribed with the names of the deities in Manchu and Chinese characters, stand on high platforms in the hall, and there is a complete set of ritual paraphernalia (again in replica) laid out as if the ritual were about to take place.

To the north of the **Hall of Prayer** is the **Hall of August Heaven** (*Huang qian dian*), where the spirit tablet of Shangdi, the Pearly Emperor Supreme Ruler in the Sky, the emperor's ultimate ancestor was stored. In recent years this hall has been used for the dissemination of public hygiene information, but it now performs its original function, in replica. There are two other rectangular halls in the courtyard. The one on the west is a sometime tourist shop and that on the east has an excellent display of the musical instruments—some of them original—played during the rituals as well as a recorded reconstruction of the music. The original purpose of these two halls was to store all the tablets used in the ritual, except the tablet of Shangdi. In the Ming dynasty, these included the spirit tablets of the Ming emperors, the moon, sun, stars, oceans, wind, clouds, thunder, rain, rivers, mountains, early mythological emperors, etc. A vast quantity of these tablets had accumulated by Qianlong's day, so he burned them all leaving only five belonging to the deceased members of his own Aisin-gioro clan, including the founder and first three emperors of the Qing dynasty.

To the east of the Hall of Prayer, a lengthy covered corridor of 72 bays connects the sacrificial altar with the Sacred Kitchen, the Sacred Abattoir, and the Sacred Warehouse, where the sacrificial animals and foodstuffs for the rituals were prepared. When the offering was completed, the remnants of the sacrifices were burnt in the tiled ovens, iron censers and disposal pit located in the southeast corner of the courtyard near the Gate of Prayer for a Good Harvest. We will find similar facilities at the Round Altar. All these buildings appear abandoned now, though one of the courtyards is used for showing open-air movies. The live acoustics of the corridors attract amateur opera singers and audiences in the morning, and you might stroll over here for a rest as you observe the friendly scene. In order to return to the ritual enclosure and the Hall of Prayer for a Good Harvest, be sure to save your ticket stub.

To the south of this corridor are the so-called **Seven Star Stones**, which are not meteors as has been suggested, but they do form a pattern that resembles the Big Dipper. The legend goes that when the Ming emperor Yongle was shopping around for a location for their altar, these stars fell out of the sky and landed in this auspicious place. Their pitted surface is not extraterrestrial but rather the result of superstitious people having chipped away good luck souvenirs over the years.

We now backtrack through the Gate of Prayer for a Good Harvest and proceed south along the long imperial cat walk, pass through a gate in the semi-circular protective wall, and soon arrive at a circular walled courtyard. On the right (west) we pass a cypress tree at least 800 years old, supposedly the oldest of its species in Beijing. Continue skirting the wall until you come to the triple-arched gate that serves as the entrance to the courtyard. The building inside resembles a simplified and shrunken version of the Hall of Prayer for a Good Harvest; note the white marble platform, the single roof, and the bracket systems supporting the roof. This is the **Exalted Vault of Heaven** (*Huang qiong yu*), so named because it is designed in the shape of

Sky. Yet despite its fancy title, it was little more than a storage place for the spirit tablets that were used in the rituals held on the Round Altar. No rituals were carried out in the building or courtyard itself. In the Qing dynasty, the spirit tablets of Shangdi and of the deceased Qing emperors were stored in the round building, while the tablets of subsidiary spirits occupied the two rectangular side buildings. The round courtyard offers two entertaining acoustical phenomena:

—Two people standing at any two points along the interior of the **Echo Wall** (the circular wall enclosing the courtyard) who speak facing the wall in a normal voice with their heads at the same altitude will be able to hear what the other is saying.

—If you stand on the first of the **Three Echo Stones** at the very foot of the staircase that leads up to the Hall, and clap once, you will hear a single echo; if you clap once standing the second stone, you will hear two echos; and from the third stone, three echos.

Unfortunately, the wall and courtyard are usually so crowded with a babel of tourists that it is only possible for people with stentorian voices and palms of steel to succeed in reproducing these phenomena, which can possibly be explained by the fact that the Exalted **Vault of Heaven** does not sit in the precise centre of the round courtyard but rather slightly to the north.

We now come to the climax of our walk. Continue walking south and pass through the triple *pailou* gateway of white marble that resembles the *torana* gateways at Sanchi in India to the **Round Altar** *(Yuan qiu)*, the uncovered temple where the emperor would communicate directly with Sky. Two major rituals took place here each year: at the Winter Solstice, the shortest day of the year, the emperor would report to Sky the key events of the year in the ceremony called 'communicating with heaven'; and in the fourth lunar month, usually around May, the emperor would appeal to Sky for rain and a good harvest.

The Round Altar is encircled by two sets of walls, an outer square wall, symbolizing the earth and an inner round wall in the shape of Sky. The green-tiled structure south of the altar is the oven used for the sacrificial incineration of an unblemished ox. A number of iron censers, now here in replica, were used for burning the other objects used in the ritual, a way of delivering them through the medium of smoke to Sky.

The design of the altar itself follows a strict numero-logical-symbolic pattern, based on the odd **yang** (male, bright as opposed to dark, vigorous) numbers three, five, seven and nine. To begin with, the altar is composed of three platforms. The top platform is nine **zhang** (a measure equal to about three meters or ten feet) in diameter, the middle platform is 15 *zhang* (3 x 5) in diameter, and the lower platform 21 *zhang* (3 x 7) in diameter, which adds up to a total of 45 (5 x 9). In the *Yi Jing (I Ching), the Book of Changes*, an early treatise of divination and philosophy based on numerology, the combination 5:9 stands for the relation-ship between a man and his superior, which in turn is analogous to the relationship between the emperor and Sky. The number of panels in the three balustrades, all multiples of the auspicious number nine, is also significant. On the first platform, there are 36 (9 x 4); on the second 72 (9 x 8); and on the third, 108 (9 x 12) which make a total of 216, or 9 x 24.

Similar formulas are repeated in the stones paving the surface of the platforms. The round stone in the centre of the uppermost platform—perhaps the most sacred bit of turf in the Chinese empire—is surrounded by nine stones. Moving outward, each ring increases by nine; thus the second ring consists of 18, the third of 27, and the outer-most ring, 81 (9 x 9), a highly auspicious number. On the second platform the innermost ring has 90 stones and the outermost ring, 162 (2 x 81); on the third platform the numbers run from 171 to 243 (3 x 81).

University students studying in the park

The foods offered to Sky during the ceremonies range quite literally from soup to nuts. The following menu is taken from an illustrated ritual text from the Qing dynasty, which specifies the placement of each of 30 containers:

Grains	**Fruits and Vegetables**	**Meats**
rice	plums	fish
sorghum	dates	venison
millet	hazelnuts	hare
white cakes	salted chives	spleen
black cakes	salted bamboo	suckling pig
roast grain	salted celery	pickled venison
rice flour	salted shallots	pickled pork
chestnuts		veal

Add to this soup, rice gruel and wine served up in bronze ceremonial vessels, along with candles, lamps, incense and baskets of jade and silks, which will eventually be consigned to the flames as a burnt offering. These dishes were prepared in a Sacred Kitchen and abattoir located to the east of the altar.

The Round Altar cries out for reverent silence, but it is usually mobbed with people standing in the centre trying out the remarkable echo effect here by clapping or shouting at the top of their voices.

Round Altar Ritual: What follows is the complete script of the major sacrifice conducted here at the Winter Solstice during the later part of the Qing dynasty.

First, imagine the shortest day in the year in the cold, dry climate of North China, when the *yang* or male principle is at its nadir and begins to stir afresh. Two hours before noon on the day before the solstice, the Director of the Sacrificial Court goes to the **Gate of Heavenly Purity** (*Qian qing men*), the entrance to the palace residential quarters in the Forbidden City, to escort the emperor to the **Hall of Abstinence** in the **Temple of Sky**. Wearing a blue double-dragon robe designed exclusively for this ceremony, the **Son of Sky** mounts his sedan chair and escorted by 12 high officials proceeds to the **Gate of Supreme Harmony** (*Tai he men*), where he reviews the text of the prayer that he will deliver the next day. At the gate he changes from his palace palanquin into a larger sedan chair. He will be accompanied while he remains inside the palace by 20 men of the 'leopard-tail' guards armed with rifles and swords, and 20 others with bows and arrows. As the procession moves south through the **Meridian Gate** (*Wu men*) [During the Ming, the emperor travelled by Burmese elephant, and one Ming emperor obsessed with the notion of appearing humble, managed to make the journey on foot, considerably irritating his advisors], the bell in the gate tower sounds, and all the princes, dukes, civil and military officials who will not accompany the emperor, assemble and kneel to see off those who will. Here the procession is joined by additional uniformed men holding colourful ensigns and standards.

As the imperial procession, now 2,000 strong, moves south, 'the city seems to hold its breath'. The deep ruts in the streets formed by cart traffic have been filled in with golden sand to smooth the imperial passage, and auspicious couplets written on red paper strips have been posted on all the shops and police stations along the way. It was forbidden, upon penalty of death, for commoners to gaze upon the emperor as he passed, but this was unlikely anyway as he was cosily concealed in his sedan chair. In the 19th century all rail traffic in the south part of the city was ordered to a halt during the procession. As the entourage enters the Temple of Sky complex through the west gate, the bell in the Hall of Abstinence is rung in a continuous peal.

The emperor's first destination in the Temple of Heaven complex is the **Zhaoheng Gate** (south of the Round Altar), where he alights from his sedan chair. Escorted by the Director of Sacrifices and the Sacrificial Prompter, he proceeds to the **Imperial Vault of Heaven**, where he burns incense before the spirit tablets of Shangdi, his ultimate ancestor, and the deceased Qing emperors, and performs for the first time the ceremony of three genuflections and nine kowtows.

The emperor then goes to the **Round Altar** to inspect the lavish silken tents and shrines that have been placed there to hold the spirit tablets, the sacrificial vessels and the edible offerings. The shrine of Shangdi is placed inside one of the round tents of blue silk that stands slightly to the north of the centre of the altar; the shrines of the former emperors are placed in square tents to both sides. The emperor then climbs back into his **Jade Chariot** and returns to the Hall of Abstinence. The members of the imperial clan and the officials who take part in the sacrifice wait outside the gate of the hall as he passes and only retire after the emperor enters. They will camp out for the night in tents put up nearby.

The next morning, precisely one and three-quarters hours before sunrise, the Director of Sacrifices goes to the Hall of Abstinence and announces the time to the emperor. The emperor dresses in his sacrificial robes, mounts the sedan chair which conveys him to the gate of the Hall of Abstinence, where he changes for the Jade Palanquin to the accompaniment of a sounding bell. Bearers haul the Jade Palanquin to the Zhaoheng Gate, where the emperor alights, walks through the gate, and proceeds along the Sacred Way to the yellow silk tent set up on the Changing Platform. The emperor now washes his face and hands carefully and changes into another set of sacrificial robes.

The emperor then proceeds through the *pailou* gates set in the square and circular walls around the altar and takes up his position on the middle step of the second tier of the Round Altar. (Try it for size. Oddly enough no tourists have carved their name on it.) The Director of Sacrifices then escorts the princes, *beile* and *beizi* (high-ranking members of the imperial clan) to their respective places on the lower tier. The entire ritual contingent of about 230 people, including musicians and dancers in colourful garb, also take their places on and around the altar. All face north.

The president of the **Board of Rites** leads a small group of officials to the Imperial Vault of Heaven to supervise the transfer of the spirit tablets, in miniature sedan chairs, to the Round Altar, and sees to it that they are placed properly in their respective altars. Then the Director of Sacrifices invites the emperor to perform the three genuflections and nine kowtows again.

The ceremony that follows is divided into nine parts. Naturally it was forbidden for any of the participants to shed tears, spit or cough during the ceremony. Those who erred in the execution of the ritual, such as by allowing a candle to go out, were severely punished.

1. The officials in charge of incense approach the emperor with their incense containers. A drum is struck three times and the musicians begin to play the tune 'First Peace', accompanied by a chorus. The prompter escorts the emperor to the uppermost tier of the altar and brings him before the spirit tablet of Shangdi.

   The emperor kneels down on a yellow silk cushion and makes an offering of incense sticks to Shangdi, and then repeats this offering before the tablets of the deceased emperors of the dynasty. He then returns to his place on the second tier, where he performs 'the three and the nine'. At this point a wooden drum in the shape of a tiger (an example of this can be seen in the building to the east of the Hall

of Prayer to a Good Harvest) is sounded three times, indicating for the music to stop. The princes and other members of the imperial clan follow the emperor's example and offer incense before the shrines.

2. To the tune 'A Smooth Prospect' the emperor now repeats the ritual described above in front of all the spirit tablets, only this time the offering consists of pieces of jade and silks in baskets instead of incense. When this is over, the emperor returns to this place.

3. The large container (*cu*) is now brought in, and the musicians commence playing 'Complete Harmony'. The emperor turns to the west and receives the *cu* which has just been filled with the fresh blood and fur of a sacrificial ox. The emperor brings this reverently before the spirit tablets of Shangdi and the emperors, kneels down, and raises it over his head. The *cu* is then wiped clean three times while the emperor returns to his place. The music 'Complete Harmony' is played.

4. Martial dancers perform an interlude to the tune 'Eternal Peace' holding a flute in one hand and a baton with a feather attached in the other. The emperor ascends to the uppermost tier of the altar and offers a vessel of wine to Shangdi. He then stands nearby while the prompter picks up the tablet inscribed with the prayer they had rehearsed the previous day in the Hall of Supreme Harmony. The music and dancing cease, and the emperor kneels down and reads the prayer, an appeal to Sky to treat its subjects kindly and to provide the proper natural conditions to ensure a good year. The prompter then places the written prayer on a table in front of the spirit tablet of Shangdi.

5. An official leads the subordinate officials onto the platform. They stand before the spirit tablets of the sun, moon, and stars, and offer up incense, silk and wine. Once this is completed, they return to their original positions.

6. The martial dancers are replaced by the civilian dancers. The musicians play 'Excellent Peace' while the dancers perform their movements with feather batons and flutes. The emperor ascends to the uppermost tier and presents a second flagon of wine to Shangdi.

7. The emperor makes a third offering of wine in a similar manner, accompanied by the music 'Eternal Peace.'

8. In the next to last offering, meat and wine are placed before the spirit tablet of Shangdi. Once the offerings are properly laid out, the emperor approaches the tablet, drinks the wine and eats the meat in a climactic act of communion with Sky. The offerings are removed and the emperor kneels down. He then returns to his place on the second tier, where he performs 'the three and nine,' which is repeated by the entire assembly.

9. The written prayer, jade, silk, food and incense are removed from the table in front of the tablet of Shangdi and taken to the furnaces to the south. The emperor again leads the assembled worshippers in 'the three and nine', and the music 'Pure Peace' is played. All the spirit tablets are now replaced in the Vault of August Heaven.

   The emperor descends from the second terrace and stands before the furnace, while the music 'Great Peace' is played. The offerings are burnt, concluding the ceremony. At this time, the tail, fur and blood of the sacrificial ox are buried in the 'fur and blood pit' next to the furnace as a symbolic way of providing sustenance to the ancestor.

The emperor then changes his robes again in the golden tent, mounts his Golden Chariot and is escorted out of the Temple of Heaven to the accompaniment of the music 'Protecting Peace'. When he arrives at the Meridian Gate of the Forbidden City, the officials who did not accompany him are once again waiting in their ceremonial robes, and kneel before him. The assembled officials enter the palace and escort the emperor as far as the River of Golden Water, where they halt while the emperor disappears into the palace.

We make our own exit from the Temple of Heaven by heading south towards the parking lot.

Walk · 5

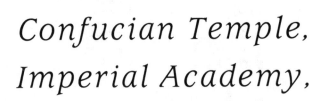

Confucian Temple,
Imperial Academy,
Lama Temple

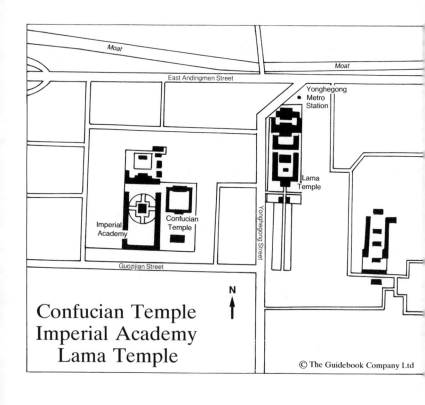

Moat

Moat

East Andingmen Street

Yonghegong
Metro
Station

Lama
Temple

Imperial
Academy

Confucian
Temple

Yonghegong Street

Guozijian Street

N

Confucian Temple
Imperial Academy
Lama Temple

© The Guidebook Company Ltd

Duration

Approximately three hours.

Description

This walk covers three destinations within a few minutes' walking distance of each other in the northeast section of the city. While the **Lama Temple** (*Yong he gong*) is a Lamaist temple both in name and superficially in practice, the **Confucian Temple** and **Imperial Academy** (*Guo zi jian*) have long been converted for other purposes only marginally related to their original functions. The Confucian Temple houses **Capital Museum**, a permanent display of artifacts related to the history and culture of Beijing from its neolithic beginnings to the present. The Guozijian houses the **Capital Library**, with rich holdings in the social sciences and Beijing local history. As the opening and closing times of these places vary, it is recommended to plan your visit between 9 A.M. and 4 P.M..

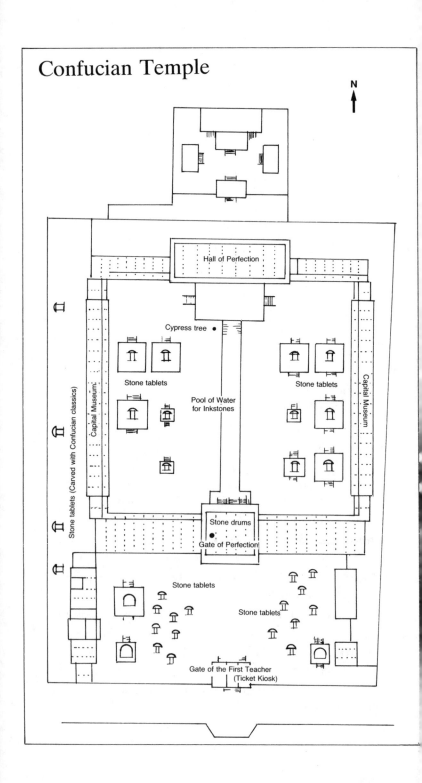

Confucian Temple

N

Hall of Perfection

Cypress tree

Stone tablets

Stone tablets

Capital Museum

Capital Museum

Stone tablets (Carved with Confucian classics)

Pool of Water for Inkstones

Stone drums

Gate of Perfection

Stone tablets

Stone tablets

Gate of the First Teacher
(Ticket Kiosk)

Starting Point
The Confucian Temple on Guo zi jian jie near An ding men.

How to Get There
Bus 13, 106, 107, 116 to Yonghegong. Take the Beijing underground train to Yonghegong station on the circle line.

How to Get Away
Take the same bus or train you came on.

Confucian Temple: The Confucian Temple in Beijing is one of the largest temples of its kind in China, and second only in importance to that in Confucius' ancestral home in Qufu, Shandong Province.

About **Confucius** (551–479 B.C.) the man little is known except what can be inferred from his principle work, the *Analects (Lun yu)*, a collection of short statements attributed to the great sage and dialogues he held with his disciples. The picture that emerges from this evidence one of an upright man with the courage to speak out against injustice yet picky in his personal habits. Living in a period of civil war, Confucius, or Kung zi as he is known in Chinese, envisioned a peaceful, ordered world run by a moral elite.

Confucius believed that men were bound together by *ren*, 'human heartedness' or 'humanity,' a quality that manifested itself in five cardinal relationships: ruler and subject, parents and children, older and younger brother (sisters were not considered), husband and wife, friend and friend. Held together with *ren*, these relationships were conducted according to a code of ritual and etiquette (*li*) that reinforced the status quo.

Confucius had his own mirror version of the Golden Rule: Do not do unto others what you would not have them do unto you. He also attached great importance to practical matters and shied away from the occult and the question of death because, as he stated, he did not, and could not know

Exercising in the early morning

enough about them. In this respect Confucianism differs from Buddhism and Taoism (pronounced Dow-ism), religions that offer salvation, self-realization through disciplined personal cultivation, and eventually enlightenment. Summing up the differences among the Three Religions of China as practised by the elite, one could say: the Chinese gentleman is a Confucian from Monday to Friday and a Buddhist and Taoist on the weekend.

The ritual worship of Confucius has been part of the imperial ritual repertoire since as early as 175 B.C. when a Han-dynasty emperor first offered sacrifices at the Kong family temple in Qufu where Confucius was born. A later Han emperor promoted this worship in schools throughout the empire, and before long Confucianism became a religious cult 'based on a kind of hero-worship and borrowing both from the cults of nature-deities and ancestor worship.' Confucian thought is also closely associated with the Chinese civil service examinations, the first practical system ever devised for staffing a bureaucracy. For 2,000 years, from the Han dynasty to the early 20th century, the Chinese examination system supplied the empire with its mandarins great and small by testing candidates' knowledge of the Confucian classics: poetry, history, rituals, the works of Confucius and Mencius, and *The Doctrine of the Mean*. Chinese government, in the ideal, was practised through moral suasion by gentlemen (no women allowed) of cultivation with good memories and the ability to write formulaic essays on didactic subjects; practical knowledge or ability was of little consequence.

Kublai Khan, the first great foreign ruler of China, established the earliest Confucian temple in Peking in the late 13th century, while the Confucian temple on the present site dates from 1306. In a curious symbolic gesture some 450 years later, the Qianlong emperor replaced the green roof tiles on all the major halls in the temple but one with yellow, thereby elevating them to imperial status; the single exception was a hall used for sacrifices to Confucius' parents and ancestors. In 1906, two years before her death, Cixi rebuilt the temple and elevated the status of the ritual worship of Confucius even higher, putting it on a par with the worship of Sky, Earth, the Imperial Ancestors, and Land and Grain.

After the founding of the **Republic of China** in 1911, the worship of Confucius continued as it had for centuries, but under the aegis of the president of the republic rather than the emperor, while the other major imperial sacrifices to heaven, the sun and the moon were discontinued.

Juliet Bredon describes her visit to a dress rehearsal of the ceremony here—foreigners and common Chinese were not allowed to witness the actual ritual—in the 1920s. In the ceremony, which resembled the imperial sacrifice to Sky in the Temple of Heaven, offerings of animals, silk, jade, grain, fruit and wine were placed before the the spirit tablets of Confucius and his key disciples. Music is played, prayers recited and the chant 'Confucius, Confucius! How great is Confucius!' is repeated by a chorus. Finally the text of the prayer is burnt, just as in the finale of the worship of Sky. Local magistrates performed a similar ritual on the same day, but on a smaller scale, at Confucian temples throughout the empire, as well as in schools.

The colourful ritual pageant is still performed every year in Taiwan by the 76th generation descendant of Confucius, who as a hereditary duke receives an annual stipend from the Nationalist government.

Confucius and his school of worldly thought have not fared well under communist rule. The Confucian temples that were a regular fixture in every country town in China were either demolished, converted into warehouses or factories, or simply abandoned and neglected in political movements that rooted out the influence of 'feudal' culture perceived as inimical to the dictatorship of the proletariat. One cloak-and-dagger campaign of the 1970s specifically attacked Confucius and Lin Biao, Mao's appointed successor, as 'feudal reactionaries,' while pointing a finger at Premier Zhou Enlai as a renegade latter-day 'sage.'

In the 1980s, Confucian studies enjoyed a revival in China. This would not have been possible without the approval of the Communist Party's most influential ideologues, who loosened up enough to be able to tout the Old Boy as a great Chinese thinker and teacher. And thus he will be until somebody in Zhongnanhai decides otherwise.

The Walk: *Guo zi jian jie*, the street running in front of the Confucian Temple and Imperial Academy, was once an enclosed area where, according to the message inscribed in six languages on the old stone tablets now stuck in the pavement, 'military officials must demount from their horses, and civil officials must descend from their sedan chairs.' Such tablets appear in front of all Confucian temples in China.

Guozijian jie is one of the only streets in Beijing where the decorative archways called *pailous* (see page 208) have been preserved. The three-character inscription on the first *pailou* reads 'Perfecting Virtue Street' as Guozijian Street was known before such idealistic concepts became intolerable to the city fathers. The inscription on the second *pailou* more laconically reads 'Guozijian.' The wall on the south side of Guozijian Street, indented for a length of about 15 meters (50 feet) in front of the temple entrance, functions as a spirit wall to protect the front entrance of the temple. Like most of the important buildings in Beijing, the temple lies on a north–south axis, with the principal buildings facing south.

Purchase your ticket and enter the Confucian Temple through the central **Gate of the First Teacher** (*Xian shi men*), built in Yuan-dynasty style, and formerly off limits to all mortals save the emperor; others would enter by side gates. The first courtyard contains an important collection of 198 stone tablets that record the names and home towns of 51,624 successful candidates in the capital (*jin shi*) examinations held during the Yuan, Ming and Qing dynasties. The earliest degree holder on record here passed his examination in 1313. During the Ming, however, most of the names of the Yuan graduates were filed off the stones and replaced with the names of Ming scholars; now only three Yuan steles remain. These tablets provide a permanent record of what is probably the oldest old boy network in the world.

In a narrow north–south corridor to the west of the first courtyard is another set of stone tablets, 189 in all. Carved on both sides by a single hand, these tablets preserve the texts of 13 Confucian classics in non-flammable, book-worm- and water-proof form. By taking page-size rubbings from the tablets—actually the only way to appreciate their contents—autographic texts can be reproduced and thus preserved in perpetuity. Artisans who specialized in carving calligraphy on stone could reproduce all the idiosyncrasies of calligraphic brush strokes with remarkable fidelity. This set of classics is a rare example of this art.

Heading north through the first courtyard we come to the **Gate of Perfection** (*Da cheng men*), where you may inspect a set of ten ancient **stone drums** surrounded by much scholarly controversy. These 'drums', carved at the behest of the Qianlong emperor in the 18th century, are copies of another earlier set of drums that date back over 2,500 years to the eighth century B.C.. The inscriptions consist of poems on hunting, a favourite imperial pastime since ancient times (the Qing emperors had several hunting parks in the Peking suburbs). The poem on the first drum reads:

> Our chariots were strong,
> Our steeds alike swift,
> Our chariots were good
> Our steeds tall and sleek.
>
> A numerous array of nobles
> With a waving cloud of banners;
> The hinds and stags bounded on,
> The nobles in close pursuit.
> The strings of black bows resounded,
> The bows held ready for use,
> We pursued them over the hills,
> Coming on with audible roll.
>
> In a close packed mass,
> The charioteers driving at full speed,
> The hinds and stags hurried on,
> We drew near upon the wide plain,

> We pursued them through the forest,
> Coming up one after the other
> Shooting at the same time the wild boars. [1]

According to one source, the original set of drums was excavated in Shanxi Province in the Tang dynasty, brought to Nanjing in the Song dynasty, shipped to Peking during the Jin dynasty and placed in the Confucian Temple here in the Yuan dynasty. In the late 1940s, the Nationalist government removed the original drums to Nanjing for safekeeping, and they are now in the collection of the Palace Museum, much of which is still stored in that Yangtze River port. The stone tablet mounted on the wall to the right (east) of the drums records a testimonial to Qianlong's good works in preserving these relics.

The courtyard beyond this gate, lined with ancient cypress trees, is the main courtyard of the temple. Of interest here are the **11 tile-roofed chambers** (there are three more in the first courtyard), each housing a giant stone tablet resting on the back of a mythological tortoise, a symbol of stability, a 'rock of ages.' The inscriptions on these tablets chronicle the military exploits of the Ming and Qing emperors at the apex of their power and glory.

Stroll north towards the **Hall of Perfection** (*Da cheng dian*); on the left of the paved path is a covered well that Qianlong dubbed the **Pool of Water for Inkstones**. The idea was that anyone who drank this water would have sage thoughts flowing from his brush, but the well dried up years ago.

One of the gnarled trees here is known as '**the cypress that struck the wicked official.**' In the Ming dynasty, a notoriously cruel official named Yan Song was worshipping Confucius on behalf of the emperor one day, when a strong wind blew up and a branch of the tree knocked off his hat.

The Hall of Perfection, the principal building in the Confucian Temple, was the venue for the annual sacrifice

---

(1) Translation by Bushell, quoted in Mrs Archibald Little
   Guide to Peking (Tientsin: Tientsin Press, 1904), pp. 31–2.

Statue of Confucius

to Confucius. In the centre of the hall is the altar where the spirit tablets of Confucius were placed during the rituals; the spirit tablets of his disciples were arranged to the side. In the early Ming dynasty, a statue of the sage stood here as the principal object of worship, but later in the dynasty it was replaced by a portrait and a spirit tablet. When the statue was later restored, it was decked out in imperial robes. Legend has it that when the Eight Allied Armies plundered Peking in 1900, the portrait of Confucius was stolen by German troops and eventually fell into the hands of a foreign sinophile, who humbly returned it to the temple. During the Cultural Revolution, the temple buildings were occupied by a printing school and a drama academy. Today copies of the ritual implements and musical instruments used in the ceremony are on display.

Another tale tells how the offering table used to hold the ritual vessels and sacrificial food presented to Confucius was at first quite low, as a way of emphasizing the elevated status of the sage. Then a Ming official pointed out that such a low table forced Confucius, or his spirit, to bend down uncomfortably when he was partaking of the sacrificial meal, and suggested that the table be made higher. Other improvements followed, such as replacing live animal sacrifices with offerings of cooked meat, and serving them up in porcelain bowls instead of wooden trenchers. At one point the floor of the hall was covered with coir matting, suggesting that the emperor perform the ritual barefoot, as in the **Temple of Sky** during the Ming.

The Hall of Perfection also houses a display of some of the ritual implements and musical instruments used in the worship, including sets of suspended jade chimes and bronze bells.

The various spirit tablets worshipped in the ritual were stored in the buildings lining the courtyard on the east and west. This space now houses the little-known **Capital Museum** (*Shou du bo wu guan*), with its display of objects related to the history of Beijing.

Behind the Hall of Great Perfection is the last courtyard of the temple, with its temple dedicated to Confucius' parents.

After a turn through the Capital Museum, make your way back south to the front entrance, turn right (west), and proceed to the next stop on our journey, the **Imperial Academy**.

Imperial Academy: The buildings flanking the courtyard house **Capital Library** (*Shu du tu shu guan*). The collection here is strong in the social sciences and there is a special section devoted to historical materials about Beijing, the finest public collection in China.

Imperial Academy (From an 18-century Chinese Plan)

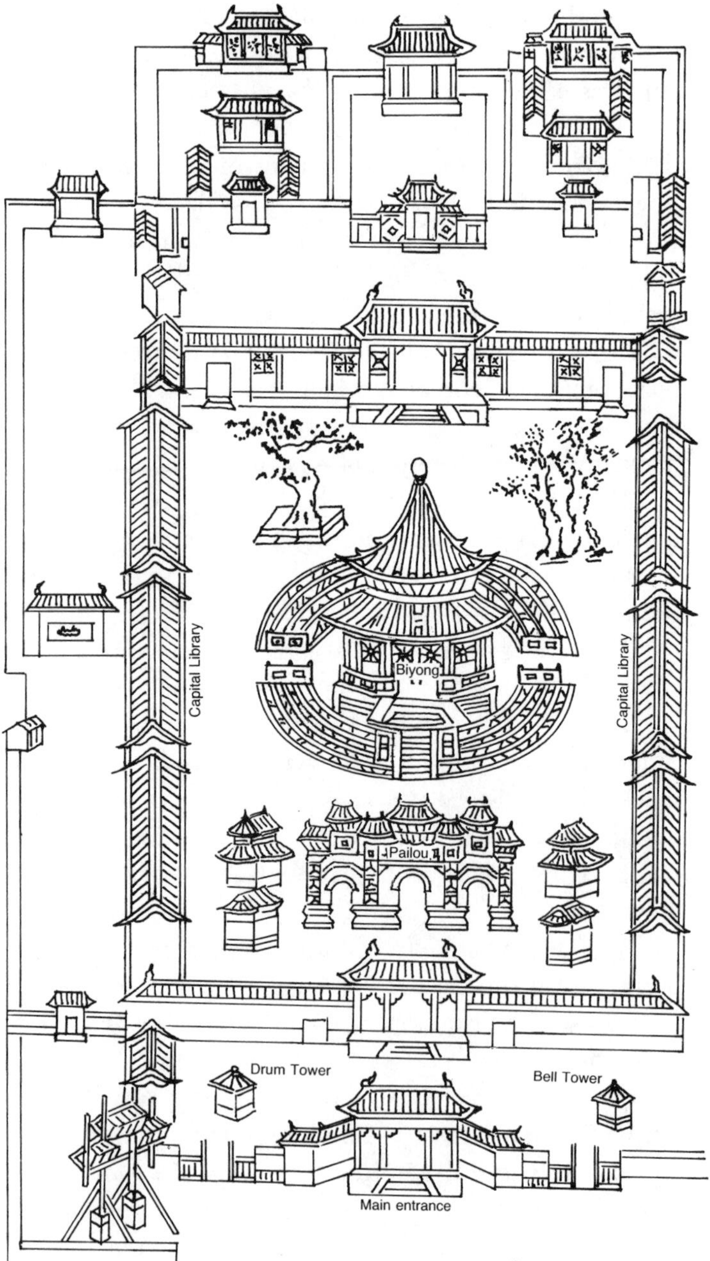

Capital Library

Capital Library

Biyong

Pailou

Drum Tower

Bell Tower

Main entrance

© The Guidebook Company Ltd

In 1306, the Yuan dynasty court founded the **Guo zi xue** ('school for the sons of the state'), a school where Mongol boys (the Yuan rulers were Mongols) studied the Chinese language and Chinese boys learned the Mongol language and the martial arts. Built in the same year as the Confucian Temple next door, its location was determined by the traditional formula, 'left temple, right academy.' which only makes sense if you are facing south. In 1313 an important library was installed here, an act repeated in the 20th century. Later that century, following the fall of the Yuan and the rise of the Ming dynasty, the school was upgraded to an institution of higher learning, with dormitories (located to the south of the main entrance) and a vegetable garden to supply the school kitchen. In 1462, the academy had more than 13,000 students. During the Yuan, Ming and Qing dynasties—from the 13th to the early 20th century—a total of more than 48,900 *jinshi* (the highest degree in the examination system, as well as the title accorded its holders) attended the school. Beginning in the Ming dynasty the academy enrolled students from the tributary states of Siam, Korea and Annam, as well as a number of Russians. In the Qing dynasty, one Manchu and one Chinese supervisor were especially assigned to take care of the Russian students.

A word about the roof tiles here and at the Confucian temple. When the Ming Wanli emperor restored the buildings in 1600, he provided them all with green glazed roof tiles. The Qing Qianlong emperor raised the status of the buildings in 1737 when, as mentioned above, he replaced the green, standard-issue palace tiles with imperial yellow,.Later, however, the yellow tiles were replaced with plain grey. But in 1783 when Qianlong built the present *biyong*, which was completed in 1784, he ordered yellow tiles once again. Was there a First Lady behind these colour changes?

The Walk: No tickets are required here, so after nodding to the gatekeeper walk right through the first courtyard with its **drum** and **bell towers** into the second large courtyard, where there is a massive **glazed-tile *pailou*** bearing an inscription from the Confucian *Analects*, 'All under heaven benefit from the teachings.' This *pailou* deeply impressed Henri Borel in 1909:

> . . .Suddenly a vivid melody resounds from
> this dead old transient mass; a glorious p'ai-
> lou of marble and porcelain with three arches,
> red, white, and yellow, lifts its song to the
> sky, filling the soul with joy, as if the immor-
> tality of life were revealed to it.
>
> This p'ai-lou is certainly the greatest wonder
> of all the stately arches of honour in Peking.
> In the midst of all the old decrepit ornamen-
> tation of the antique palace, behind these
> churchyard trees, wrinkled by the centuries,
> from the dull stillness of sombre hues, this
> miraculous p'ai-lou shouts its joy into the
> blue sky, a gleam of eternal youth, of stainless
> beauty unassailable through the ages. [2]

Beyond the *pailou* stands the Qianlong period **bi yong** (1784), where the emperor would deliver an annual spring lecture based on a subject drawn from the Confucian classics. The rest of the year the building served as a venue for a sort of graduate seminar for candidates preparing for the **capital examination** (*jinshi*), whose names, if they passed the test, would be recorded on the stone tablets in the Confucian Temple next door.

The term *biyong* dates back to the Western Zhou dy-nasty (11th century B.C.–771 B.C.) when the early kings lectured in a school of this name in the suburbs of the

---

(2) Henri Borel *The New China: A Traveller's Impressions*
(London: T Fisher Unwin, 1912), p. 202.

Official holding a tablet of audience

Lama Temple

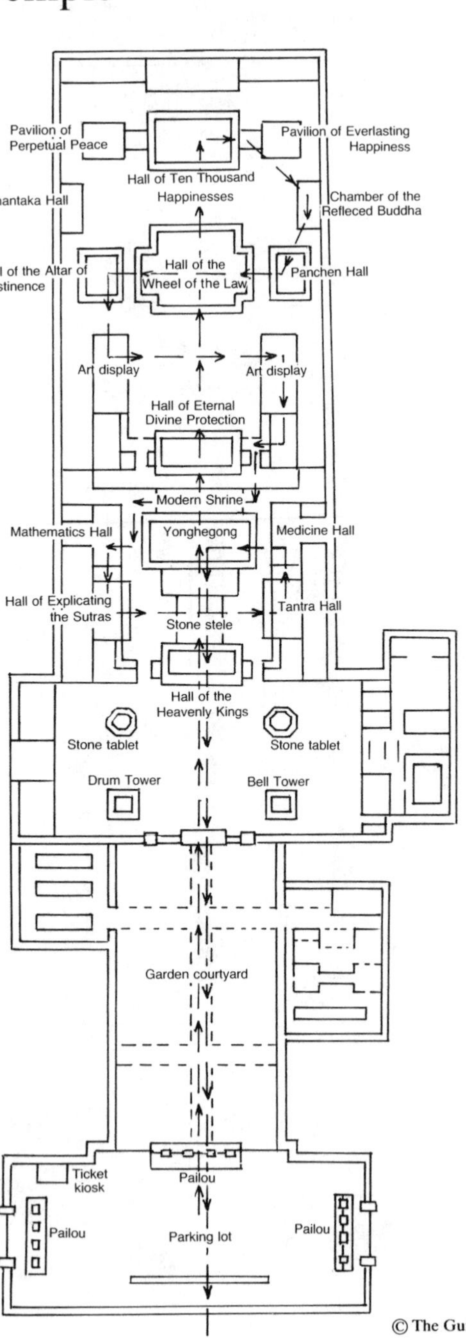

N ↑

Pavilion of Perpetual Peace

Pavilion of Everlasting Happiness

Hall of Ten Thousand Happinesses

Chamber of the Reflected Buddha

Yamantaka Hall

Hall of the Altar of Abstinence

Hall of the Wheel of the Law

Panchen Hall

Art display

Art display

Hall of Eternal Divine Protection

Modern Shrine

Mathematics Hall

Yonghegong

Medicine Hall

Hall of Explicating the Sutras

Tantra Hall

Stone stele

Hall of the Heavenly Kings

Stone tablet

Stone tablet

Drum Tower

Bell Tower

Garden courtyard

Ticket kiosk

Pailou

Pailou

Pailou

Parking lot

© The Guidebook Company Ltd

capital. The *biyong* of yore, like that in the Guozijian, sat in the middle of a round pool known as the **Crescent River**, so named because four marble bridges divide the pool into four arcs. The water in the pool is supplied by two wells and a culvert, and enters it through four dragon-head spigots of carved marble. The white marble balustrades encircling the building and the pool add a light touch to the bulkiness of the building.

The hall to the north of the Biyong sheltered the throne on which the emperor would rest before lecturing. Beyond it are a number of buildings formerly occupied by the officials in charge of the school.

Exit the Guozijian through the same gate you entered, turn left, walk to the north–south street in front of you (**Yonghegong Street**), make another left, and walk north for about three minutes. The entrance to the **Lama Temple** is on the opposite (east) side of **Yonghegong Street**.

Lama Temple: Our third and final destination today is the **Lama Temple**, or **Yong he gong**, one of the best preserved temples of any faith in China. Before entering, however, rest assured that security here is much better now than it was in the 1920s when a guidebook gave the following warning:

> Visitors are advised not to venture alone into the maze of buildings with any of the lamas. In former days the Yung Ho Kung [Yong he gong] had a very bad reputation indeed for assaults on foreigners and sometimes the complete disappearance of solitary sightseers. . . As recently as 1927 one of the authors was enticed into one of the buildings on the pretence of being shown some rare ornaments and nearly had the door closed on him. When he pulled out his revolver which from experi-

Spring Festival

ence he had taken along, the lama at once
let go of the door explaining that he had
only closed it, because he did not want the
Head Lama to see him showing visitors
around. [3]

In 1694, the Kangxi emperor built a mansion on this
site for his fourth son and successor, Prince Yong, the
Yongzheng emperor-to-be. When Prince Yong ascended
the throne and moved into the Forbidden City in 1723, a
number of buildings in the mansion were converted into a
Lama temple, while the rest became a 'detached palace,' or
pied à terre for the emperor. Fire destroyed these quarters
shortly afterwards. When Yongzheng rebuilt them he named
the place Yong he gong (palace of peace and harmony; Yong

---

(3)   L.C. Arlington and William Lewisohn *In Search of Old Peking*
      (Peking: Henri Vetch, 1935; reprinted by Oxford University
      Press, 1987), p. 195.

is the same Yong in his name) and installed his notorious secret intelligence agency and hit squad here. Yongzheng died suddenly in the **Yuanmingyuan Gardens** in 1735, and was replaced on the throne by his son Qianlong who had been born in 1711. Qianlong had his father's remains moved into the Yonghegong and ordered that the green roof tiles on all the major buildings be changed to imperial yellow within 15 days, thereby elevating their status to that of the buildings in the Imperial Palace. In 1744, at his mother's bidding, Qianlong formally consecrated the Yonghegong as a lamasery, enlarged the southern section, and invited 500 lamas from Mongolia to staff it. Several factors have been suggested as an explanation for this:

- Qianlong's mother wanted to atone for the deaths of all those murdered by her husband Yongzheng's hit squad;

- Qianlong wished to show his respect for his father's belief in the Lamaist religion;

- As a boy Qianlong had studied Chinese, Manchu and Mongolian for 11 years in the company of a 'living buddha' his age, who became his friend. When Qianlong became emperor, he wanted to provide this friend with a respectable place to practise his religion;

- Qianlong sought to conciliate the powerful Mongols and Tibetans by displaying a deep interest in their religion; and

- According to imperial usage, the birthplace of an emperor cannot be inhabited by his descendants or relatives.

The late 18th century was the golden age of the Lama Temple. Lamas of Tibetan, Mongolian and Manchu origin numbering in the thousands studied here alongside Chinese eunuch monks who served in the palace and imperial tombs. In the 19th and early 20th centuries, the monastic population diminished rapidly. The majority of monks who remained were Mongol, as they are today. Curiously, the chief lama of the temple was required to have had smallpox, because the sixth Panchen Lama died of this disease in Peking during the Qianlong reign.

After Qianlong's death, the five subsequent Qing emperors personally performed rituals in the Yonghegong three times a year: on Qianlong's birthday, on the day of his death and immediately after carrying out the sacrifice at the **Temple of Earth** (*Ditan*).

During the Qing dynasty, the Lama Temple was closed to the public except for the annual performances of the 'devil dances' (see page 226). In 1900 the Eight Allied Armies picnicked in the temple, and during the early Republican era it came under the auspices of the Bureau of Mongolian and Tibetan Affairs. Poor management and corruption among the monks during the ensuing decades resulted in the loss of many precious relics.

Few foreign writers had anything nice to say about the inhabitants of the Lama Temple. The following, written in 1888, is typical:

> These monks are Mongol Tartars of a very
> bad type, dirty and greedy of gain; and,
> moreover, are known to be grossly im-
> moral. They are generally offensively
> insolent to all foreigners, many of whom
> have vainly endeavoured to obtain access
> to the monastery—even the silver key,
> which is usually so powerful in China,
> often failing to unlock the inhospitable
> gates. [4]

---

(4) C.F. Gordon Cumming *Wanderings in China* (Edinburgh and London: William Blackwood & Sons, 1888), p. 392.

Ten years later, the situation had hardly improved:

> . . .Here twelve hundred lazy monks, filthy
> and vicious, are housed in the palace of a
> prince, who, on coming to the throne, gave
> them his dwelling and ordered them to be
> fed at his expense. So greedy are these
> recluses, whose first law is self-abnegation,
> and so indelicate is their mode of picking
> pockets, that a visitor always departed with
> the conviction that instead of visiting a
> house of prayer he had fallen into a den of
> thieves. [5]

Lamaism, the principal religion of Tibet, Mongolia, Sikkim and Bhutan, has never been widely practised or generally understood in China proper. Unlike Mahayana Buddhism, which underwent sinicization from the Han through the Tang and became the dominant school of Chinese Buddhism, Lamaism is relatively free of Chinese content, although the Lama Temple has some of the features commonly found in Chinese Buddhist temples. And while a vast corpus of Mahayana scriptures has been translated into Chinese, the Lamaist canon (written in Tibetan) has not been, and there were few Han Chinese followers of the faith. On the other hand, Indian and Tibetan influence could be seen in Chinese sculpture and architecture in Peking beginning in the Yuan dynasty; the **Western Yellow Temple** (*Xi Huang si*) and the **Five Pagoda Temple** (*Wu ta si*) are two such examples.

Before Buddhism entered Tibet from Nepal and China in the seventh century, Tibetans practised an ancient shamanistic cult known as Bon. The advent of the faith suppos-

---

(5) W.A.P. Martin *A Cycle of Cathay, or China, South and North* (New York: Fleming H Revell, 1897), p. 144.

edly took place when the first historical king of Tibet, Songtsen Gampo (608–650 A.D.), wedded two Buddhist princesses, one from China and the other from Nepal, who converted him to their beliefs. Lamaism, which replaced and to some extent absorbed elements of Bon, consists of three strands of Indian Buddhism: Hinayana, the monastic teachings of the Buddha, Sakyamuni (fl. *c.* 500 B.C.); Mahayana, a later popular elaboration of Hinayana; and Vajrayana, esoteric practices that make use of sounds, visual symbols and meditation.

Believers in Buddhism use a variety of means on their search for **nirvana**, an indescribable state in which the individual transcends pleasure and pain, life and death, by stepping beyond the cycle of death and rebirth.

The word 'lama,' from which the religion derives both its English and Chinese names, means guru or teacher in Tibetan. But a lama is not necessarily a monk, and most monks are not lamas.

Several other curious customs were practiced here besides the well known devil dances. Once a year in winter, the monks in the Lama Temple cooked up cauldrons full of a sweet porridge of rice, fruit and nuts called *La ba zhou. La* refers to the twelfth month of the lunar calendar, *ba* means the eighth day of that month, and *zhou* means 'gruel' or 'porridge.' Buddhists celebrate this day because it marks the Buddha's attainment of enlightenment, but there is another story behind it.

For six years before he attained nirvana, the Buddha lived a life of austerity. He had grown gaunt and his clothing was in tatters. One day he was sitting on a riverbank, begging for something to eat, when a girl cowherd brought him a bowl of fresh milk. After drinking it, the Buddha recovered his strength rapidly. Buddhists in ancient India celebrated this event by distributing food to the poor. In China Buddhists and especially the monks in lamaseries commemorated the day by preparing a pot of this delicious mush.

During the Qing dynasty, all the ingredients, pots and serving bowls used to prepare the super-stew in the Lama

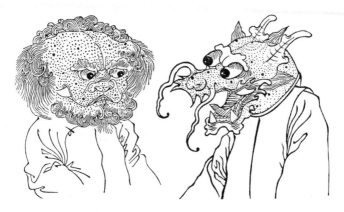

Devil dancers, Lama Temple

Temple were supplied by the imperial palace department of domestic affairs, which would also despatch a supervisor and numerous underlings to help in the kitchen, a hall to the east of the **Hall of Heavenly Kings** (*Tian wang dian*). In fact, one of the pots used to cook the brew still stands in the courtyard before this hall today.

In the early Qing dynasty, the monks prepared a total of six vats of gruel with different ingredients. Three of the vats were made with huge dollops of butter combined with dried fruit. Of these, the contents of one were presented as offerings before all the supposedly-hungry Buddha images in the temple; the second went to the emperor and his ladies in the palace; and the third was decocted to Mongolian VIPs and high-ranking lamas. Bowl number four was made with butter but without the dry fruit, and went to some lucky civil and military officials, while the fifth vat, made of rice and red dates without butter, went to the hundreds (and sometimes thousands) of monks who lived in the Yonghegong. A sixth small pot of gruel had bits of mutton added to it. The custom as practiced in the Lama Temple ceased in 1937 at the start of the Japanese occupation, but local residents continue to make **Labazhou** before the **Spring Festival** (Chinese New Year) for their friends and family.

Another delicacy made in the Lama Temple was **Dragon Whiskers Noodles**, superfine pasta made out of special wheat flour. At the summer solstice, the emperor sacrificed at the Temple of Earth (Ditan), just as he would do at the Temple of Heaven at the winter solstice. After completing the sacrifice, the emperor would proceed to the Yonghegong, where he placed stalks of freshly picked wheat before all of the Buddha images as a way of thanking them for the harvest. Then he would remove his sacrificial robe, don a more mundane costume, and eat a bowl of cold Dragon Whiskers noodles seasoned with sesame sauce before returning to the palace.

The Walk: The **Lama Temple** stands on a long north–south axis. The itinerary takes you through the main ceremonial buildings on the central axis and then back through the auxiliary halls, all of which contain interesting displays of Tibetan art, including many bronze images and *tanka* scroll paintings.

Purchase your ticket in the kiosk on the north side of the parking lot, a square flanked by three *pailous* and a spirit wall. The columns supporting these *pailous* were originally made of *nanmu*, a precious hardwood, but during the Japanese occupation (1937–45), troops removed them and shipped them to Japan. Since then they have been replaced with columns of concrete.

Head north through the long garden courtyard. To the east of here once stood the beehive-like complex of residences for the hundreds and sometimes thousands of monks who lived in the temple. Pass through the first gate into the first courtyard, which contains the standard Chinese-style drum and bell towers that are found in the front courtyards of Buddhist temples, Taoist monasteries and even the Forbidden City, two tall pavilions holding carved stone tablets, and a pair of bronze lions. The inscriptions on the stone tablets (in Chinese and Manchu on the left, Mongol and Tibetan on the right) are the text of Qianlong's essay 'On Lamaism.'

Following the pattern of most Chinese Buddhist temples, the first building in the complex is the **Hall of the Heavenly Kings** (*Tian wang dian*), where an image of the Buddha of the future, Maitreya, in his manifestation as the Laughing Buddha, is guarded by four giant heavenly kings. Note how this quartet of Subcontinental bruisers, responsible for keeping the peace in the four directions and throughout the four seasons, are engaged literally in stamping north in the direction of incarnations of evil. Guarding the rear entrance of this hall is a statue of Weida holding a sceptre and facing north in the direction of the next courtyard. Weida's job is to protect the image of Sakyamuni located in the next hall.

The second courtyard contains a **square stone stele** inscribed on four sides, again in four different languages, with an essay by Qianlong. Here the emperor outlines the origins of Lamaism, candidly explains how his own belief in the religion stems from a practical need to assuage the Mongols, and acknowledges the importance of the Lamaist practice of selecting 'living buddhas' to act as spiritual leaders. The elaborate incense burner to the north of the stele, manufactured in 1747 by the imperial foundry in the Forbidden City, is regarded as one of the finest works of art in the temple. It was designed to represent **Mt. Sumeru** (*Xu mi shan* in Chinese), a microcosm of the world. Its rare 'eel green' colour was achieved by melting down several ancient bronzes in the imperial collection. It is composed of three levels: sea, land and sky.

The next hall, the **Yong he gong** (palace of peace and harmony), where Prince Yong held official audiences before he became emperor, is now the main hall of the temple. The three presiding images here are the Buddha of the Past (left), the saviour of the world before the birth of Sakyamuni; the Buddha of the Present (centre), Sakyamuni himself; and the Buddha of the future (right), here making his second appearance in the temple. Sakyamuni is attended by his two loyal disciples, the young Ananda and the older Kasyapa. Up against the walls are 18 statues of *lohan*, or arhats,

Sakyamuni's disciples. The paintings on the rear walls depict Sakyamuni in his various manifestations. There is a fascinating clutter of ritual implements and containers crowded onto the tables before the images.

The small courtyard behind the Yonghegong contains an odd shrine that appears to have descended from outer space, though in fact it is a gift from two patriotic Hong Kong Buddhists who had this image of a four-headed Guanyin (or Avalokitesvara, the Goddess of Mercy), made in Thailand and installed here in 1987.

The next building is the **Hall of Eternal Divine Protection** *(Yong you dian)*, originally Prince Yong's residence. When the Yongzheng emperor died in 1735, his sarcophagus was laid to rest here before being buried in the western tombs of the Qing dynasty emperors. (Nine of the ten Qing emperors are buried at two mausoleum complexes to the east and west of the capital; Puyi, the last emperor, who died in 1967, was the only Qing emperor, to be cremated.) Later the images of the Amidha Buddha (centre); a reincarnation of Tsong Khapa, the 14th-century founder of the Yellow Sect of Tibetan Buddhism (right) and the Medicine Buddha (left), were placed here. A set of the 'eight precious objects' of Buddhism, each symbolic of one aspect of the Buddha's teachings, stands before each image.

The next hall, the most spacious in the Lama Temple, is the **Hall of the Wheel of the Law** *(Fa lun dian)*. The elaborate roof is a combination of Tibetan and Chinese architectural elements. Here, five times a day, the resident lamas would attend religious and philosophical lectures seated on the cushions set out in long rows. The large image is of Tsong Khapa, who established the Ganden Monastery in Tibet and who is considered the founder of the Yellow Hat Sect. Tsong Khapa was the teacher of the first Dalai and Panchen lamas, whose successive incarnations have continued to act as the leaders of the sect. The Dalai and Panchen lamas, like all other living buddhas, reveal themselves to the world in their childhood after undergoing a series of religious tests.

The throne to the left of Tsong Khapa's image is set aside for the Dalai Lama, that to the right for the Panchen Lama. Both lamas conducted religious services here in 1954. The Dalai Lama fled from Tibet in 1959 and has lived in exile in India since then. Much to the chagrin of the Chinese Government, he was awarded the Nobel Peace Prize in 1989, several months after the Tiananmen Massacre. The last Panchen Lama (whose claims to this title are doubted by some) stayed on in China and accepted a sinecure in the Chinese government. He only spent brief periods in Tibet and died there of a heart attack in 1988.

The wall paintings in this hall depict events in the life of Sakyamuni, beginning with his birth from his mother's armpit. Here also is the large carved *nanmu* wood basin in which the infant Qianlong was bathed on his third day. Another important artifact is the diorama of the **Mountain of Five Hundred Immortals** in the northern part of the hall. Five hundred is a magical number in the lore of India, like three and its multiples in Chinese numerology. The mountain itself is carved of hardwood, and the figures on the mountain are crafted of gold, silver, bronze, tin and iron. The walls of this hall are lined with stacks of cloth-covered Tibetan Buddhist scriptures, printed from woodblocks on long rectangular sheets that are left unbound.

The hall in the next courtyard, the **Pavilion of Ten Thousand Happinesses** (*Wan fu ge*), houses an awesome image of Maitreya, here making his third and final appearance in the Yonghegong. The entire statue is 26 meters (85 feet) tall, though one third of its length is below ground to prevent it from toppling over in the event of an earthquake.

The story goes that in 1750, Qianlong sent troops into Tibet to quell an uprising but they arrived long after order had been restored. To express his gratitude, the seventh Dalai Lama offered a gift of Buddhist images and other precious relics to the emperor. At the time, Qianlong had been concerned that the northern section of the Yonghegong, then occupied by a temple to the Goddess of Mercy, needed a tall building to prevent evil influences from the north from

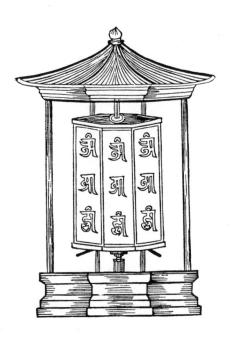

Prayer wheel with Tibetan inscription

entering the Yonghegong, and he decided to erect a giant image there. Coincidentally, at this time the king of what is today Nepal was shipping a huge cedar trunk 2.7 meters (nine feet) in diameter from India to Tibet, and when the Dalai Lama learned of Qianlong's intentions, he traded a quantity of precious jewels for this tree and had it shipped to Peking; it took three years to reach its destination. Qianlong demolished the Goddess of Mercy temple occupying this spot in the northern section of the Yongdegong, laid the foundation for the new pavilion, had the huge image of Maitreya carved out of the tree trunk by artisans from the Forbidden City and built the pavilion around it only after it had been set on its base. The '10,000 happinesses' refer not only to Maitreya and his good works but to the innumerable Buddha images of clay, wood and stone found on the second and third storeys of the pavilion.

The 'flying bridges' that connect the Pavilion of Ten Thousand Happinesses to the two tall towers to the east and west are unique examples of a form of architecture seen only in frescos in the Dunhuang Caves dating back to the Han and Wei (fourth–sixth centuries) dynasties.

The east tower, the **Pavilion of Everlasting Happiness**, contains a giant prayer wheel set in an octagonal pavilion and suspended on a steel axle that runs through the wheel from the floor to the ceiling. This is a jumbo version of the standing prayer wheels found in other places in the temple, and of the miniature hand-held prayer wheels common in Tibet. The significance of the prayer wheel can be explained in three ways: it symbolizes the 'wheel of the law,' the ceaseless cycle of death and rebirth; it symbolizes an altar where Sakyamuni is preaching—every time it is spun the Buddha's blessings absolve the spinner of all his sins; and it can confer instant merit on whoever turns it. As the interior of the prayer wheel is filled with Buddhist scriptures, one revolution of the wheel is equivalent to reciting all the scriptures contained inside. The giant prayer wheel was spun when the emperor came to worship Maitreya.

The west tower, the **Pavilion of Perpetual Peace**, houses a huge wooden automaton lotus with petals that open and close around a baby-faced seated image of Sakyamuni. This bit of side-show ingenuity was originally a product of a Qing-dynasty palace workshop. Now restored, it still 'performs' on certain holidays.

To the west of this courtyard there was once an interesting complex of buildings that were mostly dismantled after 1949 when the road beside the temple was widened. It contained a small **Hall of the Four Heavenly Kings** and shrines to the Goddess of Mercy and to Guan Di, the god of war and patron saint of the Qing dynasty. Here also were the headquarters of Yongzheng's hit squad, staffed by monks trained in the martial arts and other professional thugs. But Yongzheng cleverly disguised this organization as the office responsible for providing the imperial household with pet animals and insects, including fish, cicadas and dragonflies. It is said that for reasons of security these buildings were connected to Prince Yong's residence by an underground passageway. The guides won't reveal if this 'top secret' is true or not. This area now contains a pay toilet.

Finally, to the north of the Pavilion of Ten Thousand Happinesses is a courtyard with three buildings in which were kept the masks, costumes and other paraphernalia used in the famous 'devil dances' performed here once a year and revived in the 1980s . They are not open to the public.

Having seen the giant Maitreya, all other buddhas may seem anti-climactic, but don't overlook the image in the **Chamber of the Reflected Buddha** (*Zhao fo lou*) on the east side of the courtyard in front of the Pavilion of Ten Thousand Happinesses. The Chamber was the private chapel of Qianlong's mother.

A legend surrounds the name of this place: when Sakyamuni, the original Buddha, was about to ascend to heaven to deliver a scripture to his mother, his disciples asked him to leave an image of himself in the mundane world. To satisfy their request, Sakyamuni invited an artist to paint his portrait. The painter, however, was unwilling to gaze directly upon the Buddha's countenance, and asked his subject to stand on the shore of a river so that he could paint his image from the reflection in the water. From then on, all images of Sakyamuni were copied from this reflected likeness. The image in this hall is cast of bronze, crafted to resemble wood. The two figures accompanying him are the young Ananda and aged Kasyapa. Note the intricate wooden carving decorating the niche, with its 99 golden dragons disporting in the waves—carving 100 dragons, a perfect sum, would have been considered presumptuous.

On the west side of this courtyard is the **Yamantaka Hall**, now closed but once home to a grotesque image of a god who, like Guan di, was worshipped as a god of war. The Qing emperors kept weapons here that had been captured on military campaigns in the border districts as well as Tibetan weapons received by the court as tribute. They are now on display in the **Hall of the Altar of Ordination**.

Working your way south you may stop in some of the less important buildings lining the sides of the courtyards that have been converted into museums containing excellent displays of Tibetan art.

To the west of the **Hall of the Law** is the **Hall of the Altar of Ordination** (*Jie tai*; extra ticket required), where Qianlong celebrated his 70th birthday in the company of the sixth Panchen Lama. The wooden throne, set on a square three-tiered marble platform that nearly fills the room, was used by Qianlong when he took part in Lamaist rituals. Numerology inspired the unique design of this building: the upper storey is 3 x 3 bays, and the lower storey 5 x 5 bays. Both this and the **Panchen Hall** (see below) are museums today. The **Altar of Abstinence** contains a number of valuable relics associated with Qianlong and the later inhabitants of the temple, including ceramics, bronzes, cloisonné, ritual implements, snuff bottles, skull drums, trumpets, robes and hats worn by the Dalai Lama in each of the four seasons.

Across the courtyard to the east of the Hall of the Wheel of the Law is the **Panchen Hall**, built to celebrate the sixth Panchen Lama's visit to Beijing in 1780. Identical in design with the Hall of the Altar of Ordination, it contains a throne and platform on which the Panchen Lama sat when holding formal audiences. This throne had first been used by Qianlong when he sat atop the Altar of Abstinence. When Qianlong moved the throne to the Panchen Hall, he had a copy made for himself.

The buildings flanking the next courtyard to the south contain numerous interesting items. The east hall features a group of Tantric images veiled in yellow sheets. These are the famous Joyful Buddhas, bronze gods and their consorts welded in sexual embrace. The guard explains that they are kept under wraps because Chinese people cannot understand their esoteric significance: they are cosmic symbols of the unity of opposites. In the old days, the monks could be persuaded to lift these veils for a penny or two. One guidebook commented, 'the figures are very crude indeed and, as a pornographic exhibition, disappointing.' The two large stuffed bears on display here are believed to have been shot with bow and arrow by Qianlong in one of the imperial hunting parks in Manchuria.

The hall on the west side of the courtyard contains a number of buddhas of lesser interest as well as *tanka* paintings. Unfortunately most of these displays are so poorly lit it is difficult to appreciate them.

The first of the **Four Study Halls** set around the four corners of the Yonghegong is, moving counter-clockwise, the **Hall of Mathematics** (northwest), where the monks learned astronomy and geography. There is an image of Tsong Khapa here, and some astronomical instruments. Proceeding counter clockwise we come to the **Hall of Explicating the Scriptures** (southwest), the **Hall of Tantra** (southeast), where the precepts of this branch of abstruse learning were studied, and the **Medicine Hall** (northeast) where traditional Tibetan medicine, with its vast pharmacopoeia of plant and animal drugs, was studied. This brings us back to the Hall of the Heavenly Kings.

The Tibetan 'devil dances'—a Peking 'entertainment' mentioned by nearly all early foreign visitors as an event not to be missed—took place on the last day of the first lunar month and marked the conclusion of the new year celebrations. If you happen to be in Beijing at this time of year, consult a lunar calendar as they are mentioned in the press only *after* they have taken place.

There are several interpretations for the devil dances. Scholars of Buddhism believe that they are an object lesson in vanquishing symbolic 'devils,' here referring to and a particular sextet of human weaknesses: wine, sex, covetousness, anger, recklessness and killing. These evils are attributed to the followers of the Red Hat Sect of Lamaism, and hence the protagonist in the dances is the founder of the opposing Yellow Hat sect, Tsong Khapa. Another traditional view, held primarily by Manchus in old Peking, is that the hero in the dances is the Kangxi emperor, who twice in his reign sent troops to Tibet in support of the Dalai Lama. A third view popular among monks is that the devil dances are an ancient Indian form of ritual opera, symbolizing the union of opposites, or resolution of contradictions, similar to the message concealed in the Joyful Buddhas. Chinese scholars set little store on this theory. H.Y. Lowe, in his *Adventures of Wu*, described the dances in the 1930s:

> The front court of the temple would be crowded to capacity with sight-seers from early morning. To prevent mobbing of the inner precincts, where most of the temple's images and various religious and sacrificial attributes are kept. . .these are forbidden to the visitors of the day. By noon the dance party would come out to the front court for their mystic antics, performed in full public view.

> To get a vantage point to watch a Devil Dance is not an easy matter. . . [Some 'reserved seats' are on the walls or in the trees where Tarzan-the-Apeman youngsters perch.] In the center of the courtyard the attendant priests with the help of the police manage to make a clearing with the help of long whips and the tossing of handfuls of lime powder, and within the cordon thus thrown are seen the various characters of this colourful paganistic show, all clad in conventional garbs of rich embroideries though shabby from age and wearing big,

top-heavy masks of various kinds, some
representing the various Lamaist deities
and others the devilish members with ugly
faces, some with their hats decorated with
facsimiles of human skulls and others
brandishing short religious weapons and
others wearing the heads of cows and deer.

In the center is the figure of buttered
dough painted red and carried ceremoni-
ously on a small wooden stand—the
embodiment of the devil. Chanting of
Tibetan scriptures and playing of religious
music, echoing drums and horns, accompany the mimicry subduing process. A few
minutes later the entire group form into a
procession and make for the gate of the
temple where the dough figure is cut into
pieces and burned, thus ending the Devil
Dance. [6]

Richard Wilhelm, the German sinologist and translator
of the *I Ching* who lived in Peking in the 1920s, compared
these Devil Dances to the gyrations of another sort of devils:

. . . When, to the accompaniment of a jazz
band, the foreigners perform on hot
summer nights their negro dances on the
airy roof of the Hotel de Pekin, there is not
a very great difference from the cult dances
in the Yong Ho Kung [Yonghegong]
Temple in the north of the town, according

---

(6) H.Y. Lowe *The Adventures of Wu: The Life Cycle of a Peking Man*
(Peking: The Peking Chronicle Press 1940–41; Princeton
University Press, 1983), II, pp. 188–9.

to Chinese ideas. There the Mongols dance in the winter and their Lamas are wrapped up and are masked, so that almost nothing of their original appearance can be seen and the horn and skull-drums beat the rhythm to it. Here, in the summer, the Europeans dance and their ladies are so décolletées that almost nothing [everything] of their original figure can be seen, and the negro saxophones and wooden rattles beat the rhythm. Of course their gods are different. . . . [7]

---

(7) Richard Wilhelm *The Soul of China*
      (London: Harcourt Brace Jovanovich, 1928), pp. 264–5.

Walk · 6

Yi He Yuan, The Summer Palace

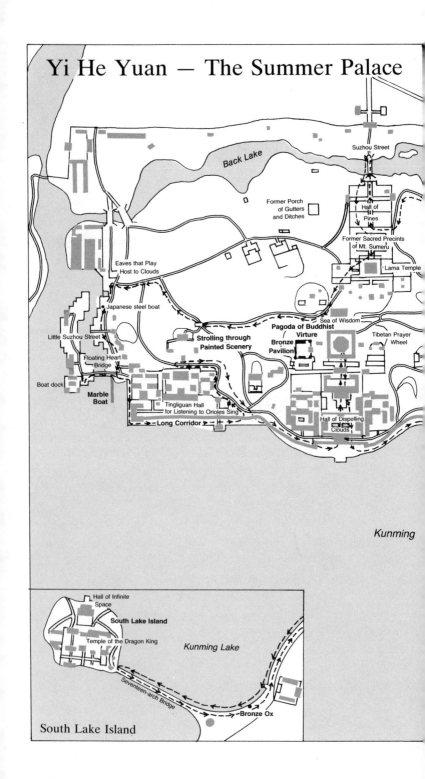

Yi He Yuan — The Summer Palace

Back Lake

Suzhou Street

Former Porch
of Gutters
and Ditches

Hall of
Pines

Former Sacred Precincts
of Mt. Sumeru

Lama Temple

Eaves that Play
Host to Clouds

Japanese steel boat

Sea of Wisdom

**Pagoda of Buddhist
Virture**

Little Suzhou Street

**Strolling through
Painted Scenery**

**Bronze
Pavilion**

Tibetan Prayer
Wheel

Floating Heart
Bridge

Boat dock

**Marble
Boat**

Tingliguan Hall
for Listening to Orioles Sing

Hall of Dispelling
Clouds

Long Corridor

Kunming

Hall of Infinite
Space

South Lake Island

Temple of the Dragon King

Kunming Lake

Seventeen-arch Bridge

Bronze Ox

South Lake Island

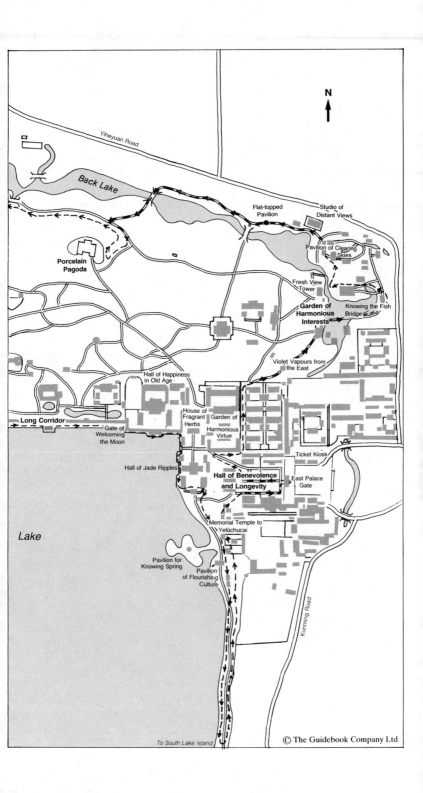

N

Yiheyuan Road

Back Lake

Flat-topped Pavilion

Studio of Distant Views

Pavilion of Clearing Skies

Porcelain Pagoda

Fresh View Tower

Garden of Harmonious Interests

Knowing the Fish Bridge

Violet Vapours from the East

Hall of Happiness in Old Age

Long Corridor

House of Fragrant Herbs

Garden of Harmonious Virtue

Gate of Welcoming the Moon

Ticket Kiosk

Hall of Jade Ripples

Hall of Benevolence and Longevity

East Palace Gate

Lake

Memorial Temple to Yelüchucai

Pavilion for Knowing Spring

Pavilion of Flourishing Culture

Kunming Road

To South Lake Island

© The Guidebook Company Ltd

Duration

Approximately five hours.

Description

This walk holds many a pleasant surprise in store. We visit the **Summer Palace** ceremonial quarters; a garden-within-garden; and the relatively wild north side of the man-made mountain *before* exploring a huge abandoned **Lama Temple** and viewing **Kunming Lake** from the highest point in the park. We then view the famous **Marble Boat**, stroll along the **Long Corridor** and visit the other major buildings on the south face of the mountain, before rounding the east shore of the lake and crossing the **Seventeen-arch Bridge** as the sun sets over the **Western Hills**. The idea is that as the crowds disperse you will have the Summer Palace almost to yourself—as it was meant to be.

This is perhaps the most physically demanding walk in this book, and includes a bit of hill climbing. It is suggested that you wear hiking boots or running shoes and begin no later than noon. You may also want to bring a picnic lunch, as the only decent restaurant on the premises, the Hall of Listening to the Orioles Sing (*Ting li guan*), is often fully booked by tour groups, and may be reluctant to accommodate à la carte diners, though it is certainly worth a try.

Starting Point
The East Palace Gate of the Summer Palace.

How to Get There
Buses 332, 333, 346, 362, 374, 375. Bus 332 begins at the Beijing Zoo. There are numerous 'wildcat' mini-buses that run from the Beijing Railway Station directly to the Summer Palace. Some of them go along Chang'an Boulevard and pick up passengers on the way. By bike it takes a little over an hour to get from the Summer Palace to Tiananmen Square.

How to Get Away
The same way you got here, as the walk begins and ends at the East Palace Gate.

> . . .'See the Summer Palace,' said an old Pekinese, 'and you will have seen all that China has to offer in art and architecture', and we found verily that not only in the tout ensemble but in every detail of porcelain roofs, canopied walks, marble caves, arched bridges, lotus ponds and rockeries, there was a plan apparent which showed that a whole empire had been drawn upon to furnish the scheme of this gigantic effort of man to combine the beauties of his craft with those of nature's own art. [1]

---

(1) Paul Myron *Our Chinese Chances through Europe's War* (Chicago: Linebarger Brothers, 1915), p. 87.

Plan to begin your visit to the Summer Palace by noon in order to catch the sun setting over the Western Hills at the completion of the walk. By five o'clock the swarms of local visitors evaporate without a trace to take their dinner as there is no place for them to eat on the grounds. The Summer Palace is at its best in spring and summer, when the willows cast their shadows on Kunming Lake, and the resident staff and neighbourhood folk come out to enjoy the cool breezes in the lakeside pavilions and take part in improvised performances of Peking opera and ballads. When Kunming Lake freezes over in the winter—nowhere is it deeper than two meters (six feet)—skaters by the hundreds defy safety warnings and spin circles in the lip-cracking air. Though Beijing has four clearly demarcated seasons, spring and autumn are painfully fleeting. The Summer Palace is a perfect place to spend these elusive days in relative solitude.

During the Qing dynasty there were five imperial gardens in the northwestern suburbs of Peking. The Manchus also built a summer getaway at Chengde (Jehol) and a palace in honour of the founding of the dynasty at Shenyang (Mukden). The extant Summer Palace, or *Yi he yuan* (**Garden of Peace and Harmony in Old Age**) was known to foreigners as the **New Summer Palace** after it was rebuilt in the late 19th century, to distinguish it from the even more splendid *Yuan ming yuan,* the Old Summer Palace, which had been destroyed in 1860 and was never rebuilt.

The Chinese names of both of these gardens—*yuan* in fact means 'garden', not palace—contain no references to summer; their English names derive from the fact that several of the Qing emperors, and the Empress Dowager Cixi, often spent all but the coldest months of the year in them. The *Yi he yuan* was twice destroyed (in 1860 along with the Yuanmingyuan, and in 1900) and twice rebuilt (1888 and 1902). It was renovated on both occasions in accordance with Cixi's instructions and by dint of her shrewdness in controlling the imperial purse. Its present incarnation still bears the personal stamp of this remarkable and notorious woman, and indeed much of her career as the virtual ruler of China was played out on these grounds. The Swedish art historian Osvald Siren wrote:

> Tzu Hsi's [Cixi's] summer palace was the last product of a tradition that can be traced back to the beginning of our era, a last attempt to render in concrete form a phantasmagoria of art and Nature which might serve as a residence for the divine ruler of the Middle Kingdom. It is easy to understand that she loved this place above all others, and accounted the periods she spent here as the best in her life. [2]

All that remains of the original Yuanmingyuan, the **Garden of Perfection and Light**, are a few sadly crumbled stone columns and plinths. The three contiguous gardens designated by this name were built during the reigns of the Kangxi, Yongzheng and Qianlong emperors (grandfather, son and grandson) in the 17th and 18th centuries. One of its best-known sections, the well-documented Western Buildings, was designed in Italian baroque style by the Jesuits Castiglione, Benoist (who was in charge of the fountains) and Sichelbarth, who as some of the earliest 'foreign experts' in China, served the emperor at the Manchu court. The Yuanmingyuan was sacked and burnt in 1860 by the English and French troops but was never significantly restored. The idea of reconstructing it has been proposed several times in recent decades. Conservative opinion holds that not rebuilding it is a more persuasive historical lesson in the subject of foreign imperialism than fabricating a shiny-new, or fake-old, park on the theme of imperial extravagance. Now both 'imperialism' and extravagance seem to have won the day. With the assistance of a French team of scholars and architects, the European-style maze was rehabilitated and opened to the public in 1988.

---

(2)   Osvald Siren *The Gardens of China*
        (New York: Ronald Press, 1949), p. 134.

Another noted garden in the western suburbs, now off limits to visitors, is **Jade Spring Mountain** (*Yu quan shan*), with its fine porcelain pagoda, which stands about one and a half kilometres to the west of **Longevity Hill**, the principal protruberance in the Summer Palace grounds. The Qianlong emperor built himself a cozy summer retreat here, and for centuries the water from its numerous springs was transported daily by donkey cart to the **Forbidden City** to fill the imperial teapots. Jade Spring water was so highly regarded that the emperors also had large jugs of it transported along with them on their journeys away from the capital. In Republican days **Jade Spring Mountain** was converted into a spa, and a soft-drink bottling plant was built nearby. Since its occupation after 1949 by the Chinese air force, it has served as a watering place for high ranking commissars.

According to an unsubstantiated but widely circulated report, it was on the southwest slope of Jade Spring Mountain that Mao Zedong arranged for his appointed successor, Lin Biao, to be 'liquidated with rocket launchers' after a failed coup. If this is true, Lin did not die in the officially publicized and 'carefully documented' air crash in Inner Mongolia when his plane ran out of fuel during his escape flight to the Soviet Union. [3] There is a military airstrip about a mile southwest of Jade Spring Mountain, one of several Peking airstrips used for civil aviation before 1949. Both this and another runway at Nanyuan several miles south of the city, now used regularly by tourists flying in chartered military planes, are curiously eliminated from all currently available Beijing maps, and do not even appear in a reconstructed 1947 map of Peking published in a 1988 'historical' atlas of the city.

The earliest imperial parks in the western suburbs of Peking date back to the 12th century, when a Jin-dynasty emperor built a summer retreat in the Western Hills.

---

(3)   Yao Ming-le *The Conspiracy and Murder of Mao's Heir* (London: Collins 1983), pp. 160–3.

Around 1190 he diverted a stream from Jade Spring Mountain to provide water for the urban centre in the southeast, and at the same time dredged a lake in the marshy land immediately south of Jug Hill, the molehill that eventually became today's Longevity Mountain.

In the 13th century, the hydraulic engineer Guo Shoujing built canals from the Western Hills and nearby Changping County for the purpose of supplying sufficient water to the Yuan-dynasty capital, **Khanbaligh** (*Dadu* in Chinese), to enable the urban waterway system to be linked to the Grand Canal. The lake was considerably enlarged at this time.

Though the Ming emperors were not active suburban garden builders, one of them erected a temple on Jug Hill. Centuries later, in 1750, Qianlong of the Qing dynasty enlarged this temple and the hill it stood on (using mud dredged from the marsh) on the occasion of his mother's 60th birthday. He called it the **Temple of Mercy and Longevity**; renamed **Jug Mountain** as **Longevity Mountain** in her honour; and radically remodelled the lake with dykes and bridges after the **West Lake** in Hangzhou, which he had admired on his trips to the south. He dubbed the new body of water Kunming Lake, after a pond of the same name in the Tang-dynasty capital of Chang'an where the imperial navy had conducted war games nearly 1,000 years before. Qianlong built a fleet of boats for the same purpose and recruited seamen from the coastal areas to man them. Construction lasted 11 years; Qianlong called his creation the Garden of Pure Ripples.

Qianlong's birthday greeting to his mother is a model of modesty and hyperbole fueled by filial piety:

> My Holy Mother, the Empress Dowager,
> Eminently Fortunate, Manifestly Merciful,
> Peaceful and Gracious, Sincerely Agreeable,
> Liberal and Venerable, is naturally kind and
> benevolent ... meets all under Heaven with
> justice wherefore all within our realm
> honour her . . .

An elderly gentleman

I, who have sometimes failed to be a filial
son . . . have built this temple and assembled priests to chant their scriptures . . .
hoping to requite my Mother's goodness . . .

Before the temple spreads a lake, sweet as
koumiss [fermented mare's milk]. [My
mother] is charmed with the scene, she
clasps her hands in devotion, and her face
beams with joy, a joy which comes partly
from what I have done for her. [4]

In 1860 the Garden of Pure Ripples was destroyed by
the British and French armies as an afterthought to their
looting and burning of the Yuanmingyuan. This violence
was an act of revenge arising from disputes over trade,

---

(4)   Carroll Brown Malone *History of the Peking Summer Palaces Under
      the Ch'ing Dynasty* (Urbana, Illinois: University of Illinois, 1934),
      pp. 110–1.

diplomacy and the question of foreign residence in China. The troubled dynasty remained without a suburban summer palace until 1873, when the Tongzhi emperor reached his majority and ascended the throne, whereupon the Empress Dowager Cixi began to carry out repairs to provide herself with a place for her retirement. When Tongzhi died in January 1875, the work came to a halt. In 1886, with the young Guangxu now on the throne, Cixi procured funds that had been earmarked for the Chinese navy and started work again on the garden, which she renamed—one might say rather indulgently—*Yi he yuan*, **The Garden of Peace and Harmony in Old Age**. The work was completed in 1891. Cixi concentrated her efforts on the south face of the mountain, leaving most of the ruins on the north face untouched. China's crushing defeat in the war with Japan in 1894–5 turned out to be an excellent lesson in naval strategy for the rapidly weakening Manchus.

In 1900 Russian, British and Italian troops visited destruction upon the Yiheyuan once again in the wake of the **Boxer Uprising** and siege of the Peking legations, and occupied the garden for a year. But in 1902 Cixi returned from her temporary exile in Xi'an and in two years restored the garden, for the most part, as it stands today. As before, Cixi was cramped by limited funds and directed most of her attention to the south face of Longevity Mountain. In 1905, Cixi erected the tall walls that surround the palace and installed a telephone as well as troops to guard her. Cixi died in 1908, and the Qing dynasty fell in 1911. In 1914, the grounds were opened to the public for the first time, although the high price of admission was beyond the means of the average Peking family. Several years before this, visiting the Summer Palace presented other problems, as Henri Borel wrote in 1909:

> The summer palace is no longer open daily
> to tourists: they damaged, and even robbed
> it. Visitors are admitted on two Wednes-
> days of each month, provided they can

present an order for admission, applied for
by their Legation. These Wednesday
visitors are solemnly received at the palace
entrance by mandarins of the Wai-wu Pu,
the Foreign Office, on behalf of the Chinese authorities. They thereby display the
diplomatic courtesy that so often is the
gilded shell of distrust and contempt. Their
Chinese hosts, after conducting the visitors
into a reception-room where tea and
refreshments are offered, then show them
over the palace, ostensibly to be of service
to them by giving information, but in
reality to watch them so that they may not
do more damage or steal. [5]

Major rebuilding and dredging of Kunming Lake was
carried out in 1959–60, and in 1966, at the start of the
Cultural Revolution, the Summer Palace was renamed
'People's Park'. However, this name did not stick for long.
Kunming Lake was drained and dredged again in 1991.
This time the crews discovered 'foreign' bullets attributed
to the Eight Allied Armies, Qing porcelain that had once
graced the Yuanmingyuan and an inexplicably large number
of wedding rings.

While the grand symmetry of the Forbidden City and
the Temple of Heaven can be best appreciated from the air,
the Summer Palace is a visual feast for earth bound strollers.
As Juliet Bredon observed:

Unlike the Forbidden City, the Summer
Palace is not a collection of remarkable
buildings, impersonal, aloof, almost cold,
which seem to look down contemptuously
on the tiny ant-like humans that hurry

---

(5)   Henri Borel *The New China: A Traveller's Impressions*
      (London: T Fisher Unwin, 1912), p. 228.

between them. But what [Yiheyuan)]loses
in magnificence, it gains in sympathy. [6]

When you are there, remember that this huge complex was designed for the pleasure of a single imperial person and his (and in Cixi's case, her) retinue rather than for millions of tourists who visit it every year.

The Yiheyuan has several 'controlled views'—pavilions, terraces and windows so designed that an observer standing in the proper place is presented with a 'framed' picture of a fine landscape. The best example of this is the pavilion appropriately named Strolling through Painted Scenery, described below. Another such view is obtained from the terrace of the **Hall of Infinite Space** (*Han xu tang*) on the north shore of South Lake Island.

As in all gardens in China, the whole of the Summer Palace is greater than its parts. Many of the buildings, under close scrutiny, are tiresome Qing kitsch, a judgement that applies to the period furnishings as well as the several post-Mao paint job. But Thomas Cook's guide to China noted in 1917: 'The [Summer Palace] might be garish in any other part of the world but it is a fairyland in China.'

On the other hand, the relatively neglected section of the Summer Palace on the north side of Longevity Hill is especially quiet and very much off the beaten path. Here, where wheat, millet and vegetables were once grown to supply the imperial kitchen, one can feel pleasantly alienated from the hustle and bustle of Beijing.

The Walk: The Summer Palace contains more palaces, temples, *pailous*, summer-houses, tea booths, terraces, pagodas, studios, gardens, lakes and bridges than can possibly be described here or visited in a single day. The walk that follows is a selection of highlights rather than a complete inventory.

---

(6) Juliet Bredon *Peking* (Shanghai: Kelly and Walsh, 1931;
     Oxford University Press reprint, 1982), p. 297.

Buy a ticket in the kiosk on the north side of the smaller, inner parking lot near the **East Palace Gate** *(Dong gong men)*. This was the entrance most frequently used by foreigners after 1902, on the several occasions when they were invited to the Summer Palace to meet the Empress Dowager and the Guangxu emperor. The slab of carved marble set in the staircase that leads up to the gate was moved here from the Yuanmingyuan, and the two bronze lions date back to the days of Qianlong's Garden of Pure Ripples.

The emperors travelled to the palace by an interesting water route. Boarding a boat immediately outside the northwest corner of the city walls, they would often make a two-day journey of it, stopping for the night, or for tea, at Wan shou si, a temple to the east of today's **Purple Bamboo Park**, where there was a lock which made it necessary for the imperial entourage to change boats. (Wanshousi, which had been occupied by the People's Liberation Army since the Cultural Revolution, has been entirely refurbished and is now the Beijing Art Museum.) They continued their floating journey northwest on the still-extant canal that runs for 24 kilometers (15 miles) to the southernmost corner of Kunming Lake, whence they passed under a lovely camel-back bridge, called the **Bridge of Embroidered Ripples** or the **Hunchback Bridge**. They would then proceed to South Lake Island in the centre of Kunming Lake, disembark, and offer a prayer of gratitude to the Dragon King for having kept the waters calm along the way. There is talk of reopening this water route to tourists.

Upon entering the East Palace Gate, proceed through a tree-shaded courtyard (where there is a map of the grounds) to the first *pailou*–style gate (of Benevolence and Longevity), which leads to a courtyard and the **Hall of Benevolence and Longevity** *(Ren shou dian)*. In addition to the huge, much-photographed Lake Taihu stone, taken from the Shaoyuan Garden (presently on the campus of Beijing University), and much-rubbed bronze incense burners now encaged in wire, note the delicate stone carving on the gates and the stands on which the bronzes sit.

Guides and guidebooks tell you that in the Hall of Benevolence and Longevity, burnt to the ground by foreign troops in 1860 and rebuilt in 1888, the young Guangxu emperor held court while Aunt Cixi 'ruled the empire from behind a curtain'. While a similar curtain can be seen in both the Forbidden City and the Summer Palace, the phrase is actually a classical metaphor for a female regency; the expression originated with the Empress Wu Zetian of the Tang dynasty, a dragon-lady in her own right. By the end of the Qing dynasty, Cixi hardly required a curtain.

In this hall Cixi also entertained members of the Peking foreign diplomatic corps on several occasions. Today, the refurbished (1991) building contains some authentic *objets d'art* from the late Qing dynasty which are worth inspecting. The small chambers to the side of the throne area were lounges where the emperor and the dowager rested when not holding court. In order to visit this and several other important buildings in the Summer Palace, purchase, comprehensive ticket at the kiosk in front of the building (or at kiosks near the other buildings where it is required).

To the northwest of this hall is a group of buildings called the **Garden of Harmonious Virtue** *(De he yuan),* including a multi-tiered theatre (like the one in the Forbidden City) that is said to be one of the finest old opera houses in China. Admission is by yet another special ticket (not included in the above-mentioned ticket) and inside, you may see young Beijing girls dressed up as Manchu palace maidens. Their gowns are polyester, the colours loud, their hair ornaments preponderantly plastic, but their Manchu high heels (Manchu women did not bind their feet) are authentic in design. Cixi would attend operatic performances here beginning on the second day after her arrival in the garden. On her birthday, performances by her troupe of 380 singers and musicians, etc., would last for as long as eight days. Each of the three stages is equipped with pulleys and traps in the floors and ceilings that made it possible for performers dressed up as immortals to drop down from heaven and ghosts to pop up from the underworld.

From the theater we backtrack a few steps, circumnavigate the large semi-circular planter, where there is a well from which Cixi drank before fleeing Peking for Xi'an in 1900 after the Boxer Uprising, and proceed north through an alley that separates the theater (on your left) from a complex of buildings, formerly the imperial kitchen, now being rehabilitated into a tourist hotel by a Hong Kong–China joint venture. Turn right at the end of the alley, continue on the path (don't climb the stairs) until you come to the fortress-like gate tower, dubbed **Violet Vapours from the East**, one of several such towers in the Summer Palace that were 'manned' by eunuch guards responsible for keeping the peace. Pass through the tower and down the slope until you come to the **Garden of Harmonious Interests** (*Xie qu yuan*), first built in 1754 by Qianlong in imitation of a garden favoured by his father, Yongzheng, in Wuxi, Jiangsu Province. The present reincarnation dates from the 1860s. The 'interests' referred to in the garden's name are:

Stone detail, the Summer Palace

1. *Water*: in the northwest corner of the garden, there is a stepped fountain with nine levels that produces gurgling background music, a highly desirable sound effect in a northern Chinese garden. The water is the overspill from the lakes to the north of Longevity Mountain, where the water level is more than two metres (seven feet) higher than that in this garden.

2. *Buildings*: one of the several halls built in the southern style, the **Fresh View Tower** (to the west of the pond) appears to have two storeys when viewed from inside the garden, but only one when seen from outside.

3. *Bridges*: can you count five bridges in this compact garden? The longest one, **Knowing the Fish Bridge** (*Zhi yu qiao*) stretches diagonally across the pond, and has a *pailou* named after a famous Taoist anecdote that is a fine example of Zen irreverence:

The philosopher Zhuangzi (Chuang Tzu) was once standing on a bridge over the Hao River with his disciple Huizi.

Zhuangzi: Sir, do you see how the fish are enjoying themselves?

Huizi: You, sir, are not a fish. How dare you claim to know that the fish are enjoying themselves?

Zhuangzi: But sir, since you are not me, how do you know that I *don't* know the fish are enjoying themselves?

Huizi: Indeed I am not you, and cannot know what you are thinking. But I know that you are not a fish, and thus you cannot know how happy they are.

Zhuangzi: Do you recall when we began this discussion, you asked me how I knew the fish were happy? By saying that, you implied that I had this knowledge.

> Actually, I know that the fish are happy for no other reason than because I am standing on this bridge over the River Hao.

We will come across another reference to the Hao River in another garden-within-a-garden in Beihai Park.

Walk counter-clockwise three-quarters of the way around the lake, climb the steps behind the **Hall of Far Vistas**, and wind your way northwest past the walled compound of the **Pavilion of Clearing Skies** *(Ji qing xuan)*, where Reginald Johnston, English tutor, tennis and bicycle instructor, and political advisor to the last emperor, Puyi, lived in 1919 after he was made the nominal supervisor of the Summer Palace and Jade Spring Mountain. It is now one of the two walled residential compounds in the Summer Palace that until 1989 had been leased to Club Med (the other is on South Lake Island) for use as a tourist hotel. You can try to talk your way in for a look around this day-dreamy place. Johnston's three-room flat on the top of the hill is worth a visit. Descend from here to the north shore of the easternmost section of the **Back Lake**, a large man-made extension of the waterways on the other side of the mountain.

The big hall, the first that you come to, set against the north wall of the Summer Palace and facing north is the **Studio of Distant Views** *(Tiao yuan zhai)*, which over-looks the road that leads to the Western Hills and beyond. In her heyday, Cixi would arrange for command performances in the road by the stilt-walkers and other performing troupes passing by here on their way to the annual Taoist temple fair at Miao feng shan.

In the smaller, rather unpretentious buildings west of here, the Summer Palace caretakers today make and store their own straw brooms.

Continue west on the path along the north shore of the lake until you come to the second bridge that spans the lake. On your way you will pass a uniquely designed pavilion with a rectangular flat roof contiguous with another hexagonal pavilion. Cross this bridge, and when the path reaches a junction, backtrack a bit to the southeast, and follow the path up and around in the direction of the **Porcelain Pagoda**, an immaculate relic from the Qianlong period, despite a few missing Buddhas. The crescent-shaped promontory here, scattered with ruins and the plinths of buildings no longer extant, offers a fine view of the Western Hills.

Wind your way back down the mountain and follow the path west until you get to the **Hall of Pines** (*Song tang*), a large square patio at the foot of the Lama Temple. From here we can visit Suzhou Street (extra ticket required).

Rebuilt and opened for business in 1990, this area on the shores of the rearlakes is an idyllic reconstruction of the canals and shops of Suzhou, the Venice of China. Suzhou Street was a Qianlong brainstorm, one of several souvenirs of his excursions to southern China that he brought to Peking. (There is also a smaller Suzhou Street with a number of curio shops to the north of the Marble Boat.) Here the cloistered denizens of the palace would gather to enjoy a taste of the real (commercial) world. Eunuchs and palace maidens played the role of shopkeepers, shouting their wares at the top of their squeaky voices as the Son of Heaven walked by. The shops were fully stocked with goods imported from the South at great expense. The eunuch Li Lianying revived this precursor of Disneyland in the late 19th century to relieve the boredom of the Empress Dowager Cixi. The shops today range from two-storey teahouses, wineshops and traditional Chinese snackbars to millinery shops, shoe makers, kite sellers and tobacconists. The young merchants are dressed in (polyester) traditional merchants' costumes. Beware that the pavement lining the water is treacherously narrow in places. This is wonderful place to break up the afternoon's trek and rest for a few moments with a cup of tea.

To the southwest of Suzhou Street further up the mountain here once stood a place called the **Porch of Gutters and Ditches**, described in *In Search of Old Peking*:

> There are numerous small water-courses
> running round and under this building.
> The floors are made of glass through which
> fish may be seen darting about, something
> after the style of the glass-boats on the
> Californian coast. [7]

But Chinese sources suggest that there was little left of this 'Porch' even before *In Search of Old Peking* was written in the 1930s, and only its ruined foundation remains today.

The **Lama Temple**, looking as if it were pinned to the north face of the mountain and preventing it from collapsing, dates from the 18th century. In 1752 Qianlong sent a delegation of four—two officials, a painter and a draughtsman—to the Samye Monastery in Tibet, and upon their return, had them install smaller versions of the monastery here and at the **Mountain Retreat for Avoiding Summer Heat** (*Bi shu shan zhuang*) in Chengde (formerly Jehol), some 250 kilometers (155 miles) north of Beijing, incidentally an excellent day-away journey from the capital.

Much of the temple, including the building called the **Sacred Precincts of Mt Sumeru** (*Xu mi ling jing*), which once occupied the large courtyard at the lowest level of the temple, was destroyed in 1860 by the English and French armies. What remains clinging to the hill today are the results of repairs made from 1888 to 1903 during Cixi's heyday. Buddha statues that had been brought here at that time from a temple Qianlong had built elsewhere for his mother were ravaged by Red Guards during the Cultural Revolution. The three large images on view today in the main hall are new, and very much look it.

Nothing inside any of these temples is of much interest—most of the buildings are sealed up anyway—so after exploring the temple briefly you can follow the rather steep

---

(7) David Kidd *Peking Story: The Last Days of Old Peking*
     (New York: Clarkson N. Potter, 1988), pp. 77–80.

path leading up from the highest point in the southwest corner (facing the mountain, the upper right hand corner) of the temple complex to the **Sea of Wisdom** (*Zhi hui hai*), the treasure-chest of a shrine covered entirely with green and yellow glazed tiles. The Sea of Wisdom is built of brick and stone, and thus only suffered minor cosmetic deface- ment when the Summer Palace was occupied by foreign troops in 1900; for target practice they decapitated many of the 1,008 moulded Buddha images in their niches. David Kidd, an American who lived in a spacious apartment in the north gatehouse of the Summer Palace between 1946 and 1950, mentions in his delightful memoir, *Peking Story* that the three bronze Tibetan Buddhas originally in the Sea of Wisdom, one of them two storeys tall, were victims of Red Guard fury in the Cultural Revolution. [8]

From here, the highest point in the Summer Palace, you obtain your first panoramic view of Kunming Lake and the surrounding countryside. On a clear day, you can see the skyscrapers of Beijing, as well as obtain a fine view of the Western Hills. Stake out a pavilion nearby for a picnic or a rest; there is an outhouse not far to the west. If you are in a hurry, you may descend the south face of the mountain from here, skirting the giant pagoda (*Fo xiang ge*, the **Pagoda of Buddhist Virtue**), and ending up in the **Hall of Dispelling Clouds** that encrouches onto the shore of the lake. Otherwise continue on the walk by working your way down the mountain by following the path that heads directly west, bearing right at the first intersection and left at the second until you come down to water level again.

By taking a left at the first intersection, a short climb brings you to the pavilion named **Strolling through Painted Scenery**, which offers a fine controlled view of **Jade Spring Mountain** (*Yu quan shan*).

Continuing your descent, within minutes you will come to an intersection where another fortress gate, the

---

(8) L.C. Arlington and William Lewisohn *In Search of Old Peking* (Peking: Henri Vetch, 1935; Oxford University Press reprint, 1987) p. 290.

Eaves that Play Host to Clouds (*Su yun yan*), rises up to your right. Turn left here and head south past the old Japanese steel-hull boat in its dry berth. This boat was a gift from the Japanese Government to the Empress Dowager in 1908, who had supplied several thousand tonnes of salt to the Japanese when they were at war with Russia in 1900. The boat was moored in the nearby canal until it sank in 1921. In 1941, during the Japanese occupation, the tourism department of the Japanese Ministry of Railways awarded a local foundry a contract to have it salvaged and repaired.

The area we are passing through is **Little Suzhou Street** and dates back to Qianlong times, though the antiques emporia and fast-food outlets that occupy the buildings here are of more recent vintage. On your right the lovely covered bridge, called **Floating-heart** (a water plant) **Bridge** (*Xing qiao*), is another quaint reminder of that Yangtze-delta town. Cross the bridge over the inlet called Little Suzhou Creek. From here you can get an excellent view of the lake and the famous Marble Boat.

It is a well-known story that Cixi used funds earmarked for the Chinese navy to renovate the Summer Palace in 1888, but only after her other sources of garden-building money dried up. To provide an anodyne to the endless harangues about the Old Buddha's evil ways, David Kidd wrote in her defense:

> Chinese and Western historians [who] talk
> about it in tones of outrage . . . do not see
> that this navy, had it been built, today
> would be lying at the bottom of the China
> Sea, sunk on its first encounter with a
> foreign power, while the empress's extrava-
> gance still stands, a delight to all who see it
> . . . [9]

The notorious yet innocuous **Marble Boat** (*Qing yan fang* or *Shi fang*)—only the hull is marble—was first built on

---

(9) David Kidd *Peking Story,* p. 77.

this spot in 1755 by Qianlong (not by Cixi, as is often stated), who fitted it out with a Chinese-style superstructure. As a 'ship of state' it symbolized the stability of the dynasty, yet as Qianlong reasoned in an essay on the subject: 'Water (the people) keeps the boat (the empire) afloat; yet it can cause the boat to sink as well.' In the Ming dynasty this had been the site of a Buddhist temple, where live animals were set free in an annual merit-obtaining ritual. Qianlong and his mother would perform this act of piety here with birds and fish. Qianlong's ship was scuttled by the French and English armies in 1860.

Cixi rebuilt and modernized the boat in 1893, adding the paddlewheels and a Western-style cabin. She also installed a large mirror before which she would sit on rainy days, sipping tea and gazing at the mirror as if it was a painted scroll. She also listened to the trickle of rain draining from the boat through the mouths of the four store dragons chaperoning it through the seas. In 1903 a second storey with stained-glass windows was added to the superstructure, the model for the present refurbishment, and in Republican days (1911–49) it was open to the public as a European-style teahouse that was frequented by the Chinese middle classes. From the dock west of the Floating-heart Bridge it is possible to catch a boat back to the

The Marble Boat, the Summer Palace

park entrance, but you would miss several sights on the south side of the mountain if you did so. The boats are usually rented by tourist groups but charters are also available.

Retrace your steps over the **Floating-heart Bridge** and continue south until you come to the western end of the **Long Corridor** (*Chang lang*), erected by Qianlong to enable his mother to enjoy the scenery on the lake in rain and snow without mussing her elaborate Manchu hair-do. Burnt to the ground by foreign troops in 1860, it was reconstructed in 1888, and restored by the Japanese during their occupation of Peiping (1937–45), and by the communists in 1959 and again in the early 1980s. The corridor links up the many buildings scattered along the south face of the mountain, and frames the **Hall of Dispelling Clouds** (*Pai yun dian*) like a pair of lengthy neatly plucked eyebrows as it skirts the delicately arched contour of the lake. In tourist season both railings of the Long Corridor are normally full up with 2 x 728 meters of local tourists munching on their lunches or resting. Inspired by a bad case of *horror vacui*, the overhead beams are decorated with a total of 14,000 southern Chinese landscapes and scenes from Chinese myths, fiction, drama and the lives of famous people, for the most part rather mechanically painted by art-academy students. The large panels in the four midway gazebos display brushwork of a much higher quality. During the Cultural Revolution, all the paintings (bourgeoise reactionary) of figures were covered with white paint in anticipation of replacing them with revolutionary heros, but this was not carried out.

As you proceed east in the corridor (or alongside it if the human traffic makes you claustrophobic), the first set of buildings on your left up on the hill is the **Hall for Listening to Orioles Sing** (*Ting li guan*), formerly a small-scale concert hall Cixi built in 1892 especially for ballad performances. It now houses a tourist restaurant which, despite the large number of meals served every day in two sittings, maintains a remarkably high standard of cuisine. The menu includes a number of palace favourites.

During the Qing dynasty, thoroughbred carp for the imperial table were raised in the Summer Palace lakes. In the 1950s, a carp with a gold ring inscribed with the Empress Dowager's name clipped to its gills was allegedly discovered there, and in recent years a privileged few have continued to savour the scions of this imperial school.

Continuing along the Long Corridor you come to the **Hall of Dispelling Clouds** (*Pai yun dian*) complex and its crowning glory, the **Pagoda of Buddhist Virtue** (*Fo xiang ge*), one of the tallest wooden buildings in China. As stated above, this is the site on which Qianlong chose to build a temple for his mother's 60th birthday. Here too, in 1894, Cixi celebrated her own 60th birthday by rebuilding the entire complex at immense cost. To decorate the Hall of Benevolence and Longevity (near the Summer Palace entrance) alone, a tent of silk was erected that made use of 17,500 bolts of silk, which if laid end to end would extend 230 kilometers (144 miles). As the contents of the Hall of Dispelling Clouds were sacked in 1900, the present display here consists mostly of gifts Cixi received on her 70th birthday in 1904.

You can now climb to the top of the pagoda, rebuilt in its present form in 1891–4, for a glance at the lake, but if you made it up to the Sea of Wisdom when you were exploring the other side of the mountain, you have been there before. On the first and 15th day of the first lunar month, Cixi would burn incense in this 41-meter (135-foot) tall pagoda and make obeisances to the huge Buddha image here. The Buddha with 1,000 eyes and 1,000 hands now on display is not the original inhabitant of the pagoda but was recently discovered in a dusty store room in a temple near the Rear Lakes, and moved here. To the west of the pagoda is the famous **Bronze Pavilion** cast by the Jesuits in Qianlong's day. To the east is a group of buildings centred around a **Tibetan Prayer Wheel**.

We now proceed along the east section of the Long Corridor. On your left you will pass several self-contained residential courtyards closed to the casual public, but in recent years rented out to foreigners, as they had been before 1949. The painter Zhang Daqian (Chang Ta-ch'ien) stayed here at one time, as did Chiang Kai-shek, although his visit only lasted three days. Two other groups of courtyards that have been converted into hotels flank the Hall of Dispelling Clouds. During the Cultural Revolution, Peng Zhen, the mayor of Beijing, and Mao's wife Jiang Qing lived in the Summer Palace. Madame Jiang supposedly rode her pony up and down the Long Corridor on rainy days, but as the Summer Palace was closed to the public then, evidence for this is hard to come by.

The end of the east section of the Long Corridor is marked by the **Gate of Welcoming the Moon** (*Yao yue men*), after which the corridor takes a sharp turn to the right and cleaves to the shore of the lake for a few meters from where in summer, a dense crop of lotuses can be viewed through the curiously shaped windows. These pedigree lotuses on view today were transplanted from the Chengde Retreat for Avoiding Summer Heat in 1976. Presumably the former stock had died of neglect during the Cultural Revolution. Here too is the dock, marked by two tall flagpoles, where Cixi finally landed after her journey from the city. George Kates records an exquisite vignette of imperial decadence set in these precincts:

> I once heard a story of how, during the season of the lotus, the Empress had her tea perfumed in this place. The large rose flowers, when first they come to bloom, close their petals each night, to open them the next morning. At dusk, therefore, ladies-in-waiting, from shallow skiffs that could make headway through the thick round leaves, deftly placed within them little packages of tea wrapped in soft paper. These were left during the night in the hearts of the flowers, to be gathered when they opened at dawn again. They then would be delicately perfumed with that scent so difficult to describe, and yet so

fragrant that it almost may be said to
represent by itself the dignity, display and
beauty of the Chinese ideal of life. [10]

The adjacent courtyard belongs to the **Hall of Happiness in Old Age** (*Le shou tang*), Cixi's private residence, where she was served by a staff of 48.

The largest of the gewgaws on display in the courtyard is a giant hunk of gnarled Taihu stone that Qianlong was only able to transport here by having the doorway broken down, an act that incited his mother's displeasure because she believed that destroying anything in the palace was inauspicious. The rock is inscribed with Qianlong's own calligraphy and that of several other famous scholars of the day. In this courtyard Cixi planted her favourite flowers, movingly described by Juliet Bredon:

> Oleanders, pink as painted lips, pomegranates, red as wounds, and chrysanthemums, like groups of ambassadors in full dress, stood outside the latticed windows of the Dowager's own pavilions. [11]

In 1903, despite Cixi's initial objections, a German firm installed electric lights in the Hall of Happiness in Old Age, and a generator to supply them. It is said that Li Lianying, the immensely wealthy and corrupt eunuch who was Cixi's favourite, gave the go-ahead for the project after accepting a bribe from the Germans. Li's own courtyard residence stands immediately to the east of Cixi's, and he owned another larger residence to the north of the Summer Palace on the campus of the **Instutite of International Relations**, commonly known to be a school for spies.

Continuing east the corridor runs into the **House of Fragrant Herbs** (*Yi yun guan*), the living quarters of

---

(10) George N. Kates, *The Years that Were Fat: The Last of Old China* (New York: Harper & Brothers 1952) pp. 207–8.

(11) Juliet Bredon *Peking*, p. 299.

Guangxu's empress. Attached to it to the south is the **Hall of Jade Ripples** *(Yu lan tang)*—extra ticket required). This was the place where Aunt Cixi held Guangxu under house arrest after he had lent his support to the Reform Movement of 1898. Traces of the brick walls she built to make him stay put can still be seen. The Hall of Jade Ripples contains a number of authentic relics from the Qianlong and Guangxu 'occupation periods.' Between the two imperial residences is a spacious courtyard containing a large walk-through maze, constructed of Lake Taihu stones, called the Forest of Lions. One can easily imagine the emperor and empress of China playing hide-and-seek here on a summer night. There is a more elaborate Forest of Lions in a garden of the same name in Suzhou.

Proceed south from here past the boat docks towards the pavilion on the water, and stop in for a look at the **Memorial Temple to Ye lü chu cai** (extra ticket required) on your left. The Khitan Yelüchucai (1190–1244), personal astrologer to Genghis Khan, successfully advised the Mongol emperor on economic and political matters. His tomb, a giant inverted wok now squeezed into a room on the north side of the temple, disappeared during the Cultural Revolution, though one wonders where it could have gone. There is some lovely stone carving on the marble stands here which once held bronze incense burners.

Continuing south along the shore, pass the **Pavilion for Knowing Spring** *(Zhi chun ting)*, where impromptu performances of Peking opera and ballads can sometimes be heard on summer evenings. Pass through the tall fortified gate called the **Pavilion of Flourishing Culture** *(Wen chang ge)*, where eunuchs kept watch over the lake. Approaching the **Seventeen-arch Bridge**, you will see the famous **Bronze Ox** reclining on a stone platform. In the imperial inscription on its back (1755), Qianlong commemorates the completion of the dredging of the lake and immodestly compares himself to the ancient mythological emperor Yu, who had once recorded his own success in quelling a flood on the back of an ox. The Dutchman Borel, who perhaps was eating lotuses, had a near-religious experience here when he encountered this massive bovine paperweight:

> . . . It is an ox of bronze; but a marvel, a
> marvel on the border between life and
> death . . . There is life in each curve, in
> each flexure; but it is more beautiful than
> life, because it is art and cannot die.
> Nothing brutal is left: it is life made divine,
> immortalised in bronze. I saw many
> superb bronzes in China, but this one is
> the masterpiece. Softly and discreetly I
> stroked the smooth bronze, as if I touched
> sacred life. [12]

Stroll past the octagonal pavilion and across the **Seventeen-arch Bridge** (Borel: 'It is not like a bridge for human beings, rather for the Elysian Fields, to be trodden by none but shining angels and beatified souls.') onto the **South Lake Island** (*Nan hu dao*); in winter you may walk or skate to the island on the ice.) The **Temple of the Dragon King** (*Long wang miao*; extra ticket required), the first building on your right, dates from the Ming dynasty, when it stood on the shore of the lake. When Qianlong expanded that body of water and created Kunming Lake, he left the temple in its original place, formed an island around it, and connected it to the shore with the Seventeen-arch Bridge. Legend has it that Qianlong's son, the Jiaqing emperor-to-be, once came here from the Yuanmingyuan to pray for rain. His appeal was answered, and he left an inscription that now appears on the plaque hanging over the temple: 'The Shrine for Plenteous and Beneficent Rain from Heaven'. Qianlong also built a tower on the north shore of the island where he and his mother would go fishing and review the naval exercises conducted on the lake. Cixi followed suit and in 1899 organized similar exercises on the lake. But the miniature battleships stirred

---

(12) Henri Borel *The New China*, p. 236.

up so much mud in the shallow lake that she cancelled the entire show before it had hardly begun. The present building, the **Hall of Infinite Space** (*Han xu tang*), where Guangxu would spend time in the summer, offers a superb view of Longevity Mountain.

In Republican times, the Society for the Prevention of Vandalism held meetings in the buildings on this island, and the courtyard complexes on the west were used by the Chinese Nature Society in the 1920s and 1930s as a spa. In the mid-1980s these premises were leased for a short period to Club Med for use as a hotel.

There are two more lakes to the west of the long causeway, both with islands in their centres. The island in the southernmost lake conceals a complex of buildings called the **Seaweed-viewing Hall** (*Zao jian tang*), property of Beijing Communist Party headquarters. Strangely enough, some contemporary maps omit the recently-built short causeway that enables VIPs to drive there by car. A few other buildings in this section of the Summer Palace remain off limits to common mortals. The island in the west lake was once the site of a round fortress-like tower, but that is now in ruins.

To leave the Summer Palace you must backtrack along the west shore of the lake, while the setting sun puts its finishing touches on the day. We conclude our itinerary with Borel's parting meditation.

> I knew now that I had felt the soul of the Summer Palace. The truest beauty was not in the marvels of architecture, the jewel-like dwellings on the hill: it was in the silent, deep blue lake mirroring the azure sky, in the clear spaces of air and light, in the mountains that seemed to lift their heads in worship. In this holy solitude all that is eternal sinks away. [13]

---

(13) Henri Borel *The New China*, p. 242.

Recommended Establishments

Hotels (The Chinese name is given in parentheses if it differs from the English name.)

Luxurious and Expensive

China World Hotel *(Zhong guo da fan dian)*, China World Trade Center, 1 Jianguomenwai Dajie.
Tel. 5053167, 3168, 3169, Tlx. 211206 CWH

Grand Hotel Beijing *(Gui bin lou)*, 35 Dong Chang'an Dajie.
Tel. 5137788, Fax. 5130048, Tlx. 210454 BHPTW

Palace Hotel *(Wang fu)*, 8 Jinyu Hutong. Tel. 5128899,
Fax. 5129050, Tlx. 222696 PALBJ

First Class

Beijing Airport Movenpick Radisson Hotel, Xiao Tianzhu Village (five minutes from airport) Tel. 4565588,
Fax. 4565678

Recommended Establishments

Beijing Hotel, 33 Dong Chang'an Dajie. Tel. 5137766, Fax. 5137703, Tlx. 222755 BHCRD

Great Wall Sheraton (Chang cheng), 6A Donghuanbeilu. Tel. 5005566, Fax. 5001938, Tlx. 20045, 22002 GWHBJ

Shangri-La Hotel, 29 Zizhuyuan Lu. Tel. 8412211, Fax. 8418006, Tlx. 222322 SHABJ

Hotel Beijing-Toronto (Jinglun), 3 Jianguomenwai Dajie. Tel. 5002266, Fax. 5137703, Tlx. 210011 JHL

Jianguo Hotel, 5 Jianguomenwai Dajie. Tel. 5002233, Fax. 5002871, Tlx. 22439 JGHBJ

Jing Guang New World Hotel, Hujialou. Tel. 5018888, Fax. 5013333, Tlx. 210489 BJJGC

New Otani Chang fu Gong Hotel, 26 Jianguomenwai Dajie. Tel. 5125555, Fax. 5129813

Olympic Hotel, 52 Baishiqiao Lu, Haidian. Tel. 8316688, Fax. 8318390, Tlx. 222749 OLHTL

Swissotel Beijing, Hong Kong Macau Center. Gongren Tiyuchangbei Lu. Tel. 5012288, Fax. 5012501, Tlx. 222527

Tianlun Dynasty Hotel, 50 Wangfujing Dajie. Tel. 5138888. Fax. 5137866 Tlx. 210575 TLH

Tianping Lee Gardens Hotel, 2 Jianguomennan Dajie. Tel. 5158855, Fax. 5158533

Xin Da Du Hotel, 21 Chegongzhuang Dajie. Tel. 8319988, Fax. 83202136, Tlx. 221042, 221043 XDDH

Standard and Tourist Class

Beijing Exhibition Centre Hotel (*Zhan lan guan*),
    135 Xizhimen Dajie. Tel. 8316633, Fax. 8327450,
    Tlx. 222395 BECH

Beijing International Hotel (*Guo ji*), 9 Jianguomennei Dajie.
    Tel. 5126688, Fax. 5129972, Tlx. 211121 BIH

Capital Hotel (*Shou du bin guan*), 3 Qianmen Dong Dajie.
    Tel. 5129988, Fax. 5120323, Tlx. 222650 CHB

Friendship Hotel (*You yi bin guan*), 3 Baishiqiao Lu, Haidian.
    Tel. 8498888, Fax. 8314661, Tlx. 222362, 222363
    FHBJ

Holiday Inn Downtown, 98 Beilishi Lu Tel. 8322288,
    Fax. 8320696, Tlx. 221045 HIDTB

Holiday Inn Lido Hotel, Jiangtai Lu. Tel. 500-6688,
    Fax. 5006237, Tlx. 22618 PEGCH

Kunlun Hotel, 2 Xinyuannan Lu. Tel. 5003388,
    Fax. 5003228, Tlx. 211166 BJKLH

Landmark (*Liang ma*), 8 Donghuanbei Lu. Tel. 5016688,
    Fax. 5004075, Tlx. 210301 LTC

Le Meridien Jin Lang Hotel, 75 Chongnei Dajie.
    Tel. 5132288, Fax. 5125839

Minzu (Minorities) Hotel, 5 Fuxingmennei Dajie.
    Tel. 6014466, Fax. 6014849, Tlx. 22990, 22991
    MZHTL

Peace Hotel (*He ping*), 3 Jinyu Hutong. Tel. 5128833.
    Fax. 5126863, Tlx. 222824 BJPH

Recommended Establishments

Qianmen Hotel, 175 Yong'an Lu. Tel. 3016688,
    Fax. 3013883, Tlx. 222382 QMHTL

Taiwan Hotel (Guo mao), 5 Jinyu Hutong. Tel. 5136688,
    Fax. 5136896, Tlx. 210543 TWHTL

Traders Hotel, China World Trade Center, 1 Jianguomenwai
    Dajie. Tel. 5052277, Fax. 5050818, Tlx. 222981 THBBC

Xinqiao Hotel, 2 Dongjiao minxiang. Tel. 5133366,
    Fax. 5125126, Tlx. 222514 XQH

Xiyuan Hotel, 5 Erligou, Haidian. Tel. 8313388,
    Fax. 8314577, Tlx. 22835 XYH

Zhaolong Hotel, 2 Gongren tiyuchang Lu. Tel. 5002299,
    Fax. 5003319, Tlx. 210079 ZLH

Budget

Beiwei Hotel, 13 Xijing Road, Xuanwumen. Tel. 3012266

Guanghua Hotel, 38 Dong sanhuanbeilu. Tel. 5018866,
    Fax. 5016516, Tlx. 211234

New World Tower *(Xin shi jie)* 4 Gongren tituchang donglu.
    Tel. 5007799, Fax. 5007668, Tlx. 210530 NWTBJ

Ritan Hotel, 1 Ritan Lu. Tel. 5125588, Fax. 5128671

Tiantan Sports Hotel *(Ti yu bin guan)*, 10 Tiyuguan Lu.
    Tel. 7013388, Fax. 7015388

Yanjing Hotel, 19 Fuxingmenwai Dajie. Tel. 8326611,
    Fax. 8326130, Tlx. 200028 YJHEL

Restaurants

There are now at least 1,000 restaurants in Beijing, serving food from all over the world. The following list is restricted to locally run Chinese restaurants with relatively long histories and noteworthy specialties. No hotel or joint-venture (usually with Hong Kong) restaurants are listed, although in terms of food, service and decor they are generally considered the best places to eat in the city, despite some lack of local colour (and local hassles). While the food in the restaurants listed below is usually excellent, one goes for the atmosphere and the history as well.

Note that the hours of most of these restaurants below are restricted. Lunch is served from about 11 A.M to 2 P.M., dinner from about 5 P.M. to 8 P.M.. If you arrive at a local restaurant near closing time you risk encountering poor service, or claims that there is no food. Hotel and smaller private restaurants operate on more flexible schedules. It is best to call for exact opening and closing times and to inquire about whether reservations are necessary.

Bian yi fang kaoya dian (750–505).
2 Chongwenmenwai Dajie. Vintage Peking roast duck restaurant in a new building.

Dong lai shun (552–092) 16 Jinyu Hutong, near Dong'an Market. Muslim restaurant serving the second most famous Beijing dish, Mutton Hot Pot, also called Rinsed Mutton or Mongolian hotpot. Best in autumn and winter, but available year round.

Fang shan (441–184) On the north shore of the island in Beihai Park. Most famous imperial-style restaurant in China in a superb setting. Many find the food expensive and the service arrogant, but should be tried once. Going with a Chinese host might help.

Feng ze yuan (Garden of the Horn of Plenty; 421–7508), Xingfu sancun, Chaoyang district. The cuisine of Shangdong and North China in a new, uninspiring building. Once the best known restaurant of its type.

Hong bin lou (601–4832) 82 Xi Chang'an Dajie, near the Xidan intersection. Muslim restaurant serving Peking roast duck.

Jin yang (331–669, 332–120) 241 Zhushikou Dajie. Specialty is the hearty cuisine of Shanxi Province.

Kao rou ji (445–921) On the shores of Qianhai in the Rear Lakes area. Roast mutton and Mongolian barbecue in one of the citi's nicest settings.

The Lao She Teahouse, named after the late Beijing author of *Rickshaw Boy*, located immediately to the west of Qianmen, is an attempt to recreate a traditional Beijing teahouse. Snacks are sold all day and there are performances by elderly ballad singers in the evening.

Moscow Restaurant (894–454) Beijing Exhibition Centre, Xizhimenwai Dajie. Russian-style cooking in a 1950s time warp. An experience.

Quan ju de Peking Roast Duck. The classic outlet for the dish has three venues:

- **Qianmen** (511–2418), 32 Qianmen Dajie
- **Hepingmen** (338–031), Hepingmen. The world's largest duckery, called the Wall Street Duck as Hepingmen was the site of a gate in the former city wall, or McDonald Duck due to its size.

    – **Wangfujing** (553–310), 13 Shaifuyuan. Near the Capital Hospital, jokingly referred to as the Sick Duck.

Sichuan Dou Hua Restaurant (771–2672) Guangqumenwai. Unpretentious place for authentic Sichuan cuisine.

Sichuan Restaurant (656–810, 656–348) 51 Xi Rongxian Hutong. Popular venue for the spicy cuisine of Sichuan province, in a former mansion.

Ting li guan (Pavilion for Listening to the Orioles; 258–1955, 258–1608) On the grounds of the Summer Palace near the Marble Boat. Imperial cuisine in a former theatre used by the Empress Dowager Cixi in the late 19th century. Food can be excellent.

Zhen Su Zhai Vegetarian Restaurant (653–181) 74 Xuanwumennei Dajie. Modest outlet for Chinese vegetarian dishes. To ensure variety, let a knowledgeable person select the dishes for you, or order an inexpensive banquet.

Shopping

Beijing Arts and Crafts Service Centre, Wangfujing Dajie. Large Comprehensive showplace.

Beijing Department Store, Wangfujing Dajie. Biggest in the city.

China Bookstore, 115 Dong Liulichang. Huge complex selling all varieties of printed matter, new and old.

Dong'an Market, Wangfujing Street. A crowded bazaar from the early 20th century.

Recommended Establishments

Friendship Store, 17 Jianguomenwai. Slightly upmarket tourist and resident standby.

Huaxia Arts and Crafts Shop aka The Theatre Shop, 12 Chongwenmennei Dajie and 239 Wangfujing Dajie. Closest thing to ye olde curiosity shoppe, run by the state.

Rongbaozhai Paintings Shop, Liulichang. Paintings, woodblock prints, artists materials.

Tong ren tang Traditional Medicine Shop, Dazhalan Jie, Qianmenwai. Best known old fashioned pharmacy in China.

Rui fu xiang Fabric Shop, Dazhalan Jie, Qianmenwai. Local place for dry goods with a 1920s air.

Yuanlong Silk Shop, 55 Tiantan Lu, near Temple of Heaven. Huge selection, tourist friendly.

Antiques and Curios Market

Beijing now has three markets selling antiquities and curios. They are wonderful places to visit. Allow twice as much time as you would think, and shop with care. Popular with diplomats and long-term foreign residents.

- **Chaowai Market**. On Chaowai shichang Jie, north of Ritan Park. Furniture and antiques.
- **Hongqiao Market**. On Tiantan Lu, east of the north entrance of the Temple of Heaven. Antiques and decorative art.
- **Jingsong Curios Market** (Jingsong jiŭ huo gong yi pin shi chang). On Dong sanhuan Lu, approximately 2 kilometres south of Jingsong Lu. Wide variety of antiques.

Bibliography

There are enough books on Peking in Chinese, Japanese, Korean, English, French and German to fill a Great Wall of bookshelves, yet *the* book on the city in English remains to be written. The wealth of available data begins with early Chinese gazetteers and includes Marco Polo, Ming-dynasty novels, Korean travellers' tales, Japanese maps, Jesuits' letters to the Vatican, Manchu stone inscriptions, *risqué* ballads, imperial rescripts, *hutong* rumours, B.B.C. broadcasts, opera playbills and Peking duck menus.

Quotes from early works by European and American writers suggest the seductive effect Old Peking could have on people. Reading classics like Bredon's *Peking*, Arlington and Lewisohn's *In Search of Old Peking*, and Kates' *The Years That Were Fat* makes one impatient for the invention of the time machine.

Chinese sources have been particularly helpful. Guidebooks, specialized treatises, scholarly journals and maps were essential in assembling the unfinished jigsaw puzzle of this book.

Bibliography

Acton, Harold *Memoirs of an Aesthete* (London: Methuen, 1948)

Arlington, L.C. & Lewisohn, *In Search of Old Peking* (Peking: Henri Vetch, 1935; Oxford reprint, 1988)

Blofeld, John *City of Lingering Splendour* (London: Hutchinson, 1961)

Bodde, Derk *Peking Diary: A Year of Revolution* (New York: Abelard-Schuman, 1950; reprinted by Fawcett World Library, 1967)

Bodde, Derk (trans.) *Annual Customs and Festivals in Peking* (Peking: Henri Vetch, 1936; Hong Kong: 1965)

Borel, Henri *The New China: A Traveller's Impressions* (London: T Fisher Unwin, 1912)

Bouillard, G *Le Temple de Ciel* (Paris: 1930)

Bredon, Juliet *Peking* (Shanghai: Kelly and Walsh, 1931; Oxford reprint, 1982)

Bredon, Juliet and Mitrophanow, Igor *The Moon Year* (Shanghai: Kelly and Walsh, Oxford reprint, date of original pub. 1982)

Bridge, Ann *Peking Picnic* (Boston: Little, Brown & Company, 1932)

Buxton, L.H. Dudley *The Eastern Road* (London: Kegan Paul, 1924)

Cameron, Nigel and Blake, Brian *Peking: A Tale of Three Cities* (New York: Harper and Row, 1965)

Carl, Katherine *With the Empress Dowager of China* (1906; KPI Limited reprint, 1986)

Cook, Thomas & Son *Peking and the Overland Route* (London: Thomas Cook & Son, 1917)

Cumming, C.F. Gordon *Wanderings in China* (Edinburgh & London: William Blackwood & Sons, 1888)

Der Ling, Princess *Two Years in the Forbidden City* (New York: Uoffat, Yard and Company, 1911)

Dorn, Frank *The Forbidden City: The Biography of a Palace* (New York: Charles Scribner's Sons, 1970)

The Economist Business Traveller's Guides: China (New York: Prentice Hall, 1988)

Edkins, Joseph *Peking* in Williamson, Alexander *Journeys in North China, Manchuria and Eastern Mongolia with Some Account of Korea* (London: Smith, Elden & Co., 1870)

Fei-shi *Guide to Peking and its Environs* (Tientsin: Tientsin Press, 1909)

Fitzgerald, C.P. *Flood Tide in China* (London: The Cresset Press, 1958)

Fleming, Peter *The Siege at Peking* (London: Rupert Hart-Davis, 1950; Oxford reprint, 1983)

Goodman, David S G *Beijing Street Voices* (London and Boston: Marion Boyars, 1981)

Hsü, Immanuel C.Y. *The Rise of Modern China, 3rd edition* (Hong Kong: Oxford University Press, 1983)

Japanese Government Railways *Guide to China* (Tokyo: Japanese Government Railways, 1924)

Johnston, Reginald *Twilight in the Forbidden City* (Oxford reprint: 1985; London: Victor Gollancz, 1934)

Kates, George N *The Years that Were Fat: The Last of Old China* (New York: Harper & Brothers, 1952; Cambridge: Massachusetts Institute of Technology Press reprint, 1967 and 1976; Oxford reprint 1988)

Kidd, David *Peking Story: The Last Days of Old China* (New York: Clarkson N Potter, 1988)

Lao She *Crescent Moon and Other Stories* (Beijing: Panda Books, 1987)

Leys, Simon *Chinese Shadows* (Baltimore: Viking, 1978)

Little, Mrs Archibald *Guide to Peking* (Tientsin: Tientsin Press, 1904)

Lowe, H.Y. (*Luo Xinyao*), *The Adventures of Wu: The Life Cycle of a Peking Man* (Peking: The Peking Chronicle

Press, 1940–41; Princeton University Press reprint, 1983)

Malone, Carroll Brown *History of the Peking Summer Palaces Under the Ch'ing Dynasty* (Urbana University of Illinois, 1934)

Marcuse, Jacques *The Peking Papers* (New York: E.P. Dutton, 1967)

Martin W A *A Cycle of Cathay or China, South and North* (New York: Fleming H. Revell, 1897)

Michie, Alexander *The Englishman in China during the Victorian Era* (Edinburgh and London: William Blackwood & Sons, 1900)

Mirams, D.G.A. *Brief History of Chinese Architecture* (Shanghai: Kelly and Walsh, 1940)

Morrison, Hedda Hammer *A Photographer in Old Peking* (Hong Kong: Oxford University Press, 1985)

Myron, Paul *Our Chinese Chances through Europe's Eyes* (Chicago: Linebarge Brothers, 1915)

Nagel's *Encyclopedia Guide to China* (Geneva: Nagel Verlag, several editions)

The Peiping Chronicle *Guide to Peking* (Peiping: The Peiping Chronicle, 1935)

The Peiping Bookshop *A Guide to Peiping and its Environs* (Peiping: The Peiping Bookshop, 1946)

Quennel, Peter *A Superficial Journey Through Tokyo and Peking* (London: Faber & Faber, 1932; Oxford reprint, 1986)

Rennie, D.F. *Peking and the Pekinese* (London: John Murray, 1865)

Siren, Osvald *The Gardens of China* (New York: Ronald Press, 1949)

Siren, Osvald *The Imperial Palaces of Peking* (Paris: 1926, AMS reprint, 1976)

Sitwell, Osbert *Escape with Me!* (London: Macmillan; Oxford reprint 1983)

Trevor-Roper, Hugh *Hermit of Peking* (New York: Alfred A Knopf, 1977)

Terzani, Tiziano *The Forbidden Door* (Hong Kong: Asia 2000 Ltd, 1985)

Thomson, John *Through China with a Camera* (London & New York: Harper & Brothers, 1899)

Warner, Marina *The Dragon Empress: Life & Times of Tz'u-hsi 1835–1908* (London: Weidenfeld & Nicolson Ltd, 1972)

Wilhelm, Richard *The Soul of China* (London: Harcourt Brace Jovanovich, 1928)

Willets, William *Chinese Art, 2 vols.* (Harmondsworth: Penguin Books, 1958)

Yao, Ming-le *The Conspiracy and Murder of Mao's Heir* (London: Collins, 1983)

Zhou, Shachen *Beijing Old and New* (Beijing: New World Press, 1984)

Yu, Zhaoyun, ed. *Palaces of the Forbidden City* (London: Allen Lane, 1984)

Index

Index

THE HENRY HOLT WALKS SERIES
For people who want to *learn* when they travel, not just see.

Look for these other exciting volumes in Henry Holt's best-selling Walks series:

PARISWALKS, Revised Edition, by Alison and Sonia Landes.
Five intimate walking tours through the most historic quarters of the City of Light.
288 pages, photos, maps $12.95 Paper

LONDONWALKS, Revised Edition, by Anton Powell
Five historic walks through old London, one brand new for this edition.
272 pages, photos, maps $12.95 Paper

VENICEWALKS by Chas Carner and Alessandro Giannatasio
Four enchanting tours through one of the most perfect walking evironments the world has to offer.
240 pages, photos, maps $12.95 Paper

ROMEWALKS by Anya M. Shetterly
Four walking tours through the most historically and culturally rich neighborhoods of Rome.
256 pages, photos, maps $12.95 Paper

FLORENCEWALKS by Anne Holler
Four intimate walks through this exquisite medieval city, exploring its world-famous art and architecture.
208 pages, photos, maps $12.95 Paper

VIENNAWALKS by J. Sydney Jones
Four walking tours that reveal the home of Beethoven, Freud and the Habsburg monarchy.
304 pages, photos, maps $12.95 Paper

NEW YORKWALKS by The 92nd Street Y, edited by Batia Plotch
One of the city's most visible cultural and literary institutions guides
you through six historic neighborhoods in New York.
288 pages, photos, maps $12.95 Paper

BARCELONAWALKS by George Semler
Five walking tours through Spain's cultural and artistic center—
synonymous with such names as Gaudi, Miró, and Picasso.
272 pages, photos, maps $12.95 Paper

JERUSALEMWALKS, Revised Edition by Nitza Rosovsky
Six intimate walks that allow the mystery and magic of this
complicated city to unfold.
304 pages, photos, maps $14.95 Paper

RUSSIAWALKS by David and Valeria Matlock
Seven walks through Moscow and Leningrad, with a special
emphasis on architecture and political history.
304 pages, photo, maps $12.95 Paper